THE LANGUAGE OF THE COSMOS

Rudolf Steiner
(1915)

THE LANGUAGE OF THE COSMOS

Cosmic Influences and the Spiritual Task of Northern Europe

The Human Being as an Earthly and Cosmic Being
Father-consciousness and Christ-consciousness
The Festival of the Appearance of Christ
Cosmic New Year

Eleven lectures held in Kristiania (Oslo), Berlin, Dornach, and Basel from November 24 to December 31, 1921

TRANSLATION BY
AGNES SCHNEEBERG-DE STEUR

RUDOLF STEINER

SteinerBooks

CW 209

SteinerBooks | Anthropsophic Press
834 Main Street, P.O. Box 358
Spencertown, New York 12165
www.steinerbooks.org

Original translation from German by Agnes Schneeberg-de Steur

This book is volume 209 in the Collected Works (CW) of Rudolf Steiner, published by SteinerBooks, 2024. It is a translation of *Nordische und mitteleuropäische Geistimpulse*, 2nd edition, published by Rudolf Steiner Verlag, Dornach, Switzerland, 1982.

ISBN: 978-1-62148-342-7
eBook ISBN: 978-1-62148-343-4

Printed in the United States of America
by Integrated Books International

CONTENTS

INTRODUCTION

The stars once spoke to man,
Their silence is world destiny;
To perceive their silence
Can become pain for earthly man;

But, in the silence, there ripens
What human beings speak to the stars;
To perceive this speaking
Can become strength for spirit man.

—Rudolf Steiner, verse given to Marie Steiner
on December 25, 1922

THIS VOLUME COMPRISES eleven lectures given to members of the Anthroposophical Society in Norway, Germany, and Switzerland in November and December of 1921. In Rudolf Steiner's biography, 1921 was a year of many trials. Not only did he face external opposition in the form of unscrupulous opponents who served up malicious slander daily but he also had to deal with difficulties within the Society from members who were not awake enough to grasp the seriousness of the times and the magnitude of their tasks.

It therefore seems fitting that Rudolf Steiner's three lectures in Norway, given between November 24 and December 4, 1921, begin with a reference to the years of the First World War—recently past but very much still present inwardly—and end with a reference to the opponents of anthroposophy. This bookending of the three lectures with grave matters strikes a note of urgency that can be felt throughout the lectures in this volume. The external opposition and the internal lack of understanding would increase over the coming year. Precisely one year after the final lecture published in this volume, the Goetheanum—the house of the Word to which Steiner devoted all his forces—would burn to the ground in an act of arson. The lectures here stand between the war years and the tragic destruction of the First Goetheanum.

Some years prior, in 1910, Steiner had given a lecture cycle in Oslo on the subject of "folk souls" in an effort to awaken mutual understanding between the peoples of the world as they hurtled toward the abyss of the First World War.* In the first lecture of the present volume, given in Oslo eleven years after that folk-souls cycle, Steiner reminds his listeners of those pre-war lectures. He points out how toward the end of the war, in 1918, he gave a copy of that lecture cycle to an influential German politician, Max von Baden, in the hopes that it would awaken in him a consciousness of how things really stood in Europe and how a true peace and international cooperation could arise after the war. Alas, as Steiner remarks in that lecture of November 24, 1921, "the maturity required to develop insight into the magnitude of the forces leading into decadence, although present in a number of human souls, was not present in the souls of those in charge, who were unwilling to strive for such maturity of insight" (p. 2 of the present volume). In solemn warning, he adds:

> Today, everything depends on the awareness that the spirit, which lies hidden in European and American culture, is the important thing—the spirit from which people flee, which they would prefer to avoid for the sake of ease, but which alone can guide humanity to forces of ascent. But people like to build up foggy notions by preferring to repeat again and again that things will improve of themselves. They will not; the hour of a great decision has struck. Either human beings will resolve to elevate the spirituality of which I have spoken, or the decline of the West is inevitable. No hope, no fatalistic longing for things to right themselves will be of any help in this regard. Humanity has, after all, entered a time in which human forces are used in freedom; and it is essential that humanity actually apply these forces out of free will—in other words, it must now decide for itself whether it wants to have this spirituality or not. If the decision is affirmative, then progress will be possible; if it is negative, then the doom of the West is sealed. Then, in the wake of dire

* See *The Mission of Folk Souls* (CW 121).

> catastrophes, the further evolution of humanity will have to take a different course from the one imagined today by many people. If, however, the wish for true insight into these matters is present, then it is imperative that the soul-life of human beings in general, and of the various peoples in particular, be studied—particularly the soul-life of the peoples of the East and the West. (p. 6)

The following June, at the East-West Congress in Vienna, Steiner would expand on this study of the geographical and spiritual forces at work in the dynamic between East and West in a further attempt to awaken inner understanding among the peoples of the world.†

Steiner emphasizes the need for a penetrating understanding of the spiritual reality of the human being as a true microcosm of the spiritual macrocosm:

> People must become interested again in the whole essential nature of the human being, not merely in the outer, physical sheaths. But this can only come about when the human being will once again be regarded as belonging not only to the earth, to the cosmic "mole-burrow," but rather to the whole cosmos; when it is clearly recognized that between death and a new birth the human being passes through the world of the stars; and when this world of the stars, to which we can only gaze upward from the earth, will be known once again in its living essence, in its soul essence, and in its spiritual essence. (p. 9)

In the other lectures in this volume, given in Berlin, Dornach, and Basel, he expands on this theme—notably in the lecture of December 18, 1921, in which he describes the spiritual reality of the human being not in familiar anthroposophical terms as consisting of physical body, etheric body, astral body, and I, but rather imbues these otherwise abstract designations with inner content: the physical body is an echo of the active working of zodiacal forces, expressed as cosmic consonants, while the etheric body reveals an echo of the weaving of planetary spheres in the realm of the vowels. This interplay of the planetary forces in the vowels and the zodiacal forces in the consonants, which accompany the soul on its descent to earth, was once perceived instinctively by ancient humanity. It was understood that

† See *The Tension between East and West* (CW 83).

names are not given arbitrarily based on the whim of the parents but are designations that correspond to those planetary and zodiacal forces that played the greatest role in that individual's path to earthly incarnation:

> When the human being expressed the secret of his own nature, as it could be learned in the mysteries, he voiced how he had descended through Saturn or Jupiter while they were transiting the constellations of Leo or Virgo, that is, how he descended through the A or the I in the constellations of the M or the L. In that way, the human being uttered what he had experienced of the *music of the spheres*—and that was his cosmic name. And in those ancient times people were certainly aware, instinctively aware, that the human being brought along a name, while descending from the cosmos to the earth. (p. 106)

This theme of learning once again to understand the language of the cosmos continues through Steiner's Christmas lectures. It culminates in his final lecture on New Year's Eve 1921/22, in which he points to the future-bearing impulse of anthroposophy, its relation to the past and its work in preparing a new cosmic year:

> But the cosmic year has ended; the cosmic New Year's Eve is here. A new cosmic year must begin. What we were able to say about Christmas is what we also want to experience in relation to a symbolic festival such as the one that is approaching us at this moment; we want to experience it in the same way; we want, through such a festival, to experience symbolically the turning point in time—which must, even today, already be perceived as a *cosmic* turning point in time. Times have become serious; they have become so serious today that we must of necessity look upward from the narrowly defined events occurring within the limited horizon—which the majority of humanity prefers to recognize as the only legitimate one—to the cosmic expanses, also to the cosmic expanses of human soul-spiritual experiences. This is where we witness the cosmic turning point in time.
>
> If we become aware of this cosmic turning point in time, then we become aware that a cosmic New Year of the spirit must begin for humanity. Only if we learn to recognize such things will we be able

> to feel true humanity in our present era. For true humanity is experienced only when the human being, who goes through repeated lives on earth, finds the possibility in each single earthly life not only to feel as a human being in general, but as a human being with specific tasks related to the specific epoch during which one of these lives is taking shape.
>
> Human beings can live with eternity only if they find the possibility of living in time in the right way. For the eternal should not only be revealed to the human being in time; rather, through the human being and through time, the eternal should become something that can be experienced by the human being. The eternal holds sway in timeless duration; it also holds sway in timeless duration through all human existence. But its pulsations are seen in the events of each single epoch, and in how they impact the human experience. And it is only when we experience these pulse beats and are able to unite them into a comprehensive rhythm that we will experience the eternal through time. Duration belongs to our true human nature. We can only experience duration if we lovingly, and with inner strength, let the individual pulsations of the eternal cosmic essence become our own experience. (p. 182)

Thus on the very last day of this year of difficult trials—one year before the burning of the Goetheanum—Rudolf Steiner left those who were seeking to work toward a new human community, however modest their efforts may have been, with a challenge, a mighty task: to learn to understand the nature of our age, its needs and possibilities, and to strive toward the light of a cosmic New Year.

The Editors

THE LANGUAGE OF THE COSMOS

Rudolf Steiner

I

COSMIC INFLUENCES AND THE SPIRITUAL TASK OF NORTHERN EUROPE

Lecture One

KRISTIANIA (OSLO), NOVEMBER 24, 1921

As I AM now able to be with you here again, I would like to welcome you in the most cordial and inwardly heartfelt way. You will understand that my words of welcome are even more tinged with special feelings because of the fact that, unfortunately, we were not able to be together for such a long time.[†] I believe, however, that our hearts, as they found each other in looking up to the spiritual worlds, felt nonetheless quite connected in these especially difficult times[†]—even though we were physically separated from each other—and it is out of this common bond that I speak these words of welcome.

It has indeed been a very difficult time we have experienced, a time of undergoing severe tests, and only if it is widely recognized as a time of trial and testing will it be possible for something propitious to emerge from it. I, too, am reminded today of the lectures I was able to give in this city many years ago, before the war, and those of you who reflect more deeply on what was said on that occasion will come to realize that certain definite indications were interspersed in these lectures that hinted at the terrible times ahead of us at that time. And even today I say, quite deliberately, that we have not completely overcome these times, that we are still in them. The lectures I gave here dealt with the folk-souls of the European peoples,[†] and—both as a reminder of them and in order that you may perhaps realize their purport more clearly—I would like, by way of introduction, to relate a certain interesting episode.

In January of 1918, I had a conversation in central Europe with a personality[†] who in the autumn of that year—when the war assumed a particularly menacing form—played a brief but significant part in these catastrophic events. As a matter of fact, those who were able to follow the course of events realized already in the beginning of that year that this particular man would be in a key position when matters would come to a critical, decisive point. As mentioned, I had a talk with him in January of that year and, in the course of our conversation, he spoke of the need for a psychology, an actual knowledge, of the souls of the European peoples; the chaos into which humanity was being thrust would make it essential—so he said—for those who wished to take on a leading role in these affairs to understand the effects of the forces working in the souls of the different peoples of Europe. And he expressed deep regret that there was really no possibility of basing any decisions regarding such public affairs upon an actual knowledge of the European folk-souls. I responded by saying that I had given lectures on this very subject here in Kristiania (Oslo), and afterwards I sent him this course of lectures, which included a foreword written out of the situation as it was at that time—in January, 1918.

I am telling you about this episode merely in order to indicate the real purport of these lectures. They were really meant, at that time, as a guiding orientation in the face of the forces that were leading straight into confusion and chaos. And it was for the same reason that I resorted to them again in the year 1918, in the way indicated. But nothing came of it. It was useless—in spite of the above-mentioned preface written in response to the immediate situation—because the maturity required to develop insight into the magnitude of the forces leading into decadence, although present in a number of human souls, was not present in the souls of those in charge, who were unwilling to strive for such maturity of insight. For today, people are still terribly afraid to place before their souls a true picture of the forces that are leading straight into chaos. Instead of facing the reality of these forces of decadence, they prefer to spin all kinds of hazy notions, believing that if they take refuge in them, life will go on quite nicely. Those, however, who refuse to accept such clouded thinking and confront the true reality of the situation, hold no such beliefs.

It was, in fact, precisely here in Norway that destiny made it necessary to speak of the relationships between the European folk-souls. You will remember that I have made a certain remark[†]—expressed in a variety of forms and either in greater or lesser detail—throughout the years. I have drawn attention to the fact that a time will come in European affairs when much will depend upon whether this northern European region, and Norway in particular, can count among its people those who will, in the fullest sense of the word, sympathize with the side of true progress and devote their powers to furthering this progress—inasmuch as the geographical position of northern Europe renders this imperative and indeed possible. Here in the north, because there is a certain detachment from European conditions, many things can develop and ripen. But what is ripening here must, gradually, develop into fruit—above all things into the fruit of a truly vibrant spiritual life. This is, after all, the reason for the name given to this anthroposophical branch,[†] which was discussed a number of years ago as well.

You yourselves will have had many things pass before your spiritual eye during the years that have passed since we last saw each other, during the years of the great European catastrophe [WW I], but it is something else altogether to be in the very midst of it. Only those who actually lived through it, or at any rate through periods of it, were able to feel and realize its full significance. It is difficult to find a word in our human language that can adequately characterize the awfulness of this catastrophe. One is tempted to use the word "senseless," because it is indeed the case that nearly everything generated in the domain of European public affairs up to the beginning of the twentieth century resulted in some form of senselessness. What went on between the years 1914 and 1918 was a kind of senselessness, and matters have not greatly improved since then. The only difference is that these senseless actions of the materialistic world are not as outwardly noticeable as they were during the actual war-years. Today it ought to be recognized—more fully than it generally is—that Europe is bound to come to grief if people do not consider the spiritual foundations of human life, if, simply for the sake of convenience, they continue to brush aside everything that actually intends to offer help by leading humanity out of this anti-spiritual turmoil.

The fact that my lectures on the folk-psychology of northern Europe were ignored by a person who was in a leading position during this period of senseless actions, seemed to me to be deeply symptomatic. And it is still basically the case today that everything is brushed aside by those holding leading positions in public life. It would be important if people in Europe understood that certain words spoken casually by a South-African statesman† are actually words of great significance for European public affairs. These words were not spoken from any great depth, but more from a feeling for the way in which humanity's affairs are developing at the present time. This statesman said that the focal point of the world-historical perspective has shifted from the North Sea—that is to say, from Europe in general—to the Pacific Ocean. One could also say that the reason for Europe's having held a kind of central position up to now, no longer exists; that today, we are living within its remains; that it has been superseded by the great global affairs transpiring between the East and the West. What is going on today in clueless fashion in Washington,† is nothing but a feeble stammering taking place on the surface, but actually surging up from those depths where—mostly still unnoticed—the important affairs of humanity are occurring.

There will be no calm on the earth until a certain harmonization will have come to pass between the affairs of East and West; however, people do not yet realize today that this harmony must first be brought about in the realm of the spirit. No matter how much is discussed regarding questions of disarmament and other "luxurious" matters in the face of these difficult times—these will amount to no more than luxuries, beautiful words, as long as the western world fails to discover the spirituality that is actually contained, but not sought, in our culture as it has been developing since the middle of the fifteenth century. For this culture does indeed contain a store of such treasures.

Humanity has acquired a magnificent scientific knowledge of the natural world and has achieved marvelous achievements in technology. We are surrounded by it. All of this is truly splendid, but dead—dead as compared to the great currents of humanity's evolution. And yet in this very death there is a sparkle of life, a living spirituality that can shine into the world even more brilliantly than anything brought to humanity through oriental wisdom—which, however, must never be belittled in its own right. This is the kind of feeling that I would like to describe to you, the feeling that is present in an unbiased observer.

One can turn to the great wisdom-treasures of the East, which are contained—albeit merely as a reflection—in the Vedas and in the wonderful Vedanta philosophy,[†] and so on. One can be filled with enthusiasm for everything that was revealed in them, as though from heavenly heights, to humanity. It has undoubtedly experienced a certain deterioration since then, but even in that form, in which it still lives in the East, it arouses the wonder and admiration of anyone who has a feeling for such things.

In contrast, there is the purely materialistic culture of the West—of Europe and America. Yet this purely materialistic culture and its equally materialistic mode of thinking should not be belittled either. At the same time, it must be said that what initially appears to us as materialistic culture does indeed resemble a hard nutshell—a dying nutshell. Nevertheless, it contains the nut, the living kernel; and if this nut can be uncovered, what will then be exposed is something that will outshine all the radiance of the oriental wisdom that once came down to humanity. But let us not misunderstand the reality of the present situation. As long as the dealings of Europeans and Americans with Asia are confined to purely economic and industrial interests, there will be no trust among the peoples of Asia, no matter how many discussions take place about disarmament, about the desirability of ending wars, and so on. A great war between the East and the West is inevitable, in spite of all disarmament conferences, if a particular thing does not occur—if the people of Asia cannot perceive something coming from the West, something that is in fact the spirit of the West. This spirituality of the West can shine for the people of Asia; and if it does, they will be able to trust it, because with their own inherent—albeit somewhat depleted—spirituality they will be able to understand it. The peace of the world depends upon this understanding, *not* upon the international discussions now going on among the world's leaders.

Today, everything depends on the awareness that the spirit, which lies hidden in European and American culture, is the important thing—the spirit from which people flee, which they would prefer to avoid for the sake of ease, but which alone can guide humanity to forces of ascent. But people like to build up foggy notions by preferring to repeat again and again that things will improve of themselves. They will not; the hour of a great decision has struck. Either human beings will resolve to elevate the spirituality of which I have spoken, or the decline of the West is inevitable. No hope, no fatalistic longing for things to right themselves will be of any help in this regard. Humanity has, after all, entered a time in which human forces are used in freedom; and it is essential that humanity actually apply these forces out of free will—in other words, it must now decide for itself whether it wants to have this spirituality or not. If the decision is affirmative, then progress will be possible; if it is negative, then the doom of the West is sealed. Then, in the wake of dire catastrophes, the further evolution of humanity will have to take a different course from the one imagined today by many people. If, however, the wish for true insight into these matters is present, then it is imperative that the soul-life of human beings in general, and of the various peoples in particular, be studied—particularly the soul-life of the peoples of the East and the West.

This is the reason for the preliminary remarks made here. They are based on my firm belief that if those qualities to which the Nordic spirit is especially inclined can be cultivated in this particular region of Europe, then it will be possible for insight to ripen, which, in turn, can also work fruitfully upon the rest of the western world. Indeed, any spiritual movement can only be taken very seriously when people are inclined to credit it, in the sense here indicated, with a mission that includes this kind of understanding.

It is, after all, a fact that our modern civilization regards everything in the universe scientifically, that is, strictly as a matter of mathematics and mechanics. We look at the stars through telescopes, examine their substances by means of the spectroscope and so on; we then convert what has thus been observed into calculations and formulas, and we finally arrive at the idea of "the universe as a great machine" into which our earth is inserted like a cogwheel. We develop fantastic notions about the habitability of other planets, but do not attach great significance to them because we limit ourselves to mathematical-mechanical formulas to express what is contained in the universe. And humanity has gradually restricted itself to experiencing life on earth just as a mole—if it had a human soul—might experience itself within its burrow during the winter. In a manner of speaking, the earth has become like a mole's burrow in the universe. Nowadays, people tend to look back with a certain superciliousness to "primitive" cultures, such as the culture of ancient Egypt, where people did not speak of a "great world-machine" but, rather, of divine-spiritual beings who existed outside in space as well as beyond space—beings to whom they knew themselves connected in the same way as they were connected to the beings of the three kingdoms of nature on earth.

The ancient Egyptians had attributed the soul-spiritual nature of the human being to the higher hierarchies, to supersensible worlds, in the same way as they attributed the human bodily-physical aspect to the kingdoms of nature, to the mineral, plant, and animal kingdoms. In our age, if people speak of extra-earthly realms at all, they do so based on a belief-system that has grown ever paler and would not stand up to scientific scrutiny. Scientifically, people speak only of a great world-machine that can be defined through mathematical formulas, and of anything related to human and earthly matters as something that is supposedly confined within the human and cosmic "mole-burrow"—which is ultimately what earthly existence has now become in relation to the cosmos.

Yet there is a profound truth—one that can hardly be expressed too poignantly—namely this: When humanity loses the heavens, it loses itself. For it is simply a fact that the most important aspect of human essential nature belongs to the realm that lies beyond the earth; and that, if we lose sight of this realm, we lose sight of our own true being. Then we wander across the earth without knowing what kind of beings we really are. And this is basically how human beings today are relating to their earthly existence. We know—but even so, only from tradition—that the designation "human being" applies to us, that this name was originally given to us to indicate a being that stands upright in contrast to the four-legged animals. But our scientific view of the world and our technical culture curb our ability to recognize the true content of the designation "human being"; for this content ought to be derived from the realm beyond the earth, and this realm, this universe, has been turned into a great "world-machine." As human beings, we have lost ourselves; we no longer have insight into the true nature of what it means to be a human being.

It is definitely a painful, but unavoidable, experience to realize that the height of the culture to which the West has risen since the middle of the fifteenth century has actually brought human beings to the point of tearing out their own true nature and wandering the earth essentially as "non-human" beings divested of their soul-spiritual essence.

I mentioned yesterday, in the lecture I gave for the teachers,[†] that we tend to speak rather one-sidedly—and mostly based on tradition—of only one aspect of the eternal nature of human beings. We speak of human eternal nature only insofar as it reaches beyond death, and for that reason we have the word "immortality" (*Unsterblichkeit*, literally, "deathlessness") in modern languages. We do not speak, however, of a human eternal nature reaching beyond birth, of an existence *before* birth. Nor do we speak of how the human being has descended from divine-spiritual worlds into physical, sense-perceptible existence, and of how the human being becomes part of this physical, material existence on earth. As a consequence, we do not even have a word that corresponds, at this other pole, to "immortality." We speak of immortality, but not of "unbornness" (*Ungeborenheit*), and it is only when it will become natural to speak of "unbornness," of a pre-birth existence, that it will be possible to understand again the true, eternal essential nature of the human being.

Why do we even still speak of immortality today? In reality, when the word "immortality" is used nowadays, it is done in a very different sense from how it was done in times when people still spoke of "unbornness." Just listen to the innumerable sermons preached today on the eternal nature of the human soul—and these are sermons that are actually spoken out of a certain subjective honesty—and try to get a clear sense of the prevailing tone contained in them. For they count strongly on the egotism of human beings. They speculate on the fact that we long for immortality; that, because of this egotism, we abhor the idea of perishing at death. They presume that such egotism is present among the faithful. Just ponder the words spoken along these lines on many occasions, and you will realize that they count on this kind of egotism. When it comes to the question of pre-existence, of life before birth, one cannot reckon with human egotism in the same way. When anything is said about a life before birth today, it does not trigger a response from egotistic human souls, because people will say—albeit not always quite articulately—to themselves: Why should we take an interest in a life before birth? For, even if it exists, we are now living in its continuation. We are in existence now! Why, then, is it necessary to speak of what happened before? We are, after all, absolutely certain that we are here now.

Our egotism only lets us entertain the notion that death does not bring annihilation. One must therefore, when speaking of a life before birth, appeal to selflessness, to the quality of "non-egotism." And, when speaking of the life after death—which is, of course, quite valid as well—one can indeed do so by appealing to the egotism of the soul. That is the great difference. This also shows clearly that egotism has indeed gripped humanity right down to the deepest layers of the soul. And the outright dismissal of the idea of a pre-existence is a consequence of the egotism in the human soul.

It is important that these things—more than any other things—be understood by those who are earnest in their striving for spiritual insight. Human beings must find themselves again as regards their true, innermost being. People must become interested again in the whole essential nature of the human being, not merely in the outer, physical sheaths. But this can only come about when the human being will once again be regarded as belonging not only to the earth, to the cosmic "mole-burrow," but rather to the whole cosmos; when it is clearly recognized that between death and a new birth the human being passes through the world of the stars; and when this world of the stars, to which we can only gaze upward from the earth, will be known once again in its living essence, in its soul essence, and in its spiritual essence.

The first thing that appears to us when we observe a human being is his outer, physical structure; but we do not generally pay particular attention to its principal feature, namely its form. And yet, this form is assuredly the main thing when it comes to the physical human being. Now, when we embark upon a theme like this—which, incidentally, touches on many things contained in other lecture cycles—it will be obvious at once that initially only brief indications can be given. But, from what you have already gained from anthroposophy—both as regards its spiritual content and its way of thinking—you will be able to recognize that what I am about to say now is something that represents not merely a series of fleeting analogies, but rather something that is, in fact, derived from a deeper knowledge of the world.

When we observe the human form, we essentially see a marvelous structural organization of the human being. To begin with, we have the human head. It is actually modeled after the cosmos. It bears the form of the cosmos. To begin with, its form is spherical, round. This spherical form is only subject to a certain modification at its base where it is linked to the other components that make up the physical human being—in other words, this spherical form is modified at its base in order to be joined to those parts that do not constitute the human head. In principle, however, the human head is modeled after the spherical form of the universe, as you can observe for yourself even already from the basic shape of the human embryo. Linked to this head-formation we have another structure which—although in a much more hidden and not immediately apparent way—still retains something of the spherical form, namely, the chest-structure of the human being. In this chest-structure—please try to picture this spiritually in your mind—we have something that is like a spherical form squashed and elongated by a variety of other forces, like a sphere having undergone a substantial metamorphosis. And when, finally, we observe the limb-structure, the third component of the human being, we can only just perceive something of the original, embryonic-like, spherical form of the human being. It is only through true spiritual science that we are alerted to the fact that even the limbs still contain certain traces of a spherical form, although this is not very obvious in their outer shape.

When we study the threefold human configuration in its relation to the cosmos, we can say that the human being is formed out of forces coming from the cosmos, but that these forces work upon us in many different ways. Think of the different ways in which the human being is subject to the influences of the fixed stars. Throughout the various epochs, people have viewed the changing position of the sun in the zodiacal constellations as an indication of how different forces are working down from the world of the fixed stars. Even today, our mechanistically-inclined astronomy speaks of the fact that the sun rises in a particular constellation in spring, at the vernal equinox; that in the course of time it will move through other zodiacal signs; that during the day it passes through certain constellations and during the night through others, and so on. But there is no awareness of the relationship that exists between the human being and this whole extra-earthly universe. For example, it is not really known today that when the sun is shining upon the earth from the constellation of Aries in the spring—that is, when the vernal equinox is in Aries—the effect of the solar forces upon human beings is different in certain parts of the earth due to the fact that the sun's forces are modified by the influences emanating from the region of the fixed stars that is represented by the constellation of Aries. Nor is it known that these forces are especially suited to working upon the human head in such a way that, during their life on earth, human beings can develop a certain faculty of self-observation, self-knowledge, and consciousness of their own I.

There is a special significance to being exposed to the forces coming from Aries. As you know, it was particularly during the Greco-Latin cultural epoch[†] that the sun stood in the constellation of Aries at the vernal equinox, and that it was therefore principally during this time that humanity, especially in western regions, was subject to the Aries-forces. This situation—that is, humanity being exposed to the forces coming from Aries—meant that the human head-organization could be developed in such a way that a certain I-consciousness, a certain faculty of self-contemplation, could unfold.

Even when the zodiacal signs are discussed today from a historical point of view, the crux of the matter is not always recognized. Historical traditions point to the signs of the zodiac—Aries, Taurus, Gemini, and so on. Images are shown, but few people know what these things really mean. In old calendars we frequently find the symbol of Aries, but very few people realize the point of greatest significance, namely, that the ram is depicted in such a way that the head is looking back. What this picture was meant to indicate is that the Aries-forces work upon the inner aspect of the human being, as the ram does not look forward, out into the wide world, but rather looks back—that is, toward itself, toward its own being. This reflecting-upon-itself depicted in the figure of the ram is full of significant importance. We must find our way again—and this time in full consciousness, *not* with the instinctive clairvoyance people had in olden times—to this cosmic wisdom. We must come to know again that the forces of our head-organization are predominantly developed through the forces of Aries, Taurus, Gemini, and Cancer; that the forces of our chest-structure are formed through the forces of the four constellations in the middle—that is, Leo, Virgo, Libra, Scorpio. We must come to know again that our head receives its form from the cosmos, through the influence of the forces coming from Aries, Taurus, Gemini, and Cancer; and that, if we want to comprehend the human head-form, these forces must be thought of as radiating from above downward, whereas the zodiacal forces working upon the human chest-structure—Leo, Virgo, Libra, Scorpio—must be thought of as working laterally.

And then, situated beneath the earth, there are the other four constellations—their influences blanketed by the earth, as it were. These four constellations work through the earth, not directly like Aries, Taurus, Gemini, Cancer, nor laterally like the other four but, rather, from below upward. They work in such a way that they cannot sustain the spherical form. These forces work upon the human limbs. The forces of the limb-organization are formed by the constellations which, in the instinctive consciousness of olden times, were envisaged to be working upon human beings in such a way that the earth is situated between the human being and these constellations. The human being stands upright on the earth; and so, when constellations are beneath the earth, they work upon the human limbs. And in these olden times there was still an awareness that the forces which give the limbs their earthly shape have a connection to these particular constellations; that the form of the limbs has its origin in these constellations.

The spherical formation of the head, therefore, was known to be connected with Aries, Taurus, Gemini, Cancer. And it was known that the forces affecting the limbs also worked in a fourfold way [Sagittarius, Capricorn, Aquarius, Pisces]. As this knowledge stemmed from ancient clairvoyance, the terminology used to describe these things also stems from the conditions prevailing at that time. Thus, in those olden times when knowledge was derived from the stars, one person might have been a hunter, an archer; in that case, the constellation that was thought to stimulate the corresponding activity in his limbs, which made him into a hunter, received the name of Sagittarius, the archer. Or someone might have been a shepherd, concerned with the care of animals; in that case, the corresponding activity was associated with the goat, with the constellation that is called Capricorn today—although it is not really a goat, as its symbol contains a fish-tail.† This illustrated the general distinction between the animal caretaker [Capricorn] and the hunter [Sagittarius].

The third constellation in this group was Aquarius, the water-carrier. But if you take a good look at the ancient symbol of this water-carrier, then it becomes clear that it does not show a water-person, in the sense of someone splattering about in water. The true image of this constellation is of a human being walking as though on firm soil, on a meadow or a field, fertilizing it, or watering it from a water vessel. It depicts a human being engaged in agriculture, as it is represented by the farmer. This was the third occupation of these ancient times when there was still an instinctive knowledge about these things—the occupations of hunter, shepherd, farmer.

The fourth occupation was that of the mariner, the sailor. In very early times, ships were built in the form of a fish; and even in later times one can still often see a dolphin's head at the prow of vessels. This is where the symbol of Pisces comes from. In depicting two ships—in the form of two intertwined fish—trading together, it represents the fourth occupation connected to the forces working in the human limbs, namely, the occupation of the merchant or trader.

This is how the human form was derived from the cosmos.† The archetypal form of the head is the spherical form. Here, the human being is directly exposed to the forces of the fixed stars or, respectively, to the corresponding representatives among the zodiacal constellations. Then, working laterally upon the chest-organization—where the spherical form is only present in an eclipsed and hidden way—are the forces of Leo, Virgo, Libra, Scorpio. And then there are the forces that do not work directly upon the human formation but, rather, in a roundabout way, through their influence upon earthly activities, through their affecting the corresponding occupations. Incidentally, the divine-cosmic entity connected to the hunter [Sagittarius] was sometimes depicted as a kind of centaur, half horse, half human being—in other words, half animal, half human being, and so on.

From this you can see—and in our present time we must again develop such insights in full consciousness—how the human being was placed within the cosmos. The form and shape of the human physical body were acknowledged to be the result of cosmic influences. The upper part of the human body was viewed as a product of the cosmos, the lower part as a product of the earth. The earth blanketed those constellations known to affect earthly activities. And we will only be able to comprehend the mysteries of the human form, and its relation to human activities on earth, when we recognize and acknowledge the inherent relation between the human being and the entire cosmos. And, to begin with, this human form indeed leads us to the zodiacal constellations.

Just as it is important for life here on earth that someone is, for example, a farmer—and in this context, only the ancient occupations are represented, but in the following lectures we shall hear how these things apply in our own time—so, in the same way, it is important that we come to realize again that, as far as earthly life between birth and death is concerned, the human being belongs to the powers of the earth; that with respect to life between death and a new birth he belongs to the heavenly powers; and that these powers initially shape the human head out of themselves and then leave it to the forces of the earth to give form to the human limbs.

This is how the human form can be studied. Similarly, we can also study the human life-forms, or life-levels.[†] To begin with, when we observe this life of the human being, we find there the same two poles. On the one side, we have the life in respect to the head and on the other side the life that comes to expression in human activities, particularly through the limbs. In between these two poles lies the aspect of the human being that manifests, and makes itself known, in the rhythms of breathing and of the circulation of the blood. But at these two poles of the human being we have, at the one end, the head-organism and at the other end, the limb-organism.

The head-organism constitutes, for the most part, the dying aspect of the human being; for, in reality, the head is perpetually dying. Our life is only possible because, throughout the whole of our earthly life, forces are continually sent upward to the head from the metabolic-limb organism. If the head were to unfold merely its own inherent forces, it would only unfold death-forces and would be in a state of dying. However, the fact that we can think, that we have a consciousness, is entirely due to this dying-process. At the very moment when an excess of pure life-forces flows to the head, consciousness ceases. For all intents and purposes, life means a dimming of consciousness, whereas death introduced into life means a lighting-up of consciousness. If, for example, only a tiny amount of what is rightly located in the stomach were to find its way to the head, the head would become like the stomach—that is to say, without consciousness. We owe the head's consciousness solely to the circumstance that our head is not permeated with life in the same way as the stomach.[†] A dimming of consciousness means that the forces of nutrition and growth are protruding too strongly into the head. On the one side, we are dying beings; on the other, we are beings who are continually coming to birth. The dying part, which is precisely the part that constitutes our consciousness, thrives primarily when it is exposed to the forces working down upon the earth from the spheres of the outer planets: Saturn, Jupiter, Mars. For, naturally, the forces that integrate the human being into the universe are not only related to the fixed stars but also to the planetary spheres.

Saturn, Jupiter, Mars—the so-called outer planets—contain the forces that work chiefly in the direction of the consciousness-pole in the human being; the forces coming from the so-called inner planets—Venus, Mercury, Moon—work in the direction of the metabolic-limb system. The sun itself stands in the middle and is mainly associated with the rhythmic system. Together, these represent the seven conditions of our life, the seven levels of life.[†] On the one hand, through the life-levels that represent an eradication, a suppression, of life—so that consciousness can come about—we are, with respect to our earthly life, more akin to heaven, akin to the more distant planetary realms. On the other hand, through the life-levels that represent the actual, unbridled life—that is, the forces of metabolism and of the movements of the limbs—we are akin to the inner planets, to Mercury, Venus, Moon. The Moon is, after all, directly connected with what is the most rampant life in the human being, namely, the forces of reproduction. Accordingly, when we study the life of the human being, we are led to the realm of the planets; and when we study the human form, we are led to the realm of the fixed stars—respectively, to their corresponding representatives in this realm, the zodiacal constellations. When we study life—whether it be a more rampant or a more dying life—we are led to the planetary spheres.

And in the same way we can study the soul nature and the spirit nature of the human being. This shall be done in the following lectures. Today, I only wanted to indicate—through this very brief exposition about the significance of the cosmos for the human being—that we must learn again to regard ourselves not merely as earthly beings, not to see our human form and life only in relation to what we encounter here on earth as the forces of wind and weather, of autumn and spring, or as the forces of heredity, digestion, and so on; rather, that we must learn again to relate both our life and our form to what is known to exist in the cosmos. We must find again what lies beyond the earthly realm—then we will find our true being, our self.

It would signify the greatest misfortune for the progress of western humanity if the notion of the "machine-like cosmos"—the product of the scientific world-view that began to develop since the middle of the fifteenth century—were to remain, and human beings were to wander on the earth knowing nothing of their true being. Because of the fact that our true being belongs to realms beyond the earth, we cannot really know anything about ourselves as long as we see only what is earthly and regard what lies in realms beyond the earth only in terms of mathematics and mechanics—as modern science does.

As earthly human beings, we can only find our true self when we are able to link ourselves again to what lies beyond the earth; it is essential that this realm be incorporated into our moral and social life—if it is to thrive. It is for this reason that, in reality, no moral-social wisdom can arise unless a link is forged to cosmic wisdom. This is why it is necessary—and, again, more will be said about this in the following lectures—that some of the things inferred by the science of the spirit, anthroposophy, be presented with respect to the moral-social domain as well; for these impulses can lead from forces of decline to forces of ascent.

Lecture Two

KRISTIANIA (OSLO), NOVEMBER 27, 1921

WE HAVE SEEN how, in accordance with anthroposophical knowledge, the true nature of the human being must be regarded in relation to the whole universe. To begin with, we considered the form and configuration of the human being. This structure had to be attributed to the fixed stars, or rather to the representative of the fixed stars—the Zodiac. We have seen how certain forces emanate from the corresponding star-constellations and, when combined with the influence of the sun, how the forces that give form to the human head and the organs connected with it, are related to the upper constellations of the Zodiac: Aries, Taurus, Gemini, Cancer. We have seen how the forces that determine the form of the human chest-organization are related to the middle constellations: Leo, Virgo, Libra, Scorpio; and, finally, how the forces that lead to the metabolic-limb system are related to the lower constellations—that is to say, to their influences while they are, in a sense, covered by the earth—to the constellations of Sagittarius, Capricorn, Aquarius, Pisces. And so, in summary, we may say that the whole sphere of the fixed stars—for the zodiacal constellations are only their representatives—works upon the human form and structure.

The planetary spheres work upon human life, upon the levels, or conditions, of life. And indeed, we must make it quite clear to ourselves that there are various forms of life within us. We would not be able to think, and our head would not be an organ of thought, if life in our head were as vigorous as it is, for example, in the metabolic system. When metabolism becomes too strong in the head, our consciousness, our ability to reason, is extinguished. It can be inferred from this, even in an outer sense, that a lowered, suppressed life, a dying life, is necessary for consciousness and for the forming of mental images. On the other hand, an intense, thriving, rampant life is necessary for that which works more out of the unconscious in us, for the will.

Accordingly, among the various levels of life within us, we have some that are more of a dying, self-extinguishing kind, and some that are true life-levels, comparable to how a strong, intense, organic life develops in a child, in whom thinking is not yet present. We have this childlike life continually within us; but the other life, the life that is progressively dying, inserts itself into this childlike life.

These different life-levels are regulated by the planetary spheres. Whereas the sphere of the fixed stars works through its physical forces upon the human being, the planetary sphere works through its etheric forces. The planetary sphere, therefore, works upon the human being in a more delicate way. And it is indeed so that the human physical body has received its form, its shape, from the fixed stars, *not* from anything earthly, and its life-levels from the planetary sphere.

In this way, we have considered the form of the human physical body and the life-levels of the etheric body. We can now proceed to a consideration of the soul-life and the spirit-life of the human being. However, here our approach must be different. What is it that our physical body and our etheric body provide for us in waking life? They facilitate what we perceive through our senses and what we can process through our thoughts. For it is only in what our senses perceive and in what we process in our thoughts that we are truly awake.

Contrast this with the life of feeling. It will be obvious, even from a merely superficial observation, that feeling does not signify wakefulness in the same sense as thinking and sense-perception. When we wake in the morning and encounter the colors and sounds of the outside world, when we become aware of the conditions of warmth around us, our fully awake state appears and we process, in our thoughts, what is transmitted by the senses. But when feelings rise up from the soul, it cannot be said that in these feelings we are conscious to the same extent. Feelings are linked and associated with sense-perceptions. One sense impression pleases us, another displeases us.

Feelings also link themselves with our thoughts. Moreover, anyone who compares the pictures we experience in our dreams with what we experience in our feelings will be well aware of the relationship between the state of dreaming and that of feeling.

Dreams must first be grasped by our waking thought-life if they are to be evaluated and understood aright. But feelings, too, must be examined by our thought-life, as it were, if we are to find the right connection to them. In our feelings we are actually dreaming. When we dream, we dream in pictures. When we are awake, we dream in our feelings. And in our will, we are asleep even when fully awake. Just consider the following. When we raise an arm, when we do something, we know through observation what movements the arm or hand is making; but we do not know how the power of the will is actually functioning in the organism. We know as little about this as we know about the conditions prevailing during sleep—that is, from the time of falling asleep until we wake up. Inasmuch as we *will* something, inasmuch as we do something, we are asleep, while at the same time we are awake in respect of our sense-perceptions and our thoughts. Accordingly, we are not only sleeping from the time we fall asleep until we wake up; we are sleeping, in part of our being, during waking life too. We are sleeping as regards our will and we are dreaming as regards our feelings.

What we experience during sleep is concealed from our consciousness. But the true nature of our feeling and of our will is also concealed from our consciousness. It is, nevertheless, important that we also become conscious of what the human being experiences in these unconscious realms, in these realms of which our ordinary life is not conscious.

You know from various anthroposophical lectures that from the time of going to sleep until that of waking, the I and the astral body are outside the physical body and the etheric body. Now, it can be especially important to become familiar with those experiences, in particular, which the I and the astral body undergo from the time of falling asleep to that of waking up. When we are awake, we meet the natural world through our sense-perceptions. One could say that with these sense-perceptions of nature we come to a barrier; that with our sense-perceptions, with our waking thoughts, we reach no further than the surface of things.

Now, someone could of course argue that one could get beyond the surface of things, for example, by cutting a piece of wood—perceptible to the senses—and one would then be inside it. This would not be correct, however, for if you slice a piece of wood, you have once again only a surface, and if you cut the two pieces again, you still have merely surfaces. Even if you were to get right to the molecules and atoms, you would again only have surfaces. You would not reach what may be called the inner essence of things, for this true inner essence lies beyond the realm of sense-perception.

We can think of sense-perceptions as a tapestry spread out around us. What lies on this side of the tapestry we can perceive with our senses; what lies on the other side of the tapestry we do not perceive with the senses. We are in this sense-perceptible world from the time of waking up until the time of falling asleep. Our soul is filled with the impressions made upon us by this sense-perceptible world. Now, when we enter into sleep, we are no longer on this side of the sense-world; for, in reality, we are then inside the things, we are then on the other side of this sense-tapestry. But human beings living in their earthly consciousness know nothing of this and dream up all sorts of things presumed to exist beyond the realm of sense-perception. They dream up molecules and atoms; but these are only dreams—dreams of the waking consciousness. People invent molecules, atoms, and the like, and believe them to be realities. But take any of the studies describing atoms—even the most recent, the most meticulous ones—and in them you will find nothing more than minute objects, described according to the criteria of what everyday consciousness experiences on the surface of things. It is all a fabrication derived from the experiences of waking consciousness on this side of the tapestry of sense-perception.

But when we fall asleep, we escape from this whole world of the senses and penetrate through to the other side. And whereas, on this side, we experience the natural world with our senses and our waking thoughts, over on yonder side, from the time of falling asleep until the time of waking, we experience the world of spirit—the spirit-world which we also go through before birth and after death. However, in this phase of human development on earth, we are so constituted that our consciousness is extinguished when we are beyond the world of the senses; human consciousness is not strong enough to penetrate into this spirit-world. But what spiritual science designates as *imagination, inspiration, intuition*[†] enables us to have knowledge of what lies on the other side of the sense-tapestry. And the first thing we find there is the lowest level of the realm that is called the world of the hierarchies.[†]

When we wake from sleep, we are placed into the world where the animals, plants, and minerals—the beings of the three kingdoms of nature—are, which belong to the world of the senses. When we fall asleep, crossing beyond the world of the senses, we are initially transported into the first level of the beings ranked above us—that of the Angeloi, or angels. And, from the time of falling asleep until waking, we are connected with the being who is allotted to each individual person as his or her angel-being—just as we are connected, through our eyes and ears, with the three kingdoms of nature here in the sense-world. Even if, at first, we are not aware of this connection with the world of the angels, it is nevertheless there. This connection extents as far as into our astral body.

If, while living in the astral body during sleep, we were to suddenly awaken in our astral body, then we would encounter the world of the angels—that is, initially, the angel-being who is connected with our own life—in the same way as, here in the earthly world, we encounter animals, plants, and minerals.

Now, even in the earthly world, in the world of the senses, it is the case that if people are attentive and discipline their thinking, they notice much more than those who are inattentive and observe only in a cursory manner. Accordingly, our connection with the three kingdoms of nature can either be intimate or superficial. And it is the same with the world of spiritual beings. But the conditions are different as regards this world of spiritual beings.

Someone whose thoughts are entirely wrapped up in the material world, who has no desire to rise above this world or to learn to appreciate moral ideals extending beyond the merely utilitarian, who has no desire to experience true human love or to develop a devout reverence for the divine-spiritual during waking life—such a person, on falling asleep, has no forces remaining that would make it possible to come into contact, in the right way, with his or her angel-being. Each time we fall asleep, our angel awaits expectantly, as it were, how much we bring with us into sleep as idealistic feelings, as idealistic thoughts; and the more we bring with us of this nature, the more intimate becomes the contact with our angel while we are asleep. And so, throughout our whole life, our waking life, we gather what we develop in ourselves above and beyond material interests; we gather that which makes the relationship to our angel ever more intimate.

Once we pass through the portal of death, anything pertaining to the senses falls away from us. The outer world can no longer make any impressions on us, for this can only be done through our senses, and the senses fall away with the body. And thoughts that are tied only to sense-perceptions are extinguished, too, for this thinking is contained in the etheric body. The etheric body remains with us only for a few days after death. We see it, as it initially is present, in the form of a tableau—a tableau which [under special circumstances] can be known and seen,[†] but which *must* be seen after death (I have also spoken about this from a different point of view in the public lectures of the last few days).[†]

One can see right away that, as the etheric body's fabric dissolves into the universe, the ordinary thoughts derived from the sense-perceptible world also depart from us. They do not remain. Everything we have thought throughout our life in relation to utilitarian matters, to circumstances regarding the sense-world, what we have thought based on the material world—all this departs from us when we pass through the gate of death. Only what we have cultivated throughout our waking life as idealistic thoughts and feelings, as pure human love, as religious reverence in the truest sense of the word—and have thus united with our angel—this we take with us when we pass through the portal of death.

Now, this causes something very important to occur in the time of our further development between death and a new birth. In fact, even during our life on earth we actually have a relationship with other, even higher, hierarchies; it is therefore correct to say that, as we fall asleep and the ideals we have cultivated penetrate through to our angel, this angel-being, in turn, communicates with an archangel, with an Archai, and so on. Consequently, we find that our existence is carried forward, as it were, into a rich, abundant world of spirit. But this rich spiritual world has no special significance for us while we are living between birth and death. It is only when this world of the higher hierarchies becomes our environment between death and a new birth that it acquires great significance for us. And, the more we have handed over to our angel, as it were, the more can this angel—even after our death when we are beings of soul and spirit—give us of the conscious life, the conscious soul-content coming from the higher hierarchies. One could put it as follows. What our eyes and ears are for us here in the physical world—this is what for our consciousness between death and rebirth in the spiritual world our angel develops, or, actually, what the other beings of the third hierarchy together with even higher hierarchies develop through our angel. And the more we have brought to our angel in the way of idealistic thoughts and feelings, of human love and pious reverence, the more does our consciousness become lighter, the more does it become inwardly radiating.

Now, there is a certain time between death and a new birth when the angel has a specific task in connection with us. This angel-being must establish an even more intimate relation with the hierarchy of the Archangeloi, the archangels, than was formerly the case. I have described the time which the human being undergoes between death and a new birth from the most diverse points of view—for this is certainly possible—most recently in a course of lectures given in Vienna in 1914.[†] Today, I will describe this matter from some other viewpoints.

When a certain, somewhat lengthy, period of time has elapsed after death, an important moment arrives when the angel must, as it were, pass on to the archangel what he has received from us through our above-characterized idealistic experiences. It is as though the human being were placed before the world of the archangels, who can then receive what this individual has cultivated as soul-spiritual experiences of this sort during his or her life between birth and death. This is where great differences become apparent among human beings dwelling between death and a new birth. In our epoch there are persons who bring very little with them in the way of idealistic thoughts and feelings, of human love, when the time comes for the angel to pass on to the archangel—for the sake of the continuing evolution of the world—what human beings have carried through the portal of death.

The interaction developing in this way between the Angeloi and the Archangeloi must, under all circumstances, take place. But there is a big difference in how we human beings experience what thus transpires between the angels and the archangels, that is to say, whether we are able to follow it more consciously, as a result of our above-mentioned experiences, or whether we only undergo it in a dull, dim state—for this is how it must be experienced by those whose consciousness had been focused only on materialistic contents. Actually, it is not quite correct to say that these experiences are dull or dim. It would perhaps be more accurate to say that these human beings experience this in such a way that they feel continually rejected by a world into which they ought to be received; that they feel continually chilled by a world that ought to welcome them with warmth. For human beings should be received with kindness and sympathy by the world of the archangels at this important point in time; they should be received with warmth. Then, they will be led in the right way toward what I have called in one of my mystery plays, *the midnight hour* of existence.[†]

Human beings are led, in turn, by the Archangeloi to the realm of the Archai. And, as we become integrated, as it were, into the realm of the Archai, we are simultaneously being integrated with all the higher hierarchies; for it is through the Archai that we enter into a relationship with all the higher hierarchies. From this realm we receive the impulse, the drive, to descend to the earth again—inasmuch as we receive the power to work once again as a soul-spiritual being in what will later be provided as physical matter by the hereditary stream.

This midnight hour of existence is the point in the life of the human being between death and a new birth which is crossed in such a way that, before reaching this point, one becomes ever more estranged from earthly existence and gradually grows into the spiritual world; *how* this unfolds depends on whether one is received with more and more sympathy (in the sense described above) by this spiritual world, drawn into it with greater and greater warmth, or is actually repelled and chilled by it. But when the midnight hour of existence has come to pass, the human being gradually begins to feel a longing, as it were, for life down below on earth again, and is then, on the second part of this journey, confronted by the world of the archangels once again. For it is really true that, between death and a new birth, human beings first ascend to the world of the Angeloi, Archangeloi, and Archai, then descend again; and, after passing through the world of the Archai, notably encounter the world of the archangels again.

Then there comes again an important point in the life between death and a new birth. If we have carried nothing through the portal of death in the way of idealistic thoughts or feelings, of loving kindness, of true religious reverence, then something of our soul-spiritual nature will have perished, as it were, due to the antipathy and the chilly response coming from the higher world; but, if we arrive in the realm of the angels with the right soul-spiritual attitude, then we will receive, implanted into our inner soul-spiritual nature, the power to work effectively in our subsequent life on earth, the ability to penetrate our body in the right way. If we have not brought along such soul-spiritual insights, the angels will have to implant—but now in such a way that it works more unconsciously—this longing for earthly life. A very great deal depends upon this process of implanting. For during this process, certain aspects of a person's forthcoming earthly life are determined—namely, into which nation, into which language, into which so-called mother tongue this individual will descend and incarnate. What is determined during this process is whether this urge toward a particular people, toward a particular mother tongue, is implanted in a more inner or in a more outer sense—so that, during this descent, a human being either becomes filled with deep and inward love for what will become his or her mother tongue, or enters more automatically into what he or she will later have to express by means of the organs of speech.

It makes a great difference *how* a human being becomes destined for a particular language in his or her next life on earth—whether this happens in the one or in the other way described. If, already before this earthly life, that is, during the second passage through the realm of the angels, our soul can be permeated inwardly, lovingly, with an inclination toward our mother tongue, then we can assimilate it inwardly, take it in as a part of our very being; we become one with it. Then, it becomes a genuine love, becomes a soul-love. And, as we then grow into our language and ethnicity, this becomes something that is absolutely natural. If, however, we grow into it in the other way—I have called this the more automatic mode—then, having descended through birth into our earthly existence, we will arrive on the earth in such a way that we only learn to develop an instinctive, compulsive love of our language. And, what we cannot generate inwardly as love, as natural love for our language and ethnicity—this gets then forced out, as it were, from our life.

It makes a great difference whether we grow into a nation and into a particular language-affiliation with the kind of tranquil, pure love of someone who is inwardly united with folk and language, or whether we grow into a language and a nation more automatically and then, out of instinct and compulsion, as it were, force out the inner love for folk and language. The former disposition will never manifest in what is called chauvinism, in what is a superficial, aggressive form of patriotism; rather, the inner soul-spiritual love for folk and language—gained as a result of previously experienced ideals and devout reverence—will come to expression naturally, and is entirely consistent with true, universal human love. A genuine cosmopolitan or global outlook can never be stunted by this type of soul-spiritual love for a nation and a language. If, however, we grow into our language more automatically, and if—as a result of this—we develop, through our instincts and compulsions, an over-fervid, base, animal-like love of language and nation, then we develop what in reality is a false nationalism, a chauvinistic disposition, with its emphatic stance on race and nationality.

It is especially important and necessary at the present time to look at what we encounter in the outer world (in the time we spend as human beings between birth and death) from the standpoint of life between death and a new birth. For, the way in which we become immersed in an ethnicity and a language—through our being linked to a particular hereditary stream by birth—depends upon how we meet and experience, for the second time, the realm of the archangels.

Someone attempting to understand life today from a spiritual viewpoint will have to recognize the importance of what human beings experience between death and a new birth when they come, for a second time, into the realm of the archangels. Today, we can see how all around the world people view their nationality, ethnicity, and language in the wrong way; and much of what has come to pass in the evolution of the western world with the catastrophic events of the second decade of the twentieth century can only become comprehensible if it is considered from viewpoints such as these. For, if we study the inner aspect of life in the light of anthroposophical spiritual science, then we must recognize that the former lives of many people today were lived in such a way that they became more and more entangled in materialism. You all know that, as a rule, the period between death and a new birth is lengthy. But—and this is especially the case in the current phase of evolution—there are many people who have only had a short time between their last death and their present birth. Already in their previous life on earth they had cultivated little in the way of human love or idealistic sentiments; even in their previous earthly life they were mostly concerned with utilitarian matters. And, as a result, the seeds were laid, during their second contact with the realm of the angels between death and a new birth, for what we see arising today in such an evil form in western civilization.

Accordingly, the human being can only be understood as a spatial being when we recognize that we must go as far as the realm of the fixed stars to trace the origin of the human physical shape and as far as the planetary spheres to trace the origin of the human life-levels; that, as a spatial being, the human being draws the forces working within the body not only from the earth but from the whole cosmos. And, just as it is necessary to go beyond the earthly realm in order to get insight into the human being as a spatial being, so too is it necessary to go beyond the life between birth and death in order to understand human life on earth in its social and nation-bound aspects.

When we study life in its manyfold aspects today, we find that, although people are often emphatically calling for freedom, they are, in reality, inwardly unfree; that there is no free life pulsating through the endeavors that bring about such obvious forces of decline nowadays; that, instead, instincts and compulsions are pulsating there, causing the misery in social life. And anyone observing these things, obviously also will want to understand them.

Now, just as there is a second meeting with the realm of the archangels, so is there also at a later time—namely, when the human being comes much closer to earthly life again—a more intimate union with the angel-being, with the Angelos. And, as one approaches earthly life again, one is pulled back, pulled out, as it were, from the realm of the archangels. As long as we dwell in the realm of the archangels, our angel is also more strongly bound to this realm. One could say that human beings then live within the higher hierarchies. But, as the time spent between death and a new birth runs its course, we come to rely more and more only on the realm of the angels, who then lead us through the world of the elements, through fire, air, water, and earth, to the hereditary stream. For it is this angel-being that leads us to physical existence on earth. Our angel can make us into a human being able to act in freedom, out of the depths of our soul-spiritual being, as long as all the above-mentioned conditions have been fulfilled through our former earthly life.

But, if things transpired in such a way that we had to be united with our language and our nation "automatically," as described above, then the angel is not in a position to guide us to a life of freedom. Then, the individual life also becomes unfree. This lack of freedom shows itself in the following way. If we do not grasp concepts freely but, instead, inwardly merely think words, then, although we will still develop an inner consciousness, we will do so only superficially and, as a result, will be made unfree because our whole thinking resolves into words. This is, in fact, a fundamental experience of people today—that their thinking becomes immersed in words. It is not possible to understand earthly life in its historical development, especially in its present state, unless we advance to the life between death and a new birth, to the world of soul-and-spirit.

And so, in order to understand the human form, we must point to the realm of the fixed stars; to understand the human life-levels we must point to the planetary spheres; and to understand the soul-spiritual life of human beings, we cannot confine ourselves to the period between birth and death, for, as we have seen, this soul-spiritual life is rooted in the world of the higher hierarchies—just as the physical body and the etheric body of the human being belong to the external physical and etheric worlds.

Similarly, in order to understand thinking, feeling, and willing correctly, we must not confine ourselves to considering the human being only in relation to the external world of the senses but also in relation to life between death and a new birth. Thinking, feeling, and willing are the forces through which our soul-being initially develops. And our idealistic thoughts—that which was implanted into our thoughts and into our soul-being out of idealistic love and piety—carry us through the portal of death. The way in which we have influenced our thoughts, how we have permeated our thinking with an idealistic disposition—this is what leads us in the right way to our first encounter with the archangels, with the Archangeloi. But, once we have passed through the midnight hour of existence, our thinking fades away, as it were. For it is this thinking which then, after the midnight hour of existence, is re-molded and adapted for the next earthly life. And, out of this, out of what formerly was our thinking, specific forces are then being formed which will permeate our physical organs of thinking in the coming earthly life.

If you observe the human head and see how forces are working in it, then you will recognize that these are not just the forces that are active in this life. These are the forces that stem from the thinking of a previous life and now give rise to the structure and form of the brain. In contrast, it is notably the *will* which, during the second meeting with the archangels, plays its own special role in the soul-spiritual life of the human being. And it is this will which then, in the next life on earth, takes hold of the metabolic-limb organism in particular. When we then enter through birth into earthly life, the will becomes the factor that makes us either well-suited or less suited for certain functions as far as the metabolic-limb organism is concerned. One could say, then, that within our head we have a physical reflection of what we have developed in our previous life as thoughts; that in the abilities of the metabolic-limb organism we see the activity of the newly acquired forces of will which, during the second meeting with the archangel, are incorporated into us either in an inner soul-spiritual way, as described earlier, or more "automatically."

If we see how contemporary life—which leads to the above-identified forces of deterioration, specifically for people in the western world—has evolved, then we will look with the greatest, ideal-filled interest at what was taking place in human beings between death and a new birth, during the life preceding this present earthly life. And what can be recognized in this respect will then give us—now that the consequences of materialism are manifesting in the life of the nations—the strong impulse to provide human beings who were already too materialistically inclined in their last incarnation, with the kind of motivation that can lead once again to a deepening of the inner life, to freedom, to a true inner (and therefore, natural) connection to language and ethnicity, a connection that does not in any way contradict internationalism or cosmopolitanism.

This, however, can only be achieved if our thinking can be set aglow by true spirituality. What does the spirit actually amount to for modern human beings? Thoughts—thoughts about something. When people today speak of their spirit, they are actually speaking only of their thoughts, of their thinking—which is either fairly abstract, or less so. What we need, though, is true spirit, the living spirit penetrating into our inner being. Anthroposophy is really about this living spirit—in the way it views the world that lies between death and a new birth. What we need today, therefore, is that we regard ourselves—in respect of our human form, our life-levels, our soul-spiritual nature—as belonging to a world that lies outside the earthly sphere. Then, we will be able to bring the right things into earthly life.

We have all experienced how the spiritual essence of human beings is gradually sucked up by various aspects of earthly existence, by political life, by economic life. What is needed is a proclivity, an affinity, for an independent spiritual life. This alone can provide the basis for the human being to be imbued with real spirituality, with spiritual substance—not merely with thoughts about one thing or another. This is why anthroposophy must be willing to work toward a freeing of the spiritual life. If this spiritual life does not create its own firm foundations, then human beings will be living more and more in abstractions; then, they will not be able to permeate themselves with a living spirit but only with a spirit of abstractions.

When here, in physical life, we pass through the portal of death, our physical corpse is committed to the earth, or to the elements. Our true human essential being is no longer within this, our physical corpse. When we pass through birth in such a way that, through the processes described, our relation to nation, language, and to our own conduct has become more "automatic," then, when we are born into the physical world, our living thinking, our living impulses of will, our living soul-spiritual nature die away; and what then emerges is a corpse of the divine-soul-spiritual human being within the realm of physical existence.

Our abstract, rationalistic thinking does indeed hold the corpse of the soul-spiritual. Just as the true human being is no longer within the discarded physical corpse, so do we actually have something like a corpse within a thinking that is abstract, within a soul-life that is not imbued with spirit—a corpse of the divine-spiritual world. Today, humanity really stands at a pivotal, decisive point where it must resolve to accept the spiritual world again—so that the human being can once again penetrate that which has become more or less like a divine-spiritual corpse within the abstract thinking of humanity, that which has yielded once more to instincts, compulsions, and automatism.

And so, you can see the profound inner truth of what I said at the end of yesterday's lecture[†] to the students here: What is needed today, if we are to go forward from a decline to a real ascent, is that human beings overcome the abstractions, the corpse-like elements in the soul—for this is what they may be called—that are prevalent in the intellectualistic and rationalistic thinking of today. What is needed is a kind of reawakening of the soul-spiritual! That such a soul-spiritual awakening is indeed a necessity can be seen from the way our social life manifests, both historically and in its present form. If we understand anthroposophy in a correct and unbiased manner, then we realize that it has a task to fulfill with respect to the human being. It has an eternal task with respect to the enduring principle in human beings that must continue throughout all ages, but it also has a current task in the present age. It must bring human beings back from superficiality, from lameness, from having the divine-spiritual life within them dying off. Anthroposophy must bring back this divine-spiritual life, inasmuch as we must learn to regard ourselves not merely as earthly but as heavenly beings, inasmuch as we learn that our earthly life can only be lived in the right way if the forces of heavenly existence, of the existence between death and a new birth, are carried over into this earthly life.

We will continue these observations next time, in order to bring them to a certain conclusion during these days, which I am able to spend in your midst in a way that is most gratifying for me.

Lecture Three

KRISTIANIA (OSLO), DECEMBER 4, 1921

THE TWO PREVIOUS lectures, which I was privileged to give here once again, covered important observations relating to the nature and destiny of the human being. What had to be considered was that the physical and etheric bodies of the human being are connected not merely with what we perceive here on earth as the external world—that this bodily nature can only be understood if we also recognize its connection with the starry heavens that surround us. We tried to clarify for ourselves how the realm of the fixed stars and the planetary spheres work upon the outer form of the human being, giving it its shape and imbuing it with life. Moreover, we tried to place before our souls how the inner spiritual essence, the individual soul-spiritual core of the human being, can only be understood if we consider it in its relation to the world of the higher hierarchies. We also pointed out that this connection with the world of the higher hierarchies becomes especially noteworthy when we observe how, through our physical life on earth, we can build a connection with the spiritual world in a moral sense, in a religious sense, in the sense of love for our fellow human beings and so on; and how, in doing so, we enable our own angel-being to work in us in a way that makes it possible for our descent to the earth—at the end of the life between death and a new birth—to proceed in such a way that we can acquire the full essence of individuality and, as a free individual, take hold again of our human nature. And it was necessary to point out that if we have not established such a relation to the spiritual world during the previous incarnation—resulting, for example, in a purely external connection to one's nation—then this, in its extreme form, can lead to a more chauvinistic relationship with one's nationality.

We can see, then, from such observations that the life of a human being can only be truly understood if this life is also considered from its other side, that is to say, from the side of the existence between death and a new birth. Whenever we approach the inner nature of the human being, we must consider this life between death and a new birth; for life here on the earth is, in fact, a reflection of the life between death and a new birth. Living in earthly substance means having a bodily existence, and this bodily existence is merely an expression of what we have developed in the world of soul and spirit, before birth. What we must acquire anew, what must be built up anew in our essential being is the will-aspect, and in a sense also the feeling-aspect. The thinking-aspect, which is tied to the head, is what we bring, to a large extent, with us from our pre-earthly existence in the spiritual world—namely, to the extent that our feeling is included in our thinking. Our thinking capacity as such comes into physical existence for us through birth and requires only that it be developed during this physical existence, or be allowed to be developed through education. But what we, in this new incarnation, acquire mainly through interaction with the outer world—namely, the element related to feeling and will—must, for that reason, play the most important part in the field of education.

For all this has a bearing on education. If, as teachers and educators, we fall short with respect to teaching children to think properly, then much may remain undeveloped which, as a result of previous incarnations, could have manifested in these children. If, on the other hand, we are unable to be effective with respect to the realm of will and feeling through our natural authority and our own example as teachers and educators, then we do not provide the children with the things they ought to receive in the physical world, which will have harmful consequences for their life after death. This is precisely what generates such profound pain today in anyone who is able to comprehend these things.

In today's world of education, people insist again and again on the idea that an intellectual understanding needs to be fostered in the child in order to stimulate its faculty of thinking. Although it is true that much of what the child brings along at birth can be exposed by these means, this can only be of real use if the reality of earthly life itself is also offered to the child in the right way—that is to say, if we are able through our example and natural authority to develop in the child the aspects of will and feeling that are not generally recognized. Most of all, we actually harm the eternal life of the child if we do not cultivate feeling and will. Our thinking, which we bring with us at birth, comes to an end here, in the material world; it dies with us. Only what we cultivate through feeling and will—even though this is then, unconsciously, permeated with new thoughts—we take with us through the portal of death. What needs to happen in our present difficult time is that religion, education, the spiritual life, indeed all aspects of life, begin to take into account the eternal nature of the human being—but not from the viewpoint of human egotism only.

Religions today cater unduly to human egotism. On the one side, they encourage inertia by not motivating people to acquire insight into the eternal through their own inner efforts involving their feeling and will; and, on the other side, they foster egotism by speaking only of an eternal life that will happen after death, *not* of the life that existed before birth—or, more specifically, before conception—and has come down with us into the physical world. I have already mentioned earlier that, in order to speak of this life before birth, one would have to turn to the selfless forces in human beings, whereas one is really only addressing human egotism when speaking of the life after death. And this speaking of life after death assumes, by its very nature, an egotistic form in the religious concepts of today. The idea is brought to people in such a way that it, above all, satisfies their yearnings. Once this kind of satisfaction has been instilled in people, resulting in a more egotistical soul-life, the religions believe that they have done what is expected of them. But what must enter into humanity as a whole, through a truly spiritual understanding of the world, is that all of human life should be viewed in a way that is eternal, free of egotism, and be molded accordingly by those who teach and educate our children.

Now, this also has significance in relation to larger, more public circumstances, and I would like to speak of these situations in this third lecture here today. For it is absolutely necessary today that we infuse our actual life situation with what we acquire through anthroposophical knowledge about higher worlds, and that we know how to present it there. With respect to actual life, abstract theories are of little use. Life on this earth is very diverse, full of variety. If, for example, we look at the life of the various peoples with this in mind, it is not only obvious that people from India differ from Americans, or from the English, but also that Swedes are often said to differ from Norwegians, although they live in such near proximity. It is simply a fact that we cannot let ourselves be guided entirely by general principles; that we encounter concrete, individual conditions everywhere and that these must be considered as such. And it is these very conditions, these concrete, individual conditions, that will not be recognized unless we consider them from the perspective of the spiritual. People today do not really know the world. They talk a great deal about the world but do not know it, for they are unaware that this soul-spiritual element extends into physical existence and that it is the spiritual which, ultimately, rules this physical existence. This is why abstract, general principles will not make a difference in this realm. It is true that these abstract principles are often quite correct, but they do not help us much in understanding the world as it actually is.

It is of course principally correct to say, "God governs the world." But it is not of much use, in light of the great diversity of the world, to simply say, "God governs the world in India; God governs the world in England; God governs the world in Sweden; God governs the world in Norway." There is no doubt that God governs the world everywhere, but in order to apply this idea to life in its immediate reality, it is necessary to know *how* God governs the world in India, in England, in Sweden, in Norway. It is necessary to identify—also in the case of spiritual observation—the prevailing, concrete conditions in every case. Of what use would it be, for example, to take people to a meadow, show them a plant with yellow flowers and round petals and merely point out, "That is a plant," and then take them to a plant with thorns and pointy, filamentary petals and say again, "That is a plant." It would be much more meaningful, instead, to explain the specific, distinguishing properties of each plant. But, when it comes to spiritual matters, people have become so easygoing in the extreme that they are quite satisfied with general, spiritual principles and only want to hear, "God governs the world," or, "we each have an angel." They have no desire for detailed knowledge of how life develops in the very diverse regions of the earth, or how its various manifestations have been formed by forces coming from the spiritual world.

The intent of today's lecture, then, is to clarify some of these matters. It is precisely in these tumultuous days—when people all over the world are so utterly at a loss in the face of public affairs, when congresses and conferences take place without producing results, where, in spite of developing magnificent programs, people disperse without having come to any real decisions—it is precisely now that deeper questions should be raised about what is becoming manifest in the various regions of the earth, under the guidance of the spiritual world.

Consider, for example, this peninsula here, which you, Norwegians, share with the Swedes as your earthly dwelling place. You will realize that there is something about it which, in a way, presents a riddle to those who do not live in Sweden or Norway, but also to those who actually live here. There was certainly a great difference in how people here have thought about the tumultuous events going on in the world since 1914, compared to how people in central Europe thought about them. These events have undoubtedly had a dreadful impact in many ways, but people today are largely unaware of their effects; they do not clarify for themselves what kind of hidden forces were at work. You were able to look south from here to central Europe, to southern Europe, to Africa, even to regions of Asia, and you will have observed that these events took their course in a way that went far beyond what you experienced here as their after-effects and reverberations. You will have observed something flaring up from violent, elemental human passions, something that may well have perplexed you here in the North, for it really was as if people had suddenly become crazed with the desire to tear one another to pieces. To those who were onlookers only, these things must certainly have appeared most perplexing, even upon deeper reflection.

But such things cannot be explained by looking only at a single time period—even a period as fraught with momentous events as this recent one. And, although it is true that those who have lived through the last few years can feel as if they had navigated several centuries, it will gradually become clear that the above-mentioned statement is true. Most people today are still living and thinking exactly as they did in 1914. But in countries such as this one here in the North, things can already be understood to some extent. It is terrible that people in central Europe still feel this way. People have undergone these events—and this is only normal—as something that can otherwise only be experienced during a span of several centuries. Everything was compressed into a few short years. You only need reflect on the fact that the events of 1914/15 embraced, within this brief space of time, as much as took place in, say, ten years of the Thirty Years' War.[†] Nonetheless, it is possible to throw some significant light on these events—if they are studied from a much wider historical perspective.

And what you can observe, especially from the vantage point of your northern peninsula, is that things have been happening further south, basically since the beginning of the present age, in which your participation has actually been different from the way in which the people of southern Europe, of western Asia, and also of central Europe have participated in these centuries-long events. One can certainly get an idea of the great contrasts between southern and northern Europe, in this respect, by studying specific time periods.

Think, for example, of the fourth century AD or, more specifically, of the period that reached its zenith in that century. In the South, on the Greek and especially on the Italian peninsulas—and also in the parts of central Europe that were already closely linked with them—one can see Christianity slowly expanding. But something else can be observed as well. Christianity had made its way from the East into the pagan world of Europe and had, during the first few centuries, established itself in a variety of ways in this pagan world. When we consider these early centuries—the first, second, and even still the third century—we find that this Christianity was imbued with an old wisdom, with a wisdom that humanity had inherited from ancient times, and that people tried to understand this Christianity through the so-called Gnosis† and penetrate it with the highest wisdom.

This began to change in the fourth century, exactly at the time when Christianity was expanding further into the regions of central Europe. The Gnostic, wisdom-filled understanding of Christianity disappeared. What could then be experienced was that a writer like Origen,† who still attempted to bring something of the old Gnostic wisdom into Christianity, was branded as a heretic, and that Julian, the so-called Apostate,† who wanted to unite the old pagan wisdom with Christianity, was shunned. In the end, this led to Christianity becoming more externalized with the formation of a politically shaped church, through the deed of Constantine.† What had set Christianity apart, what had been so full of wisdom, what had made people realize that only the highest wisdom could discern its Christian secrets—all this began to take on a less wisdom-filled character in the fourth century. Increasingly, people were called upon to relate to Christianity with a more elementary sense, with a more abstract feeling. Christianity advanced northward from southern Europe. Although it is true that the Christian life that developed between the fourth and the fifteenth centuries in the South, and especially in central Europe, was rich in soul aspects, the actual spiritual element had receded. Gnosis was regarded as something that was no longer needed in Christianity.

What has been described so far should have highlighted some of the events occurring in regions of Europe that lie further to the South.

And so, Christianity was spreading, finding its way into the Greek world, the Roman world, into the life of central Europe; and there, in a certain sense, it was stripped of spirituality. Now think of your world here in the North, say, in the third and fourth centuries, that is to say, in the early centuries of the Christian era. This cannot really be done by means of external history, which does not offer a true account of what was happening at that time. This period must be studied with the help of anthroposophy. A number of years ago we contemplated these things in relation to the European folk souls,† but today we will look at them more in relation to the external character of the peoples concerned.

At the time when, in the South, the situation became such that the spirit was retreating more and more toward the East—that is to say, shortly after the period I have described—the old philosophical schools of Athens were closed† and the last of the Athenian philosophers had to make their way to the East, where they joined the mysterious Academy of Gondishapur.† A remarkable spiritual life was spreading at that time from this academy via Africa and southern Europe toward the rest of Europe, profoundly influencing the spiritual life of later times. It can certainly be said that there, in the South, people were able to look back at what they once possessed as a lofty spirituality; that the mighty event of Golgotha had then come to pass; that, in the first few centuries, this sublime spirituality was still considered necessary to understand the Mystery of Golgotha; that this spirituality had then gradually been displaced; and that the human element had more and more taken the place of what may be called the working of the divine in human beings.

The Gnosis had still been something that helped people become conscious of the fact that there was a divine-spiritual element living within them. This divine-spiritual element then gradually receded and the human element had to emerge instead. In this respect, much has been contributed by the ethnic groups and peoples who took part in the great migrations. Through their migrations toward the South, through their conquests of the southern regions, the Germanic peoples of central Europe—whose souls were, by nature, more inherently bound to the physical—contributed to this repression of the spiritual, inasmuch as they did not understand the old spirituality and brought a more basic human element to the South. And so, the lofty primordial wisdom, which had once existed in human beings, receded gradually from the spiritual culture of the West. And in that same period, when this repression of the spiritual was occurring in the South—that is, in the third and fourth centuries AD—we find that up here in the North, teachings about the Gods were still spreading among the inhabitants of this northern region.

In that period, it was indeed still the case that those who received inspirations in an instinctive way were held in high esteem. These were times that had long since expired for the people from the southern regions. What could still be experienced up here in the North was that people would seek out and listen to certain individuals, men and women, living in solitude in out-of-the-way places. In mysterious ways, through faculties arising from their special bodily constitution, these men and women were able to give revelations concerning the spiritual worlds. Such faculties were an original, natural predisposition in these individuals who worked in this way among their fellow human beings. And as people—large numbers of people—were listening attentively to these solitary, perceptive individuals, they were quite aware, when they went into the huts of these God-inebriated, God-imbued, God-revealing men or women, that it was not really the physical man or woman they were hearing but, rather, the divine spirit itself which had descended and was inspiring such individuals so that they might reveal the teachings of the Gods to their fellow human beings.

It is very noteworthy for anyone observing European history from an anthroposophical perspective to find that, during this fourth century, the spirit gradually was becoming less prominent for the people in the South, and that the human element—which comes to expression in physical, earthly existence—began to fill their souls instead, and became more prominent in comparison to the divine. What is worthy of note here is that, while the people in the South were becoming more and more eager for human teachings, the people in the North were still so constituted—during this same, decisive fourth century—as to be able to receive divine teachings and to feel that the Gods, the beings of the higher hierarchies, were still living among them.

It is therefore important to consider in all seriousness the isolated accounts sparkling forth from the obscure depths of spiritual life, accounts that seem to refer to a time—and this is, in fact, the truth—when the Gods were walking as teachers among the still-childlike peoples of the North. This state of affairs, which could still be encountered in a particular form in the North during the first centuries of the Christian era, had long since passed in the South. But it certainly is remarkable, and very significant, how the destiny of the peoples had been charted in such a way that the people of the North should become the envoys for the people of the South, the bearers of what had been learnt *not* from human beings, but from the Gods.

It is indeed of major importance that the people who primarily belonged to the population of the western part of your peninsula—whose descendants are the Norwegians of today—journeyed toward the West, in a south-western direction and that, as a result of their wanderings, sea-voyages, and conquests, their influence reached as far south as Sicily and North Africa. The sons of the Gods went to the sons of the world, bringing them—in a very specific form—what they had still been able to learn from their Gods.

It is interesting in studying history to consider these migrations of the Nordic people toward the South-West, and to observe how the elements that were still active in the teachings of the northern Gods, flowed in this south-western direction—although, naturally, in a continually metamorphosed form—and had a profound influence on the British Isles, France, Spain, Italy, Sicily, and North Africa. The effects of this influence are actually still perceptible today. At the same time, what was making its way to the North, influenced by the Roman-Latin element from the South, became permeated with the northern element. One could say that whatever remained as an awareness of the divine in this culture-stream coming from the South, manifested as something that had been impacted by the northern teachings of the Gods. It did take on a peculiar character, however, which can only be fully appreciated if one also looks at the eastern side of this northern peninsula—at Sweden.

We only need remind ourselves of a particular fact, namely, how the peoples of eastern Europe turned to the Varangians[†]; how they became impacted by them; and how in the eastern part of this northern peninsula there was more of a leaning toward the East. The effects coming from this peninsula are quite remarkable. What later gravitates more toward the Norwegian culture, streamed toward the South-West, and what later gravitates more toward the Swedish culture, streamed toward the South-East. In all cases, however, this involved the teachings of the Nordic Gods; but they were presented in different ways.

It is a characteristic feature of the peoples who later became the Norwegians that they brought an active element, an element of strength and encouragement, toward the South-West. In this way, the flagging Roman-Latin culture was revitalized and stimulated into activity. One can see the power of the Nordic Gods working in these migrations in such a way that it stimulated the whole life of the peoples and transformed it into a more active one. This can be inferred from many specific details, and it is fascinating to study these things.

But we should also note the interesting nature—perceptible even today—of the East-Scandinavian influences, the Swedish impulses, working in an eastern direction. This is, of course, partly due to the geographical conditions. These geographical conditions, however, must also be reflected in the character of the people, for the human being does not grow out of the earth but is born onto the earth, having come down from worlds of soul-and-spirit; and it makes a difference whether one is born as a Norwegian or as a Swede. Accordingly, it does not suffice to focus only on the geographical conditions; instead, we must investigate further why some souls have the urge to become Norwegians, while other souls have the urge to become Swedes.

And so, these East-Scandinavian peoples streamed toward the East, but wherever they moved forward, they were continuously deflected. Their impulses could not be transformed into action. They were not able to maintain their stand against what was confronting them from the East, first from other Asiatic peoples and later from the Mongols and Tartars, nor against what was coming from the South as Christianity, as the element in early Christianity that leaned more toward the East. This impulse-stream flowed toward the South-East but met with obstacles everywhere and, as it entered into this element, assumed a more passive character.

It is indeed a fact that the countries on the outer periphery were deeply impacted by what was coming from the North. But whereas the impulses flowing to the South from the western half of the northern peninsula turned into action everywhere, the impulses flowing to the East from the eastern half of the northern peninsula were seized by the inactive, more reflective, element of the East, and in a certain way became dulled into inactivity. One could say that, as the Nordic Gods sent their impulses toward the West, they unfolded mostly their will-nature; and, as they sent their essential nature toward the East, they unfolded more of their reflective, contemplative, reasoning nature.

External wars and conflicts are, in fact, merely the physical reflections of what is actually taking place in the way I have just indicated. Abstract theorists, who view the whole world from the standpoint of some theory—and the empiricists of today, proud as they are of their science, are actually the greatest abstract theorists of all, for they never get down to realities and only want to think about things, instead of knowing them from the inside—these abstract theorists will talk about all kinds of characteristics still exhibited in the Norwegians and the Swedes today. It is certainly possible to put forward all sorts of things—and the inhabitants of these northern countries themselves often emphasize the existence of such external peculiarities—simply because people today do not want to penetrate to the depths of human nature to acquire a real knowledge of life. But life must be considered in the way indicated in my two earlier lectures. In order to understand human life, also in its outer aspects, it must be viewed not only from the perspective of life between birth and death but also from the perspective of life between death and a new birth. We must consider those things that do not merely satisfy the egotism of human beings who merely want to have a blessed existence after death and are not concerned about the life before birth because physical existence is more immediately present; we must look at these things not just from an egotistical viewpoint but from the perspective of human life in general, from the perspective of how we can apply in this earthly life what we have brought with us through birth from worlds of soul-and-spirit.

Then we begin to see that there are certain connections in the life of the human being and in the life of whole peoples. But these connections are only revealed when we survey what the human being experiences through many earthly lives, when we include in this overview the periods spent between death and a new birth. Then we begin to see a remarkably special connection, and by developing insight into such special connections we are able to understand what is happening on earth.

In the Norwegians of today, for example, we can still recognize traits that are legacies of what had been developed by the peoples who once migrated toward the South-West in order to activate and enliven the Roman-Latin cultural element with the revelations of their Gods. At that time, something had been developed in the great plan of the world which gave the Norwegians their special character, their particular task. And those who are born in Norway today will only be able to understand their destiny and task in the world as a whole, if they look back with spiritual understanding to the period that caused Norway to develop in this special way at the time when the northern people went on their migratory journeys, their forays, their campaigns of conquest toward the South-West, in keeping with their task on earth. This earthly task sprang from the character of the people who inhabited these countries. Admittedly, this character was very different in those times, but some of it remains as a legacy in present-day Norwegians and endows them with special faculties that have a certain significance, also from the perspective of the eternal life, the immortal life, of the human being.

And in the eastern part of this peninsula, where the Swedish character was developing at that time, one can observe that the old teachings of the Gods were carried toward the East in a special way, which can only be described as follows. One could say that these Gods migrated to the East and encountered people there who had preserved their own religious doctrines in the form of a defined oriental mysticism. Consequently, any revelations arising more out of nature were met with little response in the East, and those who wandered toward the East were destined to lead a more contemplative life.

This, in turn, left a legacy, and this legacy has molded the character of the people. One could say that in order to understand the western and the eastern parts of the Scandinavian peninsula today, we must look back to what these peoples have experienced throughout the centuries, and what they have become today for the rest of the world as a result of these experiences. We have every reason at the present time to think about these things. And it is certainly possible today to grasp in a more elementary way how spiritual forces must indeed be working in the world, in the whole international course of events, in the whole life of the international community, and how the tasks of particular peoples should be understood from the viewpoint of spiritual investigation into the world situation.

Now, if we approach these things with the power of supersensible cognition, if we investigate this relationship between the tasks of present-day Norwegians and Swedes and the course of their historical evolution, then it becomes apparent that there is a remarkable connection. Norwegians have a certain, specific ability, and it does not strictly depend upon whether they have actually been born into a Norwegian milieu. What has been developing in this way can be seen even in the outer world; it can be described by anthropologists, historians, or even journalists. Their statements will be more or less to the point but will not account for what really wells up in the depths of the human soul. For human beings have a mission not only here on earth; once they have passed through death, they also have a mission with respect to the spiritual worlds. And this mission, which the human being has with respect to the spiritual worlds—after having passed through death—develops here, precisely on the earth.

What we experience in the first period following death is an outcome of human development on earth. And conversely, what we experience on the earth in the first period following birth is an outcome of the world of soul-and-spirit. And it is very meaningful to study—with the means available to spiritual investigation in the sense of anthroposophy—the Norwegian people's mission, particularly with respect to the period after death.

Souls who pass through the portal of death, particularly from the soil here in the western part of the Scandinavian peninsula, can—because of their inherent physical folk-constitution and the whole configuration of the brain and the rest of the body—have the destiny to stimulate the other souls dwelling with them after death, in a very specific way. I said, they *can* have this destiny. They can give to the other souls after death something that only the Norwegian folk character is able to impart; for the Norwegian character is, especially at the present time, so constituted that it gets to know certain secrets of nature in a subconscious and inner way—that is, *not* through external, intellectual knowledge but through the kind of knowledge that you develop in your spirit-body-existence between the time of falling asleep and waking, when you are outside in space, without making use of your physical senses.†

When, outside of your body, you experience the spirit in the plant world, the spirit in stone and rock, the spirit in the rustling of the trees and the sounds of the ocean, when you perceive them not with your senses but see them from outside your body, when you walk in their realms between falling asleep and waking up—then you become aware of mighty forces. Then you become aware of the real forces living in the plants, the real forces hidden in the rocks, the real forces in the ocean waves breaking in upon the shore. If you take all this that is the spirit of the roaring waves, the spirit of the sparsely flowering plants on the rocks, the spirit of this entire world-ensemble, if you take everything that this world-ensemble triggers in your souls during sleep—that is to say, if you take the intimate knowledge of nature, which remains completely unconscious to the intellect and the senses—then you have here the element that you can carry into the spiritual world, provided you imbue it with the right kind of devotion and feeling, as I described in the last lecture. And when you then create the right connection between it and the spiritual world, as you are able to grasp it, and develop what I have called the relationship with your angel-being—then you will carry into the spiritual world this unconscious nature wisdom, this concrete knowledge of the spirit of the plants, this concrete knowledge of the spirit of the stones and of all the other phenomena in nature.

Those who have, in a true sense, experienced living their Norwegian life become the inspirers of their fellow souls after death, the teachers of the secrets of nature here on the earth. For in the spiritual world, souls must be taught about the secrets of the earth, just as here on the earth they must be taught about the secrets of the spiritual world.

And if we consider the eastern half of this peninsula, where the influences from olden times are still present in the way I have described, then we find that in those regions a different mission is carried through the portal of death. What souls carry through death into the spiritual world in those regions is not so much what is experienced between falling asleep and waking up but, rather, what is experienced more through the senses during waking consciousness while connecting to the external world, what is experienced in the observation and contemplation of the outer world during waking life, and in a feeling-imbued rational understanding of this world.

But this is actually something which, strictly speaking, only has significance for life on earth. Yet it is precisely when the human being is developing this particular element in earthly life that something very special develops, during this earthly life, in the subconscious realm. I have pointed out to you that even in waking life a certain part of our being sleeps and dreams. The life of feeling is actually only another form of dream life. Inasmuch as we feel, we dream; and inasmuch as we use our will, we sleep. What we know about our will is only what our thinking illumines. But the will that is ignited in the Swedish soul is the kind of will that has less opportunity to penetrate the secrets of nature during sleep. What enters the Swedish soul's will and feeling more unconsciously during the act of perceiving and of rationally contemplating the outer world—this is what is carried through the portal of death. As a result, the souls who pass through death from the eastern part of the Scandinavian peninsula in the way described, actually have the mission to impart to their fellow souls an element related more to the will—exactly the opposite of what these northern peoples from eastern Scandinavia were able to impart to their physical fellow human beings while connected with them in historical times. One could say that this special ability related to the element of will has been developed in the eastern part of the Scandinavian peninsula, first as a primary quality and subsequently as an inherited part of the folk character.

The people of Europe have lived for a long time without asking in a concrete sense what they should actually devote themselves to after death, for they have felt quite content with the egotistical answer: "We shall be blessed." But if the world is not to fall into complete decadence, it will not suffice to merely receive this kind of egotistical answer. It will only be possible for people to lead their lives in the right way if they are willing to accept a selfless answer, when they not only ask: "How will things be after death so that we shall be happy and blessed," but when they also ask: "What am I called upon to do, in view of my particular situation in earthly life?" It is only when people are inclined to treat this question in this way, that they will be able to use their situation in life appropriately and hence prepare themselves for their mission in the right way. Then, it will no longer be difficult to prepare for this mission in this way.

In this sense, the two lectures—or indeed all three lectures—which I was privileged to hold here for you, are all connected. It is absolutely essential, particularly taking into account this special mission, that the spiritual element in the anthroposophical understanding of the world be understood here in Norway. For if you consider that it is certainly a special task to create out of the subconscious life what I would call a natural science for the hereafter—however paradoxical this may seem, it is nonetheless true—then you must prepare yourself here, in your conscious life, by involving your feelings; then your soul must be given the opportunity to fall asleep every night in such a way that it will not be unreceptive to the insights into nature that will be transmitted to it during sleep. But today, human bodies are no longer so constituted that they allow for this process of preparation.

The souls of the northern peoples are, through their ancient heritage, fundamentally suited for the spiritual world. Here, above all, human bodies must be prepared for this through a culture of the spirit. And so, a decisive question arises at this point. It is a question that can be clarified for us by comparing the mission of, say, the peoples of central Europe with that of the peoples of the North.

There is a book that describes the current state of affairs for the people in central Europe. It is described not badly at all—for those who do not accept anything spiritual—by a man who gave no thought to the possibility of a spiritual enrichment of humanity. Oswald Spengler wrote his book *The Decline of the West*;[†] it is a brilliant but thoroughly pessimistic book—even though he did repudiate this pessimism in a subsequent special booklet. Describing the decline of the West can, of course, only be pessimistic. But Spengler is actually speaking of the decline of culture, the decline of something that belongs to the realm of the soul. Without spiritual regeneration, the people of central Europe will suffer injury to their souls. But here in this corner of [northern] Europe, we have the peculiar circumstance that when human beings are injured in their soul, it is not just the soul but, in fact, their whole bodily nature that is injured at the same time. I have to say, though, what good fortune this is! For, if the people of central Europe do not accept the spiritual, then they become less human, then they degenerate in soul. The northern people, on the other hand, can only die in a bodily sense, die out; for everything here depends on the special constitution of the body, as described.

It is absolutely necessary at this time to consider this much-needed influence of a culture of the spirit. Central Europe will degenerate, will become less human, will be heading toward its own decline if it does not let itself be impacted by the spirit. Northern Europe will die out, will suffer physical death if it does not let itself be influenced by the spirit.

And so, seen from the perspective of the northern people, there is a direct connection between what is developed here during physical life and the mission of these northern souls after death. They will not be able to fulfil this mission if they allow their bodies to degenerate, for these bodies are so well-adapted for this mission—provided they are imbued with spirit.

It is necessary today to speak words of such a serious nature, for it is very much in line with the evolution of our age that we speak together of such matters—if we are to take this age, our time, in earnest. And it is for this very reason that I wanted to speak to you this time from the general, personal, human standpoint, to say to you what one says to one's fellow human beings on earth if one is profoundly concerned about the destiny of the evolution of the earth. For those who do not prepare themselves selflessly for an eternal life will not be leading their earthly life between birth and death in the right way either.

This is what I wanted to leave with you, now that we have completed this last lecture, during my time here in your midst. I wanted you to take note of the fact that those who perceive themselves as anthroposophists today should feel that, even as a tiny handful of people in this world, they should indeed apply all their energy to arousing the rest of humanity out of its lethargy and helping it move forward. Those who hate anthroposophy today—and it should be possible to say this among ourselves—hate it because they feel too contented to truly empathize and get involved with the great tasks of humanity, because they are too fearful of what they would have to overcome if they are to reshape their habitual way of thinking and feeling in order to understand something much more profound. This is why we see many a storm of opposition emerging against whatever is happening within the field of anthroposophy and developing as an outcome of it.

You, too, will have to become accustomed to the undeniable fact that anthroposophic spiritual science will be vehemently attacked by people who do not want to move forward, who love to stay with their old routines. And those who let this kind of opposition deter them from developing their own forces are not really grounded in the actual tasks of anthroposophy. When we see how anthroposophy is attacked today from all sides, we could, on the one hand, become apprehensive and fearful and say: "Would it not be better to proceed less forcefully so that the opposition would perhaps be slighter?" It is, however, possible to say something very different. For if, alternatively, we find that praise is doled out by people who in this decadent age hold leading positions, then we could say: "What have we, in reality, done wrong?" This question should really be asked from the anthroposophical point of view. If we are attacked and insulted, then this can generally be explained based on the reasons given above. But if praise were to come from the same quarters, then this would be very unfortunate indeed, for it would mean that our anthroposophical striving is in a bad state! It is precisely because the opponents of anthroposophy today are attacking it, that we can feel reassured—but only, of course, in the sense that we must apply all the more energy in order to accomplish for the world what anthroposophy is meant to accomplish *not* out of personal arbitrariness but out of a deep realization of the needs and tasks of the world.

And it is out of this feeling, out of this impulse, that I would like to conclude our working together here by expressing my deepest, heartfelt thanks for your active and energetic cooperation in everything that had to transpire here with you at this time.

Please rest assured that I mean it seriously when I say that separation in space is no separation to those who know the reality of the spiritual bond between souls. Please rest assured that in taking my leave, I do so *not* to be away from you, but in order to remain together with you. And this is something which I believe you can always hold in your souls, if you consider it desirable and wish this to be the case. You may be quite sure that there are already quite a few people in the world who feel a bond in this sense and who look with love in their hearts toward this region in the North with its very special task—the importance of which can also be keenly sensed in the field of anthroposophic research.

I take leave of you with this love in my heart for those who feel that they truly belong to us, to our anthroposophic movement. May our subsequent togetherness, too, be full of an inner strength and be carried by an awareness that is needed and right among anthroposophists.

II

FATHER-CONSCIOUSNESS AND CHRIST-CONSCIOUSNESS

A Lecture

BERLIN, DECEMBER 7, 1921

WHAT I WOULD like to bring to you today will have a certain connection with what I was privileged to present here last time, and will therefore relate to some of the things mentioned at that time. I would like to speak today of certain materialistic tendencies in contemporary religious confessions, but I would like to do this in connection with a particular aspect of the Christ-question. It is especially in relation to the Christ-question that a whole series of misunderstandings about anthroposophic research emerges, and much will depend on dispelling these misunderstandings, even if this may not do much for those who circulate them out of a particular interest; but for others it might make a difference.

In the more recent phases of the development of western culture, we have experienced a propensity, in various ways, for pronounced atheistic world-conceptions. It cannot be my task today to point out the different nuances of atheism that have emerged, but I would like to draw your attention to something that is basic to any of these atheistic worldviews. It is the failure to look at the actual source from which the idea of a God-consciousness originates. A God-consciousness cannot arise solely from the contemplation of external nature, but rather from human coexistence with external nature, with the sense-perceptible world. It may seem paradoxical for me to say that a God-consciousness in human beings has to arise from living in the world of the senses. But this awareness of God should not be seen as the fruition of a moment, so to speak, but rather as the essence of earthly life from birth to death.

In this life on earth, we experience ourselves, to begin with, as related to nature through the process of heredity. We entered this earthly existence as physical human beings by way of purely natural processes. As we pass through this earthly existence, we recognize that what we were supplied with at birth undergoes a certain development. And then it becomes a question of whether we are sufficiently diligent—naturally, I do not mean this only in an intellectual sense but also with respect to our feelings and our impulses of will, both of which are also meant to come into play and be experienced—whether we achieve a certain conscious awareness of this living together with the outer sensory world in the course of our life on earth.

If we combine, purely out of generally accepted experiences, everything that the world of the senses can give us, then this will never lead us to understand our entire human nature, unless we think of the world of the senses—and what it can become when we participate in it—as being permeated with spirit. No matter how carefully we examine all the mysteries which the outer world of the senses can give us through our physical perception, we could never come to understand the fact that the human being is also placed in this world of the senses. However, since we as physical, earthly beings nevertheless have our roots in this world of the senses—but will never be able to deduce what we are as human beings from our physical components—it follows that, in order to have a sound consciousness, this consciousness achieves its fulfillment with the being of God, or rather with the conception of the divine being.

And what natural science—notwithstanding its great, comprehensive successes—has particularly brought to humanity is the fact that, because it does not want to recognize the spiritual as such within the sensory world, it places the human being outside its comprehensive field of research, as it were. I have described this on earlier occasions when I said: "If we look, for example, at the modern theory of evolution, which is astounding in many respects, then we find that it deals with the human being not as 'the human being,' but rather as the conclusion, the culmination, the crown, of the animal kingdom." If we ask what natural science, as it is constituted today, has to say about the nature of the human being, then—understood correctly—we do not actually receive an answer. Science is really only answering the question: "Which is the highest-developed of the animals?" In other words, it considers the human being only from the perspective of being an animal. In many respects science is right in what it has to say about this topic, but in doing so, it places the human being outside its field of observation, as it were. With the means available to it, natural science is actually unable to answer the question concerning the nature of the human being. As a matter of fact, science can really only understand itself rightfully by stating that this question about the nature of the human being falls outside its domain.

It can obviously only be an indication of a specific feeling that arises from the entire makeup of a healthy human being—especially insofar as we understand ourselves to be related to the whole of nature—when it is said that the human being must, in fact, come to a God-consciousness, although initially only to a consciousness of God, not to a consciousness of Christ.

Now, it is actually not possible for someone using sound intelligence and healthy feelings to be an atheist. I already referred to this on an earlier occasion when I said: "Even if it is obvious that not every mild illness can be diagnosed with the usual available means, it is nevertheless clear to anyone who can distinguish between health and illness in human beings, that atheism can, to begin with, only become entrenched when the whole human nature has an unhealthy predisposition." It can therefore be said that denying God is actually the outcome of ill health. But what is really occurring in this respect is the following. In the present stage of human evolution, we come to this God-consciousness only in what I would call a wavering, doubtful way—if one looks at it from a wider context; for here it becomes important to draw attention to a significant deficiency in our current pedagogical methods, a deficiency which, for example, the Waldorf pedagogy[†] is trying to correct.

Whenever the decline of our present civilization is discussed, one cannot really overlook today's youth movement. This youth movement is more important than one usually thinks, and I actually consider it extraordinarily significant that at a number of recent events of our anthroposophic movement, including the last Stuttgart

Congress,† a considerable number of people belonging to the youth movement were present and, at that time, actually made the very positive decision, also seen from the perspective of the youth movement itself, to join forces with the aims of our anthroposophic spiritual endeavors.

Think what you may about certain aspects of this youth movement, but it needs to be acknowledged that for large numbers of our youth the authority of the older generation, which should provide leadership to young people, has faded. Even if there is much to criticize about today's youth, one cannot dismiss the fact that when these young people begin to say that they can no longer accept authority in what comes to meet them, then it is not only the youth who are to be blamed for this but, rather, the older people who ought to give them this guidance. Recently, during a lecture I gave in Aarau, Switzerland,† this very question regarding the lack of authority among today's young people was discussed. And then it happened that, after the lecture, a representative of a religious confession stepped forward and ranted about the youth of today.

But this kind of grumbling does not achieve anything with respect to what is actually emerging here with such elementary force. One needs to understand these things. It was interesting that, after this happened, a young lad from one of the local schools—comparable to a secondary school—stood up and gave, in my opinion, the best counter speech. He stepped up with great enthusiasm and said: "We want authority, we actually long for authority, but when we look at the old people, do we see anything besides the fact that no authority can come from these old people at all? We see them feuding at every opportunity, always at loggerheads." And then he listed all sorts of things that young people today notice about old people, and finally he said: "We thirst for authority, but we are not able to find it!"

If we evaluate what is really taking place, however, then we will find that today's civilization has become intellectualistic to a high degree, that basically everything that sets the tone today and considers itself to be the definitive authority has become intellectualistic, rationalistic. Strictly speaking, science and rationalism belong together. Natural science comprises what is objective, rationalism what is subjective.

But this rational culture, this intellectualism, emerges in a natural way only at a certain age. As a child, one cannot be rationalistic at all. Children are not intellectuals. Intellectualism can actually only arise after sexual maturity. And since humanity has completely descended into intellectualism, everything is dominated by it today. And those who repeatedly reject and scold intellectualism today, often do so all the more based on a different kind of intellectualism.

People laying claim to intellectualism today are abstract thinkers. But one can, in reality, only descend into intellectualism at a later age, and because we become so submerged in it, the children no longer understand us and have no use for the thought-forms we adopt while under the influence of intellectualism; moreover, we ourselves no longer have a sense of what we absorbed when we were children. Childhood is no longer fully alive in us. We have become so terribly clever intellectually that the child in us no longer plays any role for us. But we cannot be educators if we have been thoroughly abandoned by what we experienced as children. Consequently, we no longer know what to say to the children, and they grow up without any special care of their essential being. We proclaim that we must be transparent, but transparency is only the objective side of intellectualism. By doing this we create a chasm between us and the young people, and this is what confronts us in the youth movement. But again, nothing is accomplished by simply scolding intellectualism. For it has entered western civilization as a necessary phenomenon in the last three to five centuries, actually since the period spanning the thirteenth to the fifteenth century. This intellectualism had to develop so that humanity could really enter into the impulse of freedom. Accordingly, it is not a matter of merely criticizing this intellectualistic impulse. Rather, it is a matter of understanding this impulse in the right way so as to be able, through such understanding, to strive for continuing development in a direction different from the intellectualistic one.

And now we must ask: "What is the real meaning of this intellectualism?" An indication of this was actually already given through the fact that one can point to the connection between intellectualism and the sense of freedom. And this feeling of freedom, in turn, cannot be thought of without the whole development of the human I. The development of the I has evolved in a specific way in modern times and now works on the I through the consciousness soul. That is, in essence, what appears as the impulse of modern western civilization. But this I, which human beings have become fully conscious of over the past three, four, five centuries, can initially only develop from the human body. The experience of the I between birth and death can only arise from the human physical body; this can be verified especially through anthroposophic spiritual research.

One of the most important moments of the whole life after death is the moment of dying itself. This moment of dying is of course only known to the earthly human being from its external aspects. The inner aspects of it must be recognized out of the consciousness which the dead themselves have between death and a new birth. Exactly how soon after death this emerges is not our concern at this point. Today, we want to consider from a more general point of view the consciousness of a human being between death and a new birth. This consciousness is entirely dependent on the fact that the human being receives an extraordinarily significant impression at the moment of death. Just consider that during the whole life between birth and death, we only leave our physical and etheric bodies—with our I and our astral body—in the state of sleep, so that during life between birth and death there is a constant, uninterrupted connection between the physical body and the etheric body. In death, we leave the physical body with our etheric body—as you know, we remain together with our etheric body for a number of days—so that we have this experience of our full physical body only at the moment of death.

If one wants to have knowledge of something, there is no other way to acquire it than for the object of this knowledge to be outside of oneself. You can only have knowledge of something that is outside of yourself. You cannot see what is in your eye, only what is outside the eye. Neither can you see anything in a soul-spiritual sense of what you have within yourself. You must first go outside of yourself with your soul-spiritual being; then you can see the external aspect of your body. This is what happens at the moment of dying with respect to the separation of the etheric body and the physical body. In falling asleep, we never really have a conscious, complete view of our physical body and our etheric body. These two remain behind when falling asleep. It is for this reason that, when one attains a seeing consciousness during sleep, one can only see the human head and part of the torso and not really the human limbs during ordinary sleep. It is only in death, in dying, that the moment arrives when the human being encounters himself, in terms of his physical body, as a whole, complete object; and for the entire time between death and a new birth this impression remains as the last thing, one might say, of the aspect which a human being looks back upon after death. The human being observes this moment of dying; for we would not be able to recognize the I in relation to ourselves—in other words, we would be I-less—if we were not able to see this I as an object by virtue of the fact that what we are conscious of here in the physical world, namely the physical body as such, is now in front of us as an object of knowledge at the moment of dying.

This tremendous impression—the fact that we can say to ourselves: "What you experienced at the moment of death is what your I-consciousness made possible for you, namely, to see your whole, complete physical body!"—this impression remains and forms the content of the I-consciousness between death and a new birth, where everything becomes temporal, where in a certain sense the spatial is no longer there. The human being looks back from that particular point after death and sees this significant moment as the last thing of this whole perspective—its course continues, but the rays cross at the moment of death—namely, the moment of dying! This is what then works after death as "time organism," one might say, in the same way as our spatial, physical organism provides the I-consciousness between birth and death. Accordingly, we can say: "The I-consciousness here in earthly life actually comes from the physical body."

What is involved here is the following. You look out into outer nature through your senses. You see the three kingdoms of nature, the mineral, the vegetable, the animal, and also the physical human kingdom. You see clouds, rivers, mountains, stars, and so on. Everything you see in this way can be considered "nature," and what you see also supplies the elements that are absorbed by the human organism, both the physical and the etheric. With your food, you absorb the substances of the physical-sensory world. These substances unfold their physical and chemical forces and functions, even when they are in the human organism. One could say that, in terms of our physical organism, we are what we ingest from external nature. Minerals, plants, animals are permitted, if I may put it that way, to be "nature." They have the right to be nature. But when that which is contained in them is absorbed into the human organism—as food or through respiration, for example—then it becomes something other than nature. Then it becomes something in the human organism that can be described by saying: If the human being is to remain human, then what exists as nature is actually not allowed to remain nature. Nature entities only have the right to be "nature" outside of the human being; within the human being, nature becomes a destructive element. There, it becomes something which continually aims to dissolve and which also generates forces in the realm of the soul that work toward destruction.

What the ancient, instinctive human consciousness perceived in this sense was far more correct than what modern-day intellectualism perceives. Today's intellectualism takes its start from concepts, not from facts; and when the facts do not agree with the concepts, it reinterprets the phenomena in accordance with its concepts. Nowadays, people do not say that plants, animals, and human beings have an end, but rather that one should investigate death. People do not really consider the fact that the end of plants, of animals, and of human beings might well be something completely different, something that cannot be summed up under the common concept of "death." And if one draws attention to such things, then the world considers this grotesque or paradoxical. This is how things are evaluated today. But that would actually be like saying: "A knife is a knife," and then proceeding to carve a piece of meat with a razor blade because, "a knife is a knife"!

Nowadays, when people believe that they have both feet firmly planted in reality, it becomes a question of recognizing that reality cannot be attained with abstract concepts. This is something that intellectualism—which has concepts as its starting point, instead of facts—does not take into account. Hence, it also does not realize that the ancient people, speaking out of older forms of consciousness, were justified in saying that nature—in its activities and its processes—no longer has the right to remain "nature" once it enters the human being and continues its existence there; that, instead, it must be transformed; and that, if it wants to retain its validity as nature, it becomes "sin" in the human being. People no longer look at the concept of sin in connection with natural phenomena. They do not consider the bridge between the natural world and what is rooted in the human being as the soul-spiritual element. The animals, plants, minerals have the right to be "nature" outside; but what enters the human being from these kingdoms must be transformed by the human being, for if it were to remain nature, it would be transmuted into something destructive. In other words, if it enters purely as nature and the human being does not have the strength to transform it, then it becomes *illness*, and, inasmuch as it expresses itself in the soul, it becomes *sin*.

Now, if we are unprejudiced in contemplating our relation to the sense-perceptible world, if we truly observe ourselves, if we account for everything that can be taken into account in this realm, then we must come to the following realization: When I look out at nature and initially consider how I have developed out of it, then I cannot be an atheist. On the other hand, however, it is precisely as a human being today, as a human being of more recent times, that I must ascribe my I-consciousness only to my physical body, to nature as it exists within me.

What has been described here in thought-form is indeed present, as a perception or a feeling, in every healthy person who is not afraid of developing self-knowledge today. If we really observe our own inner self, instead of avoiding this out of fear or convenience, then we will experience a predicament that can be expressed in this way: "If I regard myself as a being of nature, as proceeding from nature, then a divine being must be at the foundation of the whole world, to which I also belong." But in reality, this healthy sense is at variance with the present-day development of the I, because this development can only arise from the nature-based existence of the physical body, and—as I have already described—through the impression that dying makes on the human being. And so, the inevitable consequence of this is that the modern human being must, quite instinctively, develop doubts regarding an awareness of God, *not* because something in the observation of nature would lead away from a God-consciousness, but because the human being of today—as a unitary being comprised of body, soul, and spirit—can actually not be entirely healthy, as a result of the I-consciousness. For, nature—if it remains as it is within the human being and then affects the soul—implies something that will cause illness, and, on the soul level, something that has the effect of straying, of sinning.

One should, of course, not view these things in a dogmatic way, but it is important to be mindful of the facts and of how they are revealed in life. In this context this means that, if we go back to ancient times, when the I-consciousness was not yet present, the divine being—regardless of how it was pictured—was always imagined based on a Father-concept. People could not imagine the divine being in any other way than as a unified God-being, who embraced all or part of the world, and whom they sought to grasp based on the Father-concept. And since the I-consciousness was not yet present, since it can only arise from the nature-based aspect, there was nothing that could interfere with this Father-consciousness. As modern human beings we can actually only have this Father-consciousness if, conceivably through moral strengthening, we nonetheless subdue our I and thus bypass something that *must* occur through the development of freedom along with the development of modern humanity. This is why, as human beings living today, we can actually not be content with the one consciousness, the Father-consciousness. We must say: "I would in fact have this Father-consciousness today if I were still able to live instinctively, as humanity did before the feeling of I became stronger. But as a human being of the present time, my I-consciousness impedes a full encounter with this Father-consciousness, because I am no longer in a state of dependence."

As modern human beings we can indeed experience what occurs in this respect—inasmuch as we think about the I, and are aware that the I is extinguished when it is not tied to the body. In falling asleep it is extinguished; in death it is able to sustain itself only because it views the body in dying. As human beings we know that it is actually our I-consciousness that leads us away from having an awareness of the divine Father. We must, however, experience this as something unhealthy, and if we experience it in the right way as unhealthy, then an impulse will arise in us that guides us to Christ, as he is present today. A Son-consciousness will have to arise from our inner soul experience to add to a Father-consciousness. This Son-consciousness can only enter us through an act of freedom. And we must indeed come to the following realization: Just as atheism is, in reality, a manifestation of illness, so is what may be called agnosticism regarding the Mystery of Golgotha—and specifically agnosticism regarding the ever-present Christ—a misfortune, a blow of fate! We can actually not be completely healthy when the Father-consciousness has forsaken us—and in this respect modern humanity is, in fact, not completely healthy—but if we want to come to Christ, then it requires an activity, a free deed, of finding the Christ-spirit-being.

Two experiences are absolutely necessary. To begin with, the consciousness with respect to the Father; but it must be realized that in the present phase of human evolution this awareness of the Father is dimmed, clouded. If we had not acquired our I-consciousness in the course of human evolution, the awareness of a divine Father would be there; but, because the I-consciousness actually wells up—*must* well up—from that which, left to itself, is sick in the human being, the awareness of a divine Father is clouded for people in the present time. And we must come to an awareness of Christ through a free deed, which is different from finding the Father.

As I had already indicated here on an earlier occasion, these two experiences are not distinguished from one another in western civilization. One will find, however, that it is particularly Solovyov[†] who, out of a different kind of consciousness, strictly distinguishes the Father-consciousness from the Son-consciousness. In the West, the distinction between the two is so miniscule that a typical portrayal, seen by many as authoritative, regarding the nature of Christianity could even state: "The Son does not actually belong in the Gospels, only the Father—the Son only insofar as he is a teacher about the Father."[†] Consequently, there is no awareness that people can have two spheres of experience: one with respect to the Father—an experience that is clouded today—and another one with respect to the Son. Now, if one has this experience of the Son, one would initially only experience an encounter with Christ as he exists today, and anyone can have such a present-day encounter with Christ—with the eternal Christ, as it were—resulting from the subjective relationship as it exists today. However, if one rejects this present-day encounter with Christ and instead lives with a dampened awareness, as humanity did in earlier times, then one will not attain the inner disposition that leads to an encounter with Christ. But if a person really senses what is possible in our time, then he or she will come to this inner deed of meeting Christ and, through that very deed, prove that Christ is here.

However, it is still necessary to study the historical Christ; but then it becomes important to be able to look at history from a different perspective than the one available to the outwardly focused consciousness of today, in this age of materialism. Here, I must draw your attention to something that should be strictly observed. The fact that light can be shed on the higher worlds is usually taken too much in an outer sense. People are still not listening carefully enough to realize that a person speaking of the higher worlds must, in fact, speak in a different style than someone speaking of the physical world—that is to say, not just in a different outer style, but in a different inner style.

When we live here in the physical world and let this world have an impact on us, we distinguish with our present-day consciousness—using what one might call logical reasoning—between right and wrong; we also may call it true and false. And we check, based on reasons that are logical and grounded in reality, whether something is right or wrong, true or false. But this is precisely how we get into abstractions, into an intellectual mode of life, because all logical distinctions as to whether something is true or false are driven by abstract concepts *if* observations and investigations are based only on external sensory perception. The process of cognition moves in abstract concepts; but this kind of abstractness with respect to concepts cannot be maintained when we ascend into the higher worlds. There, everything becomes much more alive, and also appears as something that is alive, rather than as something that has merely been thought.

For this reason, a person observing the higher worlds should not only speak of true or false, right or wrong—one must of course do that too!—but should speak, for example, of something that is correctly reflected in the physical world as healthy, and of something that is incorrectly reflected as sick. Even with respect to the lowest level of the higher worlds it is by no means correct to speak of true and false, for in this world everything is concerned with things that are healthy or unhealthy, wholesome or unwholesome. Therefore, if people, with a view to abstract logic, are speaking about the higher worlds in the same way as they would speak of the physical world, then it is obvious that they do not have a real perception of the higher worlds.

Now, something very remarkable arises as regards the historical development of humanity. If we take an unbiassed look at this history, we find that it shows ancient epochs filled with wisdom; and if one has a sound sense, one will develop a feeling of deep reverence for the primordial wisdom of these older epochs. If we look, for example, at what is reflected in the Vedas, in the Vedanta philosophy[†] from the perspective of its origin, then we will recognize that it has indeed been drawn from, and revealed out of, such deep wisdom-based foundations that we must have the deepest reverence for it. Then we approach this primordial wisdom of humanity in a different way than the abstract scholarship of today is able to approach it. But this primordial wisdom gradually dwindled, one could say, as humanity advanced in its development; and we find that the dulling of this primordial, wisdom-filled consciousness of humanity culminated in the period during which the Mystery of Golgotha took place.

It is not really necessary to take account of anything that is contained in the older external records, insofar as these records—for example, the Gospels—describe the Mystery of Golgotha verbatim. We only need to take an impartial look—but now from a higher perspective—at the historical development of humanity, and we will find that the further back we go, the more we see this primordial wisdom becoming increasingly obscured in the human soul. What eventually came to full expression in the fifteenth century had already been indicated in the Greek and Latin-Roman era. Essentially, all that humanity still had of this primeval wisdom was traditions; this wisdom was no longer experienced, and what we see increasingly emerging instead is full I-consciousness. In this respect, our external science has not discovered much of what especially needs to be studied about this era, which is also the time in which the Mystery of Golgotha occurred.

Tremendous predicaments arise today when we consider, for example, the Greek alphabet, where the letters still have names (alpha, beta, gamma) and—tracing its development through later times—the Latin alphabet, where letters no longer have names. Such transitions, which point in a profound way to historical phases of development, are not generally considered at all. For example, no attention is paid to what our word "alphabet," which is still taken from the Greek, actually means. If one looks into this—and a true science of linguistics will be able to investigate these things—then it will emerge that, essentially, the same reality is expressed with the Greek "alpha" as is pronounced in the Old Testament with the words: The human being was infused with the breath of life[†] and that, therefore, this breath must be seen as the element which, in the beginning, made the human being. If you examine the word "alpha" in the right way—and it is actually a word—then you will find that it is "the human being"! The first letter of the alphabet is nothing other than the word for the human being. And "beta" is the house; therefore, the beginning of the alphabet means "the human being in his house."

This view of the alphabet has been lost in later times, as intellectualism became more and more established. From then on, the letters were only used as a way to distinguish external things. What was contained in the revelation of the primordial wisdom became dissociated, the "word" of the primordial revelation became externalized, and people no longer understood what was revealed to humanity in the letters, that is to say, in the words. There is a lot of talk today, in the traditional Lodges and Orders, of the "hidden, secret word," but humanity knows very little of what was contained as a reality in this secret word; how the alphabet itself actually expressed the hidden word; and how it then became atomized, fragmented.

I could, of course, also begin with something else in order to show what a profoundly decisive impulse was driving evolution at the time of Greek and Latin culture. The way Greek culture, with the help of a special art form, sought to lift itself above what I would like to call this unhealthy state arising in humanity—this is palpable for anyone willing to see. I would like to draw your attention to one thing in particular.

Today, when people talk about drama, for example, they think that this is something to look at, something that belongs in the domain of life's luxuries. People watch it and then call it beautiful. But for the Greeks, the most important element in the drama was the idea of catharsis, of cleansing, of purification. This was something that signified not only an external, fantasy-filled event, but one that clearly points to its medicinal origin. Catharsis is the crisis that is overcome, and in the Greek tragedy the soul was brought into a crisis in such a way that, by experiencing fear and pity, it underwent a purification as it was exposed to the effects of these contrasting forces in the course of the drama. The Greeks did not think of this art form in a banausic sense at all, but rather as of something with definite healing qualities, for they still perceived an ancient wisdom governing it. For them, it still was filled with a healthy primordial wisdom which, however, dwindled over the course of time; and then a disease process of sorts arose. With this art form, the Greeks wanted to express more or less the following: There is something in humanity that is in need of healing. Nietzsche, incidentally, had an inkling of this—one can read about it in his book *The Birth of Tragedy from the Spirit of Music.*[†]

The Therapeutae, the Essenes,[†] always assumed that there was something in humanity that was in need of healing. And if the Mystery of Golgotha had not come to pass for humanity, if our lives were such today that I would have to speak without a Mystery of Golgotha having occurred, then I would only be able to describe a humanity affected by a disease process. This means that something about the Mystery of Golgotha is clarified for us when we apply the terms "healthy" and "sick" to the history of humanity. The important point here is that, even if you were to apply all concepts relating to right and wrong, you will come to a point in the course of development where you will have to look at things differently. For, once you come to the Greek epoch, you are coming to a time when a disease process entered humanity and health could only come from the Mystery of

Golgotha. The Therapeutae pointed this out and said: "This is where the great Therapeut emerges, the Savior[†] who, in the literal sense of the word, has to heal humanity."

It is simply a matter of delving deeply enough into the course of human evolution; of not staying with the usual abstract concepts but, rather, approaching historical life with the aid of medical concepts, according to categories of "healthy" and "sick." Then we will understand the need for a healing process and will also understand how the Savior [the Healer]—this word means nothing other than "the Therapeut"—intercedes for humanity. Then we will understand that something had to intervene in the evolution of humanity, which could not be accomplished through the forces that were present in humanity at an earlier time. A new impulse had to come from extra-earthly realms for the healing of humanity.

This is how one can look at the historical development and this is, in fact, how one *must* look at it if, without heeding the content of historical records, one focuses strictly on the configuration of the development of humanity. Then one comes to the concept of an extra-earthly Christ, who connected himself out of extra-earthly regions with the evolution of the earth through the Mystery of Golgotha. This way of looking at things must come into effect if one wants to understand history. If people do not want to adopt this way of observing—observing according to the concepts of "healthy" and "sick"—and apply it to the evolution of history, then they will have to acknowledge that history remains incomprehensible to them. They will not be able to understand what once lived in the East and how it passed over to Africa and then developed into the Greek-Roman culture.

We view the Greek development—correctly—as an exceptionally healthy one. Why? Because the Greeks had a sense that it was necessary to battle diseases and that they wanted to organize their lives accordingly. And with respect to this feeling—the sense that there was something that needed to be fought—there was a particularly remarkable harmony among the individual Greek personalities. On the other hand, the situation of no-longer-having-this-sense and of moving more and more toward abstractionism—which turned even the gods into an abstraction—became the peculiar characteristic of the Roman civilization and remained so. Europe was influenced by Romanism until the fifteenth century, after which the cosmic Christ began to enter human consciousness; before that, it was Romanism that carried Christ to the West.

I wanted to offer these few remarks here today so that we can gradually come to understand what actually stands before us in the Mystery of Golgotha and that we should not just focus on what developed from ancient times up to the time of the Mystery of Golgotha. If one proceeds in this way, it will become clear that there really is no longer any difference between what certain theologians put forward in their teachings about Jesus and what a secular historian, such as Ranke,[†] maintains; that one can no longer distinguish between what certain theologians say about the Jesus story and what a man like Ranke, for example, says about it. All this should really be based, however, on the realization that Christ as an extra-earthly being united with Jesus of Nazareth, who was born as a human being in the course of time. It is precisely at this point that something arises which has led to the greatest misunderstandings with regard to how anthroposophy must, of necessity, approach the Mystery of Golgotha.

It was an inherent part of all ancient instinctive wisdom that it did not separate the spiritual from the physical. For if these two are separated, then, in the case of the physical, one comes to an impossible concept of matter, and, in the case of the spiritual—that is, how human beings experience the spiritual—one actually comes to abstractionism, to a lifeless system of concepts. It became emblematic only of modern humanity to separate the material and the spiritual from one another in this way. And so, anthroposophy guides us to understand again how we should regard nature as a whole, or one could say, how we should look at it as a physiognomy, for we look at a physiognomy in such a way that we think of it as ensouled. We "read" from it that it is permeated with soul. This is how it used to be in the primordial wisdom, and this is how the light-imbued newer wisdom today also leads us again to a physiognomic beholding of the starry world, for example.

This then leads to something that allows us to approach Christ as the sun-being—which does not mean, however, that Christ is the physical sun-being, just as a human being is not a physical bodily being. And it is only in this way that we can understand how something extra-earthly could have dwelled in Jesus of Nazareth, who lived in Palestine. But this idea is cloaked in extreme misunderstandings, especially among theologians. People even find it "insulting" that anthroposophy connects Christ with the sun and with the external cosmic world in general. Why is this so? It is actually quite characteristic. Anthroposophy calls attention again to Christ's connection with the sun. But to these people the sun is, after all, merely a burning nebula-ball out there; hence, it is offensive to associate this burning solar nebula-ball with Christ. We know, however, that theology has become materialistic and can therefore only regard the cosmos as a material world. Anthroposophy, on the other hand, shows how this material world is permeated with spirit everywhere. But, because theology is unable to detach itself from the material, it feels offended when anthroposophy speaks of Christ as a sun-being. It is from this kind of materialism, from a profoundly materialistic view of the world, that this particular point of our Christology is considered offensive.

Here you can see how materialism digs its way into everything. It has especially taken hold of theology; and because theology has become materialistic, it contributes to misunderstandings of this type regarding anthroposophy. Coming from the ordinary world one can only be a materialist, and if anyone states that Christ descended from this world, then this can only be understood in a materialistic sense—and that is insulting. It is important to point out in this connection that our whole culture is becoming materialistic, but is afraid to acknowledge what really lies at its foundations. However, if we want to move away from this decline toward a new ascent, then we must look at these underlying foundations without bias, fear, or apprehension. We must get away from the very thing that has brought European and western humanity in general into this downward slide, which has led to these terrible catastrophes. The only suitable way to achieve this is through knowledge, fearless knowledge of everything that human beings can learn about the world. And it is also necessary, when ascending into the higher worlds, that we determine in an unbiased manner which aspects of the realm of intellectualism are really not suitable.

There are many people today who still say: "What is communicated about the higher worlds is rather strange; one cannot understand it unless one actually enters these worlds oneself." But this is not correct. People believe this to be the case because they accept only those concepts that apply to the physical world, concepts we have between birth and death. For example, there is a prevailing belief today—precisely because everything is developed from concepts, despite the fact that people consider themselves to be inductive and empirical—that it is absolutely possible to convey the complete, ultimate picture.

We must of course say that when the human being falls asleep, the I and the astral body leave the physical and etheric bodies and that the individual remains unconscious until he or she wakes up again. These words describe what is the normal, healthy situation for humanity today, but they do not apply to humanity's evolution as a whole. If we look back, for example, specifically to those times that gave rise to the Indian and the ancient Persian cultures, then we find that there was a different idea underlying everything—the idea, namely, that the human being, when falling asleep, descended more deeply with the I and astral body into the physical and etheric bodies than was the case during the day when awake. The ancient Indians did not say: "The human being withdraws with the I and astral body from the physical and etheric bodies when falling asleep," although the theosophists want people to believe that the Indians would have spoken like that. Instead, what they really said was: "When people fall asleep, they actually descend deeper into their physical and etheric bodies."

And this is essentially quite correct, for this situation is indeed comparable to someone endeavoring to say, in an absolute sense: "As far as the earth is concerned, the sun rises in the east and sets in the west." But this is not actually the case, because for the other half of the earth the process is reversed. And even though one might call it east and west, the directional relationships are different. In the same way, it is absolutely a fact that, during a certain time period, the I and the astral body went down more deeply into the physical and etheric bodies and that, as a result, the experience was quite different. It is for this reason, too, that the ancient Indians expressed themselves quite differently, because they were embedded in a different kind of consciousness, one which today's human being is not fully conscious of either, namely, what governs the rhythmic and metabolic functions. We are not conscious of these processes. To our human consciousness today, the situation is such that we are in a dream state with respect to the rhythmic functions, and in a sleep state with respect to the metabolic functions.

This is why the following can be said: It should be quite understandable that certain things which, according to some people today, can be spoken of in an absolute sense, were actually experienced very differently by people at different times; and that we can only understand the historical development if we let the facts speak about these things, *not* the concepts we might have construed for ourselves. At the present time—when West and East, Occident and Orient, are facing each other in such a fiery manner that a compromise must be found—it is important that humanity be able to explore these backgrounds. Failing this, there may be as many Washington conferences[†] as people wish—they will end in nothing, if the basic impulses of humanity's development are not addressed. People still do not really believe that today; but it is true nonetheless that we must look into what motivates humanity in its innermost being, if we want to move from manifestations of decline toward an ascent. What is required here may well appear to be impractical today. But when it comes to the truly impractical—which has turned out to be such, became even more impractical between 1914 and 1918, and still is today—people do not realize how impractical it actually is. But in addition to all this, we must also learn to recognize how a religious consciousness can also be illuminated and deepened through the anthroposophic way of looking at things.

Today, I could only describe one of the paths leading to the cosmic, extra-earthly Christ, and how it can be found. But you will be able to see how a deeper understanding of history can then develop from this, one that regards humanity as a living being. And, just as we generally speak of health and illness with regard to a living being, so must we also speak of health and illness in the case of humanity, if we want to get beyond materialism. People cannot say that it is difficult to find their way to Christ if, clearly, the corresponding paths are not followed. A concrete, reality-based contemplation of history aims to follow the path to the Mystery of Golgotha from the most varied perspectives. Today, however, since people cannot come up with valid reasons against spiritual science, they use anything possible to denigrate those who carry spiritual science: they become personal. And it is—I truly say this without resentment—a dreadful sign of inner poverty in those who turn against anthroposophical spiritual science today, that they decline to show an interest in spiritual science; that they only ever traipse around it from the outside; and that they, for example, portray the Christ event and the Christ experience as though anthroposophy were rationalizing the mysterious aspects, as though it were dragging the very thing that should be approached with pious reverence down into the sphere of ordinary rationalistic knowledge.

Just give some thought to the following. If a human being stands in front of us and we look at him, then it is not as though the mystery, which every person is to us, were to be lost just because we do not only hear things about him but can also see him. If the individual human being cannot be evaluated with rationalistic concepts, then how much less is this the case of the very event that appears to us as the highest meaning of earthly evolution: the Mystery of Golgotha! The mystery is not lost because we are led to a perception of it; and anthroposophy aims to lead from what is only communicated, or believed, to what becomes understandable through observation. Nothing is taken away from what constitutes the mystery. The mystery is there, but it should not just be "discussed"; rather, it should be put in front of a perceiving humanity.

This is how the critics talk around the subject today, instead of entering into what is actually contained in the anthroposophical literature itself. It is not necessary to go into everything that comes from this side, but there should be a strong awareness within anthroposophical circles that, as the anthroposophical movement expands and asserts itself, it will be met by a proportional increase in hatred. What we have achieved so far already contains strong bits for the opponents; but you can be assured that this will still be outdone in due course. And even if eurythmy is being criticized once again, as it has been in the last few days,† then it seems to me that we should say to ourselves: "In reality, there would only be reason for worry if praise were to come from this side." For then I would have reason to ask myself: "What should we be doing differently?" This is what should become a natural, healthy feeling in anyone who wants to be part of the anthroposophical movement in the right way.

What I have presented to you today is, in a certain sense, an expansion of what I was privileged to discuss the last time I was here.† There is, of course much more that can be said, but what I have indicated today should also help bring you a little further in the field of Christology.

III

THE HUMAN BEING AS AN EARTHLY AND COSMIC BEING

Lecture One

DORNACH, DECEMBER 12, 1921

When we initially survey the historical development of humanity, it shows us what we have spoken of earlier. We see a descending line from the primordial wisdom which was there in the beginning and which had been accepted instinctively by human beings. This wisdom had at first had an invigorating effect on humanity but had become much weaker around the time of the Mystery of Golgotha. This was then followed by an ascending stream of evolution, the one in which we are standing at present and which had its beginning with the Mystery of Golgotha, as has also been described already on previous occasions. What is important now is that we recognize what initially emerged as inner characteristic of the historical development, and then correctly assess how it applies to our own time, in which we stand at present and which we must understand.

There are many diverse phenomena in our time. They live in the feelings and perceptions of human beings and one can even say that, in a certain sense, they make people healthy and sick, but also that people are not aware of them and do not connect them in the right way with the great principles of development. We must direct our attention to these phenomena of our time, because the health of many things in the present and future evolution of humanity depends on this.

A number of things could be mentioned here, but today we want to emphasize one thing, namely, the difficulty we have in establishing a proper understanding with young people growing up today. This is, after all, also the basis of our anthroposophical pedagogical endeavors—this difficulty we have as human beings, as adults, in communicating with young people today. We see a distinct youth movement developing today. As children approach the age of sexual maturity and somewhat beyond, they acquire a life of sensations and feelings which is extraordinarily difficult for adults to understand, and which is even more difficult to deal with in a real sense. We see how downright agitational tendencies arise among the youth, how rebellious sentiments assert themselves against all parental or educational authority. But if we actually look at all this with an unbiased mind, then we can by no means deny the justification for much of it. We should maybe come to realize that there is something living in the developing human beings today that has lost its connection not only with external life but also with what manifests as inner life in the adults.

Nowadays, these things affect some single-minded persons in such a way that, once they have become aware of them, they simply begin to rant in a strange way. They may not always mean it, but they begin to rant that today's youth have lost all sense of authority; that they have almost become like rebels; that they defy anything that older people consider reasonable; that they are not obedient. These are all things that make life today appear hopeless and futile. And it is especially among teachers, among that part of the teaching staff who would like to keep the old routine going, that such statements are frequently heard. But these things can only be understood by recognizing certain impulses in the development of humanity.

Since the fifteenth century we have seen humanity developing in the direction of intellectualism, toward an intellectual understanding of the world. We are not always aware how strongly we actually live in this intellectualism today, how we are viewing the world in a purely rational way, a way that is becoming more and more abstract. And even though people always believe that they take their overall starting point from experience, from reality, from practical life, they actually base everything on concepts, on definitions, instead of on the facts. People think they have understood something when they have formed a concept of the object in question.

People speak of death—I have often mentioned such examples—and of how they understand it. Death, even if it sometimes occurs in a very complicated way, is viewed as the end of a being, of a specific form. When this form dissolves, when it no longer holds itself together, then people say that it is dying, and they form a concept that is meant to answer the question: "What is death in reality?" And then they apply this concept—which may certainly have been defined carefully and neatly—to plants, to animals, to human beings. They say, "Plants die, animals die, people die." But the fact that this disintegration of the inner cohesiveness may well be something completely different in plants, in animals, in human beings is not taken into account, because people get engrossed in the external side of things. This situation can be compared—I have often mentioned this example—to someone who states that a knife is meant for cutting meat, but is then handed a razor blade and uses it to cut the meat, because, "A knife is a knife." This is more or less how we deal with the concept of death, life, and similar topics today. We live in abstractions, in intellectualism. This is especially noticeable in scientific life, where people do not start from facts, but rather from acquiring concepts, from generating definitions.

Now, the capacities that are needed to be able to develop such a life of concepts actually only emerge around the fourteenth, fifteenth year, with puberty. It is almost impossible—provided we look at life impartially—to speak of children as though they already had the capacity of understanding the world intellectually. Children simply cannot think about the world in a way that tends toward the abstract. A completely different life develops within the soul of the child, for the child brings with it developmental forces, inner creative forces, from its life before birth, from the life between death and a new birth. These forces work—above all, in the first seven years of life, but also to a somewhat lesser, although still significant, extent until puberty—on forming the physical organism. And during the whole time that the physical organism is being formed in this way, it is completely impossible for the human being to attain the stage of pure intellectualism.

In the course of its development, humanity has increasingly reached the point where everything that we receive from the world, everything that is taught, comes in the form of intellectual concepts.

One could say that we are given these "soul garments" in such a way that we can only grow into them when we are fourteen or fifteen years old. It is only an illusion when we say, for example, that we let ourselves be guided by what we observe in children. What we then develop for the children based on these observations is something that they really only grow into when they are fourteen or fifteen years old. The result of this is that in today's adults there is no living connection between what actually exists as soul-life after puberty and what was there before. People really only remember in an outer sense what they experienced as a child. They do not immerse themselves in the experiences of being a child. They do not immerse themselves in these childhood experiences in such a way that they rejoice inwardly at the joys experienced as a child, or become intensely sad about the adverse events experienced. People actually forget their childhood—not in an intellectual sense, but in terms of feeling and will—and consequently are not able to look back to childhood in a living way.

But the child itself does not yet have a capacity for intellectualism, because within the child there are forces that are still working on the organism. Consequently, children actually constitute a completely different type of human being, and it is therefore impossible for adults to really understand children. The teachers talk to the children in a way that makes them, as teachers, appear terribly clever; but the children are wise. The teachers are clever and the children are wise, and the cleverness cannot understand the wisdom; it cannot build a bridge between the one and the other. If, with our cleverness, we had to do everything that children accomplish within their inner organism, then we would obviously not be able to manage it at all.

Jean Paul[†] rightfully said that we learn far more in the first three years of life than in three years of academic studies. Anyone who went through an academic experience with an open mind and then looks back on the early years of childhood accordingly, knows that this is absolutely true; for the three academic years focus only on cleverness—let us just call it that—in any case, they do not involve wisdom. But the years of childhood, especially the first three, really flow in wisdom. In those years, wisdom is at work in the human being, even if it remains in the subconscious; but wisdom is working upon the human being.

And even though it subsides later on, it is nevertheless still there and leads then to what we are experiencing today: the rebellious feelings of young people toward adults. We can really only understand this situation if we look back to earlier times when things were different. And it was certainly very different in the period of human development that extends into the fourth post-Atlantean epoch. I would like to describe a little bit how different it really was.

Take the ancient Egyptians of earlier times, or those belonging to the Chaldean stream of humanity—they did not experience the mineral nature as we do. They experienced this mineral nature quite differently. When they saw the common ground below them, they still experienced this as relatively neutral; but they had already a different, livelier, experience when they saw a mountain range or when they saw a river flowing. Something altogether alive then stirred in them. And through this, they received knowledge from the external world about the things that they actually needed to know of that world. They felt, when they saw a crystal, for instance, that the crystal was telling them something, that it was revealing a secret of nature to them.

Today, however, we are compelled intellectually in the direction of mineralogy, of crystallography. We are encouraged to learn all sorts of things about edges and angles and the like. There is nothing wrong with this, but it cannot be compared with what human beings used to feel when they looked at a crystal. In those days, elemental beings actually spoke to them; people felt that they were not alone in the world, that there was something within nature that spoke to them—notably when they turned to the plants. True, people experienced the grass all around them more or less neutrally, but they had a distinct experience when they saw, for example, a henbane plant on the side of the road and walked by it. Henbane has a specific shape; today, children are introduced to the specific form of this plant by their teacher, or by a botanist. This way of dealing with things is grounded in the intellect; and whenever this intellectual approach is taken, one remains more or less neutral with respect to almost all plants. One may well experience pleasure, and an aesthetic perception may come about, but the very vivid, living experience that used to ensue in earlier times does not set in. For in those ancient times, if someone—say, an Egyptian or an ancient Chaldean—had walked by a henbane plant, then that person would have turned pale, would have become a little bit pale. If people had walked by a foxglove plant, a digitalis plant, then they would have blushed; and in passing by a *Colchicum autumnale*, the autumn crocus, they would have felt their skin becoming tighter. Hence, people did not wander through the world indifferently. They felt as though they were participating, through their blood circulation and—as it may be called in today's language—through their nervous system, in those things that come to expression in outer forms. Theirs was a living participation in nature.

And particularly when people saw an animal, they had a very intense experience of the form of the animal, an experience that encompassed their whole inner life of sensations. Hence, they understood nature very differently. They understood it directly and with their whole being. When they saw a snake, for example, they felt in their whole organism something like a compulsion to wriggle and to escape in soul from those things that were unpleasant to them. Everything that is expressed in the Bible with the words "the snake was the most cunning animal" (Genesis 3:1) became an inner experience when seeing a snake. The mineral kingdom spoke to the human being from outside. The animal kingdom spoke in such a way that this speaking was tantamount to experiencing[†] the form of the animal.

All this has vanished from humanity, and what arose instead was a feeling of having been cast out from nature, a feeling that nature had closed its windows. People could no longer look out through them into nature; they stood there, isolated and alone. This is inherent to the natural development of humanity. What ancient humanity experienced in nature is still very much present in children as a longing, a need. It would be good to pay attention to how children are asking and what they actually ask. They do not ask in such a way that our present-day intellectual answers really correspond to their questions. These are, in fact, not suitable at all. So, the child will often feel unsatisfied. And if we then encounter children who do feel satisfied with the intellectual answers to their questions, then this must be seen as something that is arising particularly in today's educational system that is lopsided and flawed—to the detriment of the ongoing development of humanity. For, if the child shows itself satisfied with our intellectual answers, then this is really the result of a certain coquetry that is developing in the child. In reality, the child does not feel satisfied at all when given today's usual answers, and we are only training it to feel satisfied time after time; but in doing so, we actually make the child inwardly untrue, inwardly coquettish. It then flirts with this satisfaction. This shows us that there is something living in the child that is similar to what all of humanity once had in ancient times as an experience of living with the cosmos, an experience that has been dulled by the intellectual soul-life of the present time. If things were simply to continue as they are today, then the gap between adults and children would only get wider and wider.

A well-known progressive firebrand[†] once wrote an essay, much resented, about "revolutionizing" children. That was long before the war—at a time when people were virtually demanding that children should be revolutionized. After all, if everything is to be revolutionized these days, why not the children too? However, if all this takes place without understanding the essential nature of the human being, then it can only lead to great harm; it will, in fact, lead to the greatest harm. It needs to be realized that, although the intellectual development—the development toward abstractionism—was necessary for humanity, it nonetheless has dislodged the human being from nature. It must be recognized that we grow up today by satisfying our heads through the development of the intellect, and that the rest of the human being—especially the whole life of the soul, which works very strongly in the subconscious—is left unsatisfied. This is evident to those who are able to observe the whole human being—and particularly the sleeping human being—with the means available to spiritual research today.

To a certain extent, a sleeping human being today does not at all have access to what he or she actually needs. As human beings today we are deprived of this because, from the time of falling asleep to waking up, we do not only sleep physically, as indeed we should, but we also sleep with our soul in a certain way. In the case of the earlier human beings, circumstances were such that they would wake up in soul while falling asleep. Of course, this did not pass over into ordinary consciousness, but their souls awakened in such a way that they were aware that certain forces in their surroundings—because they were then connected with their surroundings and no longer with the body that had been left behind—that certain forces were absorbed through their consciousness which could not have been absorbed by their ordinary consciousness. These forces are lost to the human being today. We stand in the outer world, and yet are not in it with our soul. We are no longer able to blush when we look at the purple foxglove; we can no longer turn pale when we look at the henbane. We can no longer feel in such a living way how fortunate a person was to have been born near oak forests, because of the fact that oak trees pour forces of courage into human beings, as was the case with the ancient Germanic tribes. These things should not be grasped merely in the abstract, as we do today when we tell the stories again, when we speak in a rather common way of how the old Germanic tribes loved the oak trees. This is how nondescript it really is when we tell such things today, because we do not understand at all how the oak tree affected these ancient people; how it could happen that a seventeen- or eighteen-year-old boy, when he had encountered certain forces of an oak tree during the process of waking up, experienced that he had no choice but to unbend his knees, firm his thighs, and straighten his neck; and how this could be something that was self-evident to him.

Please, do not misunderstand this; I am not implying that we should aim for this again today. There can be no question of such a thing, because if we wanted to train ourselves in that way, then it would be unnatural. It is simply something that has disappeared from humanity, something that no longer exists. But we should recognize that a longing for it is still present in the subconscious life of the soul, that this need is still there.

So, what did the ancient people say in encountering nature? They said: "I was born"—of course, this is not what they literally said, but it was there as a feeling—"I was born; what lives in me is rooted in the stones that speak to me; in the plants that cause me to blush or turn pale, or to straighten myself, and so on; in the animals that fill me with inner strength or weaken me: I have my roots in them. This is where I will be received again with my soul, when my body falls away from me." It was the kind of feeling which, let us say, a plant could have when it blooms. If it were possible for a plant to develop a soul-life when it blooms, it would say: "I must now let my fruit develop the seeds; and that is the last of me, there is nothing more for me; I have to let my leaves wither and in due course let them drop down." And after that, if the plant were able to develop its soul-life, it would turn to the earth in gratitude and say: "But the earth is there, it takes up my seeds and fosters them. And there, I live on." This is approximately how the ancient human beings felt toward the whole of nature. They did not just derive their soul-existence from physical heredity but knew that they were rooted in all of nature. And inasmuch as they knew themselves to be rooted in all of nature, they also knew that they would be re-absorbed into all of nature, when their bodies had fallen away from them. They looked at the whole of nature in the same way as the flowering plant looks at the earth receiving its seeds. This world, which the ancients experienced all around them, actually no longer exists. This world has died; it is dead. And there is an underlying, elemental feeling in modern human beings—even if it is not understood—that they feel cast out from nature.

And now we want to put something completely different before our souls. Let us picture an initiate in the fourth post-Atlantean epoch, who was initiated into the beginning stages of intellectual life. What for us today is our normal intellectual life was for the fourth post-Atlantean epoch in a sense the result of a special initiation. There were certain initiations whose aim it was to lead the human being to an understanding of intellectualism. Such an initiate was actually led to the ultimate consequence of intellectualism, whereas people today are stopped by the fear of intellectualism and do not pursue it to its actual consequence. But these initiates were brought to the point of understanding it. In these ancient times, circumstances were such that human beings experienced the soul in all of nature. With respect to their own soul-life they lived in such a way that they knew that in death, the soul of the cosmos would receive them again.

However, a tragic mood already held sway over many initiations of the fourth post-Atlantean period, and the initiates of these particular mysteries had actually lost all hope as regards nature. They no longer expected anything from what nature could reveal to human beings. They said that nature had stopped speaking to human beings; that nature had stopped receiving human beings in death; that a completely different world would have to come, so that human beings could have renewed hope with respect to their life of soul. And it was made clear to these initiates that if they looked at nature, they would not find anything in it that could possibly give them such hope. They were instructed to look at nature and see that there was nothing in it that could redeem the soul aspect of human beings—as happens with regard to the physical aspect, which is governed through heredity.

These initiates learned to recognize that wisdom takes on an intellectual form. In our own time this is a triviality, but these initiates learned to know how wisdom was changed into an intellectual form. And this is what created a tragic mood in them; this is what made them feel hopeless. For there was one thing which the old initiates came to experience in full consciousness—they knew that wisdom is not just something that lives abstractly in the human being; that wisdom is light in human beings as they think or create images inwardly. For the initiates knew that what lives in the inner human being as images is the same as what in the outer world is the light that enlivens everything. "Our concepts cannot create light"—this is approximately what these initiates said to themselves—"therefore they take on the form of death; and this is why our concepts are dead." And what made the wisdom of a large part of the mysteries of the fourth post-Atlantean period so tragic was the realization that human wisdom can no longer be light—that it becomes dark in human beings, because light is a creative element, and the abstract thought is uncreative, is dead.

And now let us picture such an initiate who was schooled entirely on the basis of this view—namely, that there can be no solace for human beings again unless they can be convinced, as the result of a decisive event, that wisdom can shine again; that wisdom can become light again; that wisdom is not dead but, rather, is something that can be seen outside too; that wisdom can become light.

This is the solace, the consolation, that became Paul's[†] when he experienced the event at Damascus (Acts 9:1–9). Only then did he understand the Mystery of Golgotha. Only then did he understand that, through Christ, something has come into the world which cannot only be thought, which actually shines, which has the power of light again—that is to say, a creative power. And from then on Paul knew that, although nature has died for human beings, Christ is now on earth with his power. He has penetrated the earth. And humanity can now find in Christ what it formerly found in nature. This was the great experience of Paul at Damascus. And that is when he understood that human beings had lost nature as a consolation; that nature had become something aesthetic for them. But then Christ appeared. Christ—understood correctly—provides what previously had existed in the whole complex of the "speaking" minerals, of the plants that caused people to blush or turn pale, and of the animal realm that triggered billowing desires to ripple through the inner human being. A spiritual cosmos has united with the earth. The power of the sun, which previously appeared to human beings in minerals, plants, and animals, now is present in a moral sense. It is present for the inner experience. The kingdom of heaven has come nearer.

Much is discussed today regarding interpretations of what Christ proclaimed—that the end of the earth is near, that a new kingdom is arising. Those who understand this in the sense of grain growing five-fold in the fields, and grapes growing five times as big on the vines—we know that it has been interpreted in this way—do not actually understand the real meaning. They do not understand that what had existed purely as nature is now being permeated with the essence of Christ's descending to the earth. This is what was revealed to Paul through the event of Damascus. And so, we have to recognize that this second world—a second, completely new, world—has come with Christ. This new kingdom is more than just an abstract notion, as people frequently understand it; rather, it is a whole new world, a world which, if properly understood, will provide again what nature had previously provided.

Intellectualism can only laugh when we speak of the fact that there are gnomes in the minerals—which is actually just another way of expressing what I mentioned earlier when I said that the minerals "spoke" to human beings—or that there are undines in the plants. If people can no longer turn pale or blush at the sight of plants, then they are obviously not able to know anything about the undines either, because rational concepts—definitions—do not refer to undines. But blushing and turning pale, which are based in the blood, did convey this; they were an expression of this. Today, what is based in the blood only conveys it subconsciously. But all this can become revitalized again when Christ becomes a real experience for humanity. And in Christ it will also be possible again for older people to communicate with young people. For Christ cannot be grasped with the intellect.

In our time, as we survey the world in a rational sense, we speak of right and wrong, of true and false. But these concepts only mean something for the physical world in which we live between birth and death. People do not want to reflect on the essential aspects when we speak about the higher worlds to them. It is true that we should apply the concepts of true and false, and of what is logically correct or incorrect to the higher worlds as well. But this is not what is important. The essential thing is that a living aspect should be included as well; that, for example, the concepts "healthy" and "sick" should be introduced. Here, in the physical world, something is simply right or wrong; in the higher worlds, "right" is also "healthy." There, we experience this as vividly as we experience our state of health in our whole organism here, in the physical world. And what is "wrong," what is "erroneous" in the physical world—this is what equals "sick" in the higher worlds. It would actually be better—if we really wanted to discern things here in the ordinary world accurately—to talk about healthy and sick rather than about right or wrong. This also means that we must learn how to understand "healthy" or "sick." Here on earth, we form judgments logically according to what is right or wrong; in the higher worlds, we perceive that things are growing, that they are developing. There, we do not just speak of something as "right" but we actually experience it as "healthy." And if we form a concept about it, then we also experience this concept as something healthy, not just as something right. And in the same way, we experience something that is "wrong" in the spiritual world as "sick."

As far as the physical world is concerned, we can make do today—this is, after all, how we are constituted—with right or wrong. But this is not the case when it comes to history. With respect to history, we cannot make do with the concepts that modern historians have developed based only on the model of physics. In that case, we should be talking about the fact that there was a state of health when humanity began its development. With respect to the Graeco-Latin epoch we must speak of a disease affecting its culture. And we must speak about the therapeutic effect on history by explaining the influence of the Mystery of Golgotha. And so, we must speak of history in the same way as we speak of health and sickness in human beings—that is, we must depict history according to the pattern of an illness and a process of healing.

Consider, for example, how Ranke[†] presents history; it is presented as something that is infinitely abstract when compared with reality. And this history (according to Ranke or others), as it is written today, is very much like a doctor visiting a sick person, or encountering a healthy person, and assessing this situation strictly through logic. We must approach history through the lens of health, sickness, and healing. And this is, in fact, what happens when we survey history in such a way that we first surmise a state of health in primeval times, then observe a disease process affecting civilization, and then perceive the great therapeutic healer, who truly brought healing from realms outside the earth through the Mystery of Golgotha. In this way, any contemplation of history is enlivened. And this, moreover, is how Christ is placed into this historical development. The only way any account of historical development can come closer to Christ is when it proceeds in the same way as physiology or pathology must proceed in relation to physical matter. It must be possible to carry into the spiritual life those concepts that can only apply to physical life today—even though this is often done badly, because people study, for example, the human being after death, and then derive the most important laws about life from the corpse. So, even though it is executed badly, it is done in some measure.

But when it comes to considering history, this aspect is completely omitted. Only when people observe very unusual circumstances—when, say, a particular sect appears to be whipping itself into a frenzy, or when things reach the point where, as has happened in recent years, someone starts shooting at Venus with a machine gun in the belief that it was an enemy balloon—then people will speak of something pathological; then they will speak of a psychosis. In regard to such special situations, people may then say that something healthy or sick played a part. But they do not consider health or illness in relation to evolution as a whole. This is why people also are not able to really understand the healing principle, the great historical healing therapy that appeared with the Mystery of Golgotha.

One could say, of course, that people today are actually still very unhealthy. But this does not bear scrutiny, because one would have to have an idea of how things would be if the Mystery of Golgotha had not occurred. And even if people were to believe that this is strictly a matter of faith, then they would also be mistaken, because what matters here is the objective aspect of what happened in human evolution through the Mystery of Golgotha. It is true that in the case of a sick person, faith is also of some use, but what is essential is the artful skill of the physician. For this reason, it was also an aberration when people tried to explain the actual phenomenon of Christian piety through faith alone. This would be like saying that medicine can be left on the shelf; that all you have to do is convince the sick person that this medicine will bring about healing.

With respect to all these things, we have come to abstractions; we are no longer able to understand how the inner experiences of human beings are connected with what is objectively happening in the outer world. This is why our thoughts need to become more and more alive. For if we only use the dead thoughts, the dead mental images that are now customarily used to contemplate external nature, then the Mystery of Golgotha will not become a reality. With such thoughts, Christianity would increasingly fade away and Christ would gradually become just Jesus, the simple human being—as has indeed already happened for many theologians. Christianity would disappear. A true rejuvenation of Christianity requires that the entire development of humanity and of human views be permeated with living concepts—more alive than has been possible through intellectualism. Intellectualism was necessary for the sake of human freedom. But we must overcome intellectualism again for the sake of the essential human being, so that this essential being can be reinvigorated again. A dying process was necessary for freedom, because freedom can only come from activating the will within the dying element, that is, from exerting this will to the highest degree. If the life within us becomes too strong, if it overwhelms us, then our consciousness—which freedom needs in order to flourish—disappears. But inasmuch as intellectualism is present, it must be augmented by life, that is, the abstract concepts of "true" and "false" must be augmented by the concrete concepts of "healthy" and "sick."

And it is, above all, for the sake of history that we need to apply these concrete concepts. Then we shall be able to discover that the Mystery of Golgotha is the most important constituent of the whole history of earth evolution.

Lecture Two

DORNACH, DECEMBER 18, 1921

For some time, we have been concerned with gaining a more accurate understanding of the human being's relationship to the universe, and today we would like to bring some further insights to these earlier considerations. If we contemplate human beings as they exist in the present epoch of human evolution—taking "present" in its broadest sense, compared to the great evolution of the earth, so that it encompasses not only what is history but also some of the prehistory of humanity—then we must come to the conclusion that it is, above all, language that should be considered as characteristic of this present time in the cosmic evolution of humanity. Speech is what elevates the human being above the other kingdoms of nature.

Now, I had already mentioned in last week's lectures that language, speech as a whole, has changed in the course of human evolution; that in this field, too, humanity has undergone a development. I pointed out how, in very ancient times, language was the earliest primal capacity—of expressing inner experiences outwardly—which human beings developed; and how, as a result, human beings were able to reveal the divine-spiritual powers living in them, by means of their organs of speech. I also pointed out that during the transition from the Greek to the Roman-Latin culture—that is to say, in the fourth post-Atlantean cultural epoch—it can be clearly noticed that the individual sounds of the language no longer have names, but were simply used as sounds, as we do today. In the Greek language we still have a name for the first letter of the alphabet, but in Latin it is just "A." In the transition from Greek to Latin, a change occurred to something which, in a most concrete sense, had been alive in the language. It became abstract.

One could also say, pursuant to its real meaning, that as long as human beings called the first letter of the alphabet "Alpha," they experienced a certain amount of inspiration in doing so, but the moment they called it just "A," they began to conform to the more prosaic, external, conventional aspects of life—which then superseded the inspiration, the inner experience. The actual transition from the Greek to the Roman-Latin culture is indicated by the fact that civilized humanity transitioned from the world of the poetic-spiritual to the prose of life.

The people of Rome, as I have often emphasized, were a down-to-earth, prosaic people, a people of the law, who carried prose and jurisprudence over into the civilizations that followed. What lived in the Greek culture, on the other hand, continued to unfold in civilized humanity as a kind of cultural dream, which people reflected back on and, once they experienced its inner qualities, tried to access by expressing it in their own creations. One could say that all poetry contains something which makes it appear to Europeans as a daughter of Greece; and that all jurisprudence, all external compartmentalization, all prose of life contains something which makes it appear as a daughter of the Roman-Latin culture.

I also pointed out earlier how a real understanding of Alpha—Aleph in Hebrew—leads us to recognize that giving this name to the letter meant to express: "This is the symbol for the human being." If we wanted to approximate the meaning of Alpha in modern words, we would say: "The being who experiences his own breathing." In this designation we have a direct reference to the words of the Old Testament: "The earthly human being was created by having the breath of life breathed into him."[†] Accordingly, what had been done at that time with the breath in order to make the human being into an earthly being, the essence of what had been imprinted onto the human being and thus making him a being who sensed and experienced this breath, who received it into his consciousness—this is what was meant to be expressed in the first letter of the alphabet.

And Beta—if you look at it with an open mind, and especially if you consider the equivalent in Hebrew [Bet]—represents something like an enclosure, a covering, a house. Consequently, if one wanted to express in today's language what people had once felt when they began to say, "Alpha, Beta," then one would express it with the words: "The human being in his house." And we could go through the entire alphabet in this way and would thus be expressing a concept, a meaning, a truth about the human being simply by saying the names [of the letters] of the alphabet one after the other. In that way, a comprehensive sentence would be produced, which would, in a sense, express the mystery of the human being. This sentence would begin by referring to the human being in his house, in his temple. The following parts of the sentence would then go on to express how the human being conducts himself in his temple and what kind of relationship he has to the cosmos. In short, what would be articulated by speaking the names of the alphabet sequentially would not be the abstraction we have today when we say, "A, B, C" without giving it any further thought; rather, it would be an expression of the mystery of the human being and of his basic relationship to the world.

Today, when in various societal circles the "loss of the archetypal word" is mentioned—even though people no longer know what it means—then this refers, in reality, to what is contained in such a sentence as the one mentioned above, which encompasses the names of the alphabet. And so, we can look back on a time in the evolution of humanity when human beings, in uttering the alphabet, did not "breath out" what was related to external events, to external needs but, rather, what their divine-spiritual mystery brought to expression through their larynx and their speech organs.

One could say, then, that what innately belonged to the alphabet was later applied to external objects, and what human beings could reveal, through language, about this soul-spiritual mystery within them, was forgotten. The original human truth-filled word, the human wisdom-filled word, was lost. Language, speech, has been reduced to the matter-of-factness of life. And when we speak today, we are no longer aware that the primordial sentence—through which the divinity revealed our own being to us—has been forgotten; neither are we aware that all the words and sentences spoken today still contain snippets of that primordial sentence.

Poets—inasmuch as they do not surrender to the prose contexts of language but go back instead to the inner experience, the inner feeling, the inner shaping of language—attempt to return to its inspired archetypal element. One might even say that every true poem, the humblest as well as the greatest, is such an attempt to return to this lost word, to take a step back from a life that is only aimed at usefulness and turn toward those times when a cosmic being still revealed itself in the inner organism of speech.

Today, we distinguish between the realm of the consonants and the vowels in language. I have often spoken of what would appear, and what we would find, if we were to dive beneath the threshold of our consciousness. For our ordinary consciousness, memories—that is, thoughts of experiences occurring between birth and death—are reflected upward. With our ordinary consciousness we cannot penetrate further down into our own human essential being than to these thoughts left behind in memory. I have already indicated, from a certain point of view, that something is living below this threshold of consciousness, something that constitutes a kind of universal tragedy for human beings. This can also be described in the following way. One can say that when we wake up in the morning and our I and astral body are submerged into the etheric and physical bodies, we do not perceive this etheric body and this physical body from within. What we perceive is something quite different. We can visualize it with the help of a diagram (see Plate 1 in the appendix).

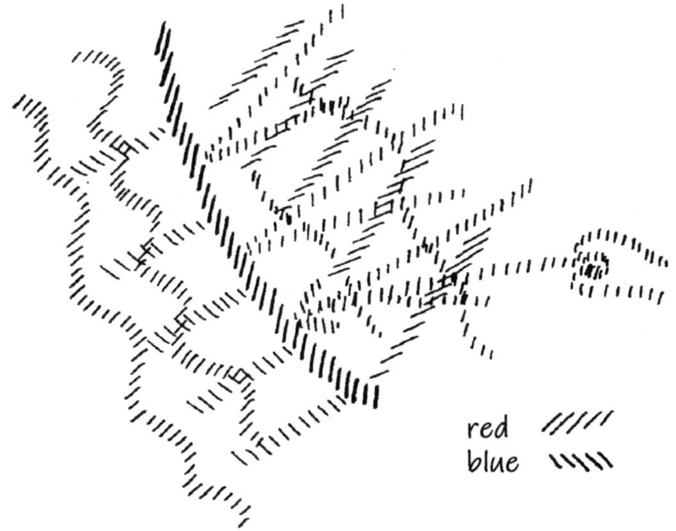

Here we have, shall we say, the boundary between the conscious and the unconscious, with red representing the conscious and blue the unconscious. Our memories are reflected back from the conscious. For it is a fact that we live with our consciousness only in this realm; the rest remains unconscious. And what we see of the outside world or even of ourselves is nothing but this. Let us say that we observe the eyes of a human being with our own eyes; what emanates as visible rays, penetrating us, is reflected back and we experience it in our consciousness. And even what we carry of our own essential being underneath the threshold of consciousness is experienced in our astral body and our I, but not in the ordinary waking state. It remains unconscious and essentially forms the actual content of the etheric and physical bodies. The etheric body is not recognized at all by ordinary consciousness, and the physical body only in its external aspects. As I previously have described, one must first dive beneath memory in order to perceive the original source of evil in human beings[†]; but then something else can also be perceived, namely, an aspect of the relationship of the human being to the cosmos.

If, through appropriate meditation, we are able to break through, as it were, to the mental images of memory, to put aside what separates us inwardly from our etheric and physical bodies, and then are able to look down into our etheric and physical bodies so that we perceive what lies underneath the threshold of consciousness—then we will hear something sounding in the etheric body and also in the physical body. And what is resounding is an echo of the *music of the spheres,*[†] which the human being absorbed in the life between death and a new birth while descending from the divine-spiritual world into the physical world in order to incarnate in what is provided, through physical inheritance, by parents and ancestors. The sounds of the music of the spheres reverberate in the etheric and physical bodies—that is to say, in the etheric body insofar as these sounds have the quality of vowels, and in the physical body insofar as they have the quality of consonants.

It is indeed the case, as you will also remember,[†] that human beings, as they progress through life between death and a new birth, ascend to the world of the higher hierarchies. We have seen how human beings join in with the world of the Angels, the Archangels, the Archai; how they live within the realm of the hierarchies, just as we live here among the beings of the mineral, plant, and animal kingdoms. After this life between death and a new birth, human beings then descend again to earthly life. And we have seen how, on their way down, they first gather the influences of the realm of the fixed stars, or more specifically its representation, the zodiac; and how they then, as they descend further, gather the influences of the planetary sphere, the moving planets.

Now just picture to yourselves this representative of the fixed stars—the zodiac. The human being is exposed to these influences while descending from the life of soul and spirit into earthly life. If we want to describe these influences according to their real essence, then we must say that they constitute the consonantal aspect of the cosmic music; and that the sounding of consonants in the physical body is an echo of what resounds from the individual configurations of the zodiac. What happens through the movements of the planets, on the other hand, constitutes the vocal aspect within this music of the spheres. This is then imprinted onto the etheric body. Therefore, in our physical body we unconsciously carry a reflection of the resounding cosmic consonants, and in our etheric body we carry a reflection of the resounding cosmic vowels.

Initially, this remains in the silence of the subconscious, so to speak. But as the child develops, certain forces—forces that reflect the formative forces of the cosmos—press upward from the body into the organs of speech, thus forming the speech organs. The organs of speech that are located more on the interior are formed out of the human being's essential nature in such a way that they can produce vowels, and the organs located more on the periphery—palate, tongue, lips, and everything else involved in forming the physical body—are structured in such a way that consonants can be produced. As the child learns to speak, something enters the upper part of its being, brought about by what is occurring in its lower part—namely, the effect of the formative forces that have been absorbed into the physical body, and also into the etheric body. (What thus enters the body must, of course, not be understood in a material sense but as something that enters as a formative activity.) Therefore, when we speak, we bring to expression what one might call an echo of the experiences which human beings undergo in relation to the cosmos as a whole, in the life between death and a new birth while descending from the divine-spiritual world. All the single details of the alphabet are actually reproduced images of what lives in the cosmos (see Plate1 in the appendix).

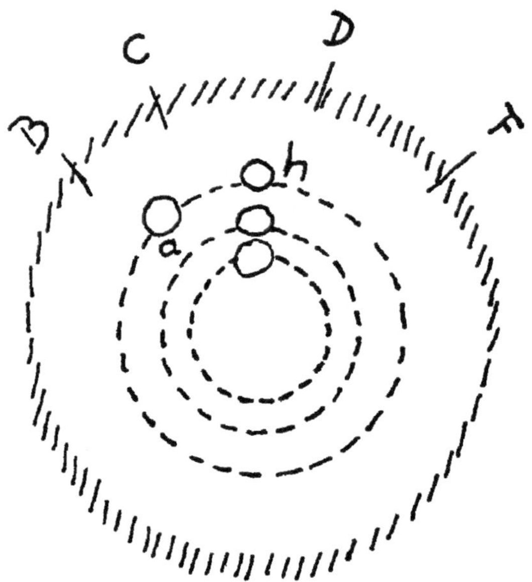

You can get an approximate sense of the signs of the zodiac if you create a connection to modern language by placing B, C, D, F, and so on, as constellations of the zodiac. You can get a sense of them by experiencing the revolution of the planets as H. H is not an actual letter like the others; H replicates the rotational movement, the circling around. And the individual planets in their revolutions always constitute the individual vowels that are placed in various ways in front of the consonants. If you imagine the vowel A to be placed in here (see diagram above, Plate 1 in the appendix), then you have the A sounding together with B and C. However, in each vowel there is also an H. When you pronounce it, you will feel it: AH, IH, EH. Every vowel has the H in it! What does it signify that H is in each vowel? It signifies that the vowel oscillates within the cosmos. The vowel is not at rest, it swings around in the cosmos. And this circling, this moving, is expressed in the H that is mysteriously contained in each of the vowels.

Imagine a sequence of vowels, sounding in harmony, being expressed in some language, for example, I, O, U, A. What is expressed through this? Through this, something is expressed that contains the cosmic influences of four planets. If a consonant was then added to a sequence like this—say, IOSUA (Joshua)—if an S was affixed and placed in between the vowels, then this would indicate that this word is not only an expression of the vowels resounding within the planetary spheres but also of the influence which the planets belonging to I, O, U, A, experience in their movements as a result of the connection made with the constellation sign S. In other words, if—at the time of ancient human civilization—someone uttered a divine name by using vowels, then a planetary mystery was expressed; the deed of a divine being within the planetary sphere was expressed in this name. And if a divine name was expressed in such a way that it contained consonants, then the deed of the divine being in question was pictured further away, as high up as the representative of the fixed stars—the zodiac.

And so, when people still had an instinctive understanding of these things—in the days of the old atavistic clairvoyance, clairaudience, and so on—they experienced the connection with the cosmos in human speech. When speaking, human beings experienced themselves within, and belonging to, the cosmos. They sensed how, as a child learned to speak, the things that had been experienced in the divine-spiritual world before birth, or before conception, were gradually evolving from out of the being of the child.

One could say that, if we were able to perceive and understand our own inner being, then we would have to acknowledge: I am an etheric body—that is, I am an echo of the resounding cosmic vowels. I am a physical body—that is, I am an echo of the resounding cosmic consonants. And inasmuch as I stand here on the earth, an echo is formed through my being, an echo of everything which the signs of the zodiac disclose; and the life of this echo is my physical body. An echo is also formed of everything which the planetary spheres disclose in their circling rounds; and this echo is my etheric body (See Plate 2 in the appendix).

1. Physical Body: Echo of the zodiac
2. Etheric body: Echo of the planetary movements
3. Astral body: Experiencing these planetary movements
4. I: Perceiving the echo of the zodiac.

Saying that the human being consists of a physical body and an etheric body does not actually say anything. Those are just vague, indefinite words. If we wanted to speak in the real language that can be learned from the secrets of the cosmos, we would have to say: The human being is constituted out of the echo of the fixed stars, out of the echo of the planetary movements, out of that which experiences the echo of the planetary movements, and out of that which cognitively perceives the echo of the fixed stars. Then we would have expressed in the real language of the cosmos what is abstractly expressed by the words: The human being consists of a physical body, an etheric body, an astral body, and an I. We remain entirely in the abstract if we say: The human being consists, first, of a physical body, second, of an etheric body, third, of an astral body, and, fourth, of an I. But we transition into the concrete language of the universe if we say: The human being consists of an echo of the zodiac, an echo of the planetary movements, an experience of the imprint of these planetary movements in the form of thinking, feeling, and willing, and a cognitive perception of the echo of the zodiac. The first version is an abstraction, the second is a reality.

When you say "I," what is that exactly? Imagine for a moment that someone had planted trees in a beautifully aesthetic order. You can see every single tree. But, if you observe them from a great distance, all those trees eventually become just a single point. Take all the individual details, everything that resounds from the zodiac in the way of cosmic consonants—and if you go far enough away, then everything that is formed as inward sound in the most manifold ways, is compressed within you into the single point, "I."

The fact is that this designation, which I give myself as a human being, is actually only the expression of what one perceives as immeasurably distant from its real place in the universe. With respect to all these things, it is necessary to go back to what, as a reflection, as an echo, appears here on earth. Then—when this matter is seen in its reality—everything that shapes our conceptions about the human being as a phenomenon, as a mere appearance, melts away before the higher and inner perception of the human being.

If we observe a human being and gradually learn to recognize the true human essential nature, then the physical body actually no longer stands there in front of us as it normally would; then our view widens, and we come to the realm of the fixed stars. And the etheric body, too, ceases to stand in front of us. Our view widens, our experience widens, and we come to a perception of the life of the planets; for this human etheric body is merely a reflection of planetary life. When a human being stands before us, what actually stands there is nothing else but the phenomenon, the appearance, the image, of what takes place in the life of the planets. We think we have an individual human being in front of us; but this individual being is an image of the whole world, seen in one particular place. What is, strictly speaking, the reason for the difference between a person from Asia and a person from America? The reason is that the starry heavens are replicated at two different points on earth, just as we have different images of some external fact from the perspective of different points. The truth is that when we observe a human being in this way, the world opens up for us; and that through such an observation, we are confronted with the great mystery as to whether, and to what extent, the human being is nothing other than a pictorial microcosm of the reality of the macrocosm.

What does modern life actually consist of? If we look back from this more current life to the life of humanity in primordial times, then we find that the human being's experience of the cosmic relationships was still present in the instinctive consciousness of these primeval times. This can be experienced in a concrete way in connection with the alphabet. When human beings intended to express the comprehensive fullness of the divine in one archetypal sentence, then they spoke the alphabet. When the human being expressed the secret of his own nature, as it could be learned in the mysteries, he voiced how he had descended through Saturn or Jupiter while they were transiting the constellations of Leo or Virgo, that is, how he descended through the A or the I in the constellations of the M or the L. In that way, the human being uttered what he had experienced of the *music of the spheres*—and that was his cosmic name. And in those ancient times people were certainly aware, instinctively aware, that the human being brought along a name, while descending from the cosmos to the earth.

At a later time, the Christian consciousness created a kind of abstract echo of this primordial consciousness by dedicating certain days to the memory of saints, who, rightly understood, are meant to be viewed as the ones who keep the connection to the spiritual cosmos alive. And, having been born on a particular day of the year, a human being was then to be given the name of the saint in question, according to the calendar of names. This was meant to express, only now in a more abstract way, what in primordial times was expressed in a more concrete way through the fact that, from out of the mysteries, the cosmic name of a human being was "found" in accordance with what he experienced, during his descent to earth, as his inner being was permeated with the resounding of the vowels [of the planets] in connection with the consonants of the zodiac. Thus, there were many names among the human race as a whole, but all these names sounding together were imagined in such a way that they harmonized with the universal all-embracing name.

Seen from this point of view, then, what was the alphabet? It was what the heavens revealed through the fixed stars and through the planets moving across these fixed stars. If people spoke the alphabet in the sense of the original, instinctive, human wisdom—then they spoke astronomy. Speaking the alphabet and astronomical knowledge were, in these ancient times, one and the same thing. In those days, people did not think of wisdom, such as astronomy, in the same way as we think today of what is taught in any branch of science—which is built up from single perceptions and concepts. It was pictured as a revelation being pressed onto the surface of human experience, either in the form of the original, archetypal sentence itself or of parts of this archetypal sentence. Accordingly, it represented a concrete experience with a part of the primordial wisdom. And we can still see signs of a very faint awareness of this situation in the fact that, in the Middle Ages, those who were led into higher education still had to learn grammar, rhetoric, dialectics, arithmetic, geometry, music, and astronomy.[†] In this ascent through the various fields of teaching there was still an awareness—albeit a faint one—of what, in more ancient times, had existed in instinctive clarity.

Today, grammar has become something very abstract. If we go back to the times of which history does not report but which nevertheless are still historical, then we find that grammar was not the abstract subject it is today, but that through grammar, the human being was led into the secrets of the individual letters. The student learned that something of the mysteries of the cosmos is expressed in the letters. Each vowel was brought into connection with its planet, each consonant with its sign in the zodiac; and so, through the letters of the alphabet, one gained knowledge of the stars. And by advancing further from grammar to rhetoric, one learned to utilize what lived in the human being as the active reality of astronomy. By ascending to dialectics, one learned to comprehend, and work through in thought, what lived in the human being as the real effect of astronomy. And arithmetic was not taught as the abstraction that it has become today, but as the real essence that comes to expression in the secrets of numbers. Numbers as such were viewed differently from how they are viewed today. I will give you just a small example of this.

How do we picture one, two, three today? It is done by thinking, for example, of a pea, then of another pea, and this makes two; then another one is added, and then there are three. It is a matter of adding one to another, of accumulation. This is not how people approached numbers in earlier times. In those times, one began with the assumption of a unit. And by splitting the unit into two parts, one arrived at *two*. Accordingly, *two* was not the result of adding one single entity to another. It was not a matter of putting together single units; rather, *two* was contained in *one*. And *three* was contained in *one* in a different way, *four* in a different way again. The unit, the oneness, encompassed all numbers and was the largest. Today, the unit is the smallest. Today, everything is pictured according to atomism. The unit is one item and then a second unit is added, and everything is imagined atomically. The original idea was organic. The unit was the largest and the subsequent numbers always appeared as something smaller and were all contained in the unit. In this way, one can come to very different mysteries of the world of numbers.

These mysteries of the world of numbers give us merely an indication of the fact that we are not dealing here with something that only exists inside the hollow human head—I say "hollow" because I have often explained that, seen from the spiritual point of view, the human head really is hollow—but, rather, that we can come to perceive in the relationships of the numbers the relationships of the objective facts of existence in the world. Of course, if we always just add one to one, then this is something that has nothing to do with the facts. Say, I have a piece of chalk. If I place a second piece of chalk beside it, then this has nothing to do with the first. The one has no relationship to the other. If, however, I assume that everything is a unit—and each thing is a unit—and then approach the numbers contained in this unit, then I come to *two* in a manner that is not inconsequential. I have no choice but to split the piece. Then I really focus on reality.

And so, after having learned to grasp the thoughts of astronomy by ascending to dialectics, one then had to go still further into the universe with arithmetic, and likewise in a similar manner with geometry. From geometry one developed the sense that the essence of geometry—if entered with real thoughts—was *the music of the spheres.* This is the difference between what exists today and what once existed in the instinctive primordial wisdom. Consider music today. The mathematical physicist calculates the pitch of a note, figuring out, for example, which pitches are working together in a particular melody. But any musical person would then actually be obliged to forget what is musical and enter completely into the abstract (unless, being a very enthusiastic musician, he or she would have already fled from the calculating mathematician to begin with). The human being would then be led away from an immediate experience and into an abstraction, which has very little to do with the experience.

It would be interesting in itself, if one had the mathematical skills, to trace the musical elements right through to the field of acoustics; but it would not yield much in the way of musical experience. As far as I know, there is nothing in the schools' curriculum today that would allow a pupil to learn geometry and then, in the course of this study, to begin to experience these geometrical forms as musical tones—in other words, in transitioning from, say, the fifth to the sixth grade, to learn how geometry is transformed into music. But this is what once was the significance of ascending to the sixth level of what had to be learned—namely, how to transition from geometry to music. Only then did the archetypal, underlying reality become a real experience. The astronomy in the subconscious then became the last thing that was consciously mastered—as astronomy, the seventh and highest grade of the so-called Trivium and Quadrivium.

The history of humanity should be studied in terms of how consciousness has progressed; for in studying this, we can get a sense that human consciousness must return to these things again. This is precisely what is attempted in anthroposophical spiritual science. It is therefore not surprising that those who are accustomed to accepting the scientific approach, as it is implemented today, cannot get a correct sense of how I have written, for example, *An Outline of Esoteric Science.*[†] It is necessary, however, that humanity return in a fully conscious way to what is the true reality—a reality which, for a certain period of time, had to recede into the background so that human beings could fully develop their freedom. Human beings would indeed have been able to develop an ever more powerful awareness of the need to be part of a divine cosmic world, if they had not been cast out of this cosmos into the realm of mere phenomena, mere appearance—an awareness powerful enough to know that the whole manifold splendor and majesty of the starry heavens had been condensed into the abstract I.

This was necessary for the sake of gaining freedom. For it is only because of the fact that the human being—albeit quite indistinctly—compressed something which fills all cosmic spaces, which flows through all time periods, into the central point of the I, that we have been able to develop our freedom. But we would lose our essential being, we would no longer know anything about ourselves, no longer be able to relate to ourselves or be active and act on our own initiative, if we were not to master the whole world again from this single point of our I, if we were not to rise again from the abstract to the concrete. It is indeed important to understand how, in transitioning from the Greek to the Latin element, abstraction took hold of European culture; and how the primordial word was lost as a direct result. The Latin language has long remained the actual language of culture and higher education. It was like a desperate clinging to what this Latin language had, in fact, already discarded. And eventually, what had originally been spoken in the Latin language-contexts remained only in the form of thoughts. What remained of the Logos was the logic, the abstract thought.

There is definitely something in the longing for knowledge of the Greek culture—Goethe, for example, had such longing—something that could be expressed as follows. It is the yearning to get away from the abstraction of modern times, from the austere "prose" of the Roman culture. Goethe wanted to reach the other "daughter" of the primeval wisdom of the world; he wanted to penetrate what remained of Greek culture. It is necessary to feel something like this if one wishes to understand Goethe's intense yearning for the South. In today's academically written biographies, however, we find nothing of all this. Only when a certain awareness begins to resound in every single thing—the awareness that the human being is an expression of the whole cosmos—only then will the foundation have been laid for the ascending forces necessary for humanity's progress, if civilization is not to decline into barbarism.

Lecture Three

DORNACH, DECEMBER 23, 1921

IN THE COURSE of these lectures, I have often mentioned that the sleep state of a human being is not something that only exists during ordinary sleep but that it also plays a role in everyday conscious life. We must distinguish, even in everyday consciousness, between the state of complete wakefulness, which is only present in relation to our conceptual life, and what we carry within us as life of feeling. This feeling life is not integrated into our waking state in the same way as our conceptual life; rather, to the unprejudiced observer, this life of feeling proves to be very similar to our life of dreams. The only difference is that dream life runs its course in pictures and that the life of feeling occurs in the way we all know it. Yet you will readily notice how dream life—which, as you know, wondrously interweaves images of unfamiliar facts, facts unfamiliar to ordinary consciousness, into everyday life—can only be evaluated with our power of conceptual discernment. And it is in the same way, in the exact same way, that the whole scope and significance of our feeling life can only be evaluated by this discerning ability of our conceptual life. And what takes place in the case of an impulse of will—in the activity and the working of will—is just as hidden from ordinary consciousness as what happens during dreamless sleep with the human being as a soul-spiritual being, from the moment of falling asleep to that of waking.

What actually takes place when we carry out the simplest act of will—when, let us say, we raise an arm or a leg through an impulse of will—remains just as hidden from us as what occurs in sleep. It is only because we can see the result of an act of will, as it were, that the act itself enters our consciousness. After having thought of raising our arm—but that is merely a thought—and after the result has come to pass, we see how the arm has indeed been raised. It is by means of our conceptual life that we get to know the result of an act of will. But what actually takes place as a fact of will remains hidden from ordinary consciousness, so that we have to designate everything that constitutes an impulse of will as a state of sleep, even during our waking hours. And everything that takes place in our life of feeling runs its course in the way of a dream.

Now, what is to be considered here is that all these facts, which I have preliminarily presented up to now, can definitely be intelligible to ordinary consciousness. If these things are presented in an abstract manner, however, they may not appear immediately understandable in every respect. But if you follow these facts, as they relate to consciousness, you will find that what has been said is absolutely correct. It is certainly the case that [someone with] a schooled consciousness is able to pursue these facts further. One can particularly trace, in more detail, how the life of concepts and of the will are formed in the course of human life. We know that it is possible to rise from ordinary, object-based cognition to imaginative cognition[†] through the exercises I have described in several of my books. It is foremost this imaginative cognition which, through its observations, can show us how these things actually relate to the human being as a whole. But it will still be useful to recall certain facts regarding this ordinary consciousness, before we continue with what imaginative cognition can reveal about the human being with respect to the forming of mental images and the will.

Let us look, then, at the actual life of thought, the life of forming mental images and concepts. One will have to acknowledge right away—if one perceives it objectively—that this conceptual life is not experienced as a reality. Mental concepts arise in our life of soul and there is no doubt that forming these concepts within the inner human being is something that is added to the actual outer course of events. The outer course of events does not directly require that it be accompanied by an inwardly experienced conception. The event, or fact, of which we form a mental image could also happen without our experiencing it conceptually. And even if we immerse ourselves in these mental images, we realize that in this world of conceptions, we actually live in something which, compared with the external world, is not real. On the other hand, it is precisely in relation to the life of the will—which our ordinary consciousness experiences in the same way as it experiences things during sleep—that we become conscious of our own reality and of the real relationship we have to the world. As long as we only form mental images about things, we must gradually come to realize that these mental images live in us in the same way as the images of objects exist in a mirror. And, just as little as we experience the images in the mirror as real—in the sense of what we usually designate as real in this world—so little will we be able to experience our mental images per se as real, provided we approach this realm with sound reason.

But there is something else that prevents us from viewing our conceptions as something real, and that is our sense of freedom. Just imagine for a moment that, in forming mental images, we lived in these mental images in such a way that they transpired within us like processes of nature; that our life of mental images was more like what occurs in outer nature, which runs its course as a matter of necessity. We would then be entrapped in a chain of necessities. We would then only be able to think what is inherently present in this chain of external natural necessities. We would never be able to have the sense of freedom which, as such, is an actual fact. We are only able to experience ourselves as free human beings if the free impulses living in us arise from images that stand outside of the usual chain of natural necessities. It is only because, in this process of conceptualizing, we live in images that are *not* integrated into a series of necessary natural phenomena, that we are able to experience free impulses of will in association with these mental images.

Accordingly, if we look at our conceptual life in this way, we perceive it in all respects as something unreal. On the other hand, it is precisely our life of will that affirms our reality for us. Whatever manifests as an act of will produces changes in the outer world—changes that must be viewed as realities. Through our will, we generate something real in the outer world. Therefore, it is only inasmuch as we are beings of will that we experience our existence in the outer world as something real.

If we now advance from these facts—which, as such, are easily ascertainable through ordinary consciousness—to what imaginative consciousness can tell us, then we come to the following. It is absolutely true that when we acquire imaginative cognition and then, by means of it, try to develop human self-knowledge, the human being appears to this imaginative cognition as a quite different being—particularly in two respects—as compared to what ordinary consciousness perceives. To ordinary consciousness, our physical body stands before us as, one could say, a self-contained entity at rest. We distinguish the individual organs of the physical body, and when we look at these individual organs of the physical body with our normal state of consciousness, we have the impression that we are dealing with autonomous bodily members, which can be outlined with definite contours and as something complete in themselves.

This ceases the moment we rise to imaginative cognition and then consider what goes on in our body from the perspective of this imaginative knowledge. What can be seen then is not something that is static, not something which, even if one wanted to draw it in a diagram, could be sketched in definite outline—although it is, of course, always possible to draw things in schematic form. We cannot depict in definite contours what imaginative cognition discloses about the lungs, heart, liver, and so on; rather, what imaginative cognition reveals to us about the physical body is that it is in a constant state of self-perpetuating motion, of becoming—not in a state of rest. It is a process, a becoming, a flowing—which we become aware of as we ascend to imaginative cognition. One could say that everything is swirling; that everything is moving internally, not only in a spatial but also in an intensive sense; that one thing flows into another. We no longer are confronted by self-contained organs at rest; instead, there is a vivid becoming, a living, a weaving. We can no longer speak of lungs, heart, liver but, rather, of the lung process, the heart process, the liver process. And these individual processes, in turn, combine to form the overall process—the human being. And the characteristic aspect here is that, as soon as we consider the human being from the point of view of imaginative cognition, he appears as something internally mobile, as something continuously in the process of becoming at every single moment.

Please note, however, the significance of this changed view of the human being. When we observe the human body with its definitely contoured members, and then direct our soul's observation at our inner soul life, we do not see anything in this life of the soul that could possibly be drawn with defined, outlined contours. In the life of soul, we see something that occurs in time, something that is always becoming and is never at rest. And even though the life of the soul presents itself to us as something that can only be perceived inwardly, as a soul-spiritual process, it is nevertheless clearly present. This process of the life of the soul—which can already be recognized by ordinary consciousness, if the inner human being is viewed without prejudice—this state of becoming of the life of the soul bears very little resemblance to the life of the body resting in itself. It is true that the life of the body also shows movement—breathing is movement, circulation is movement—but one could say that this is a transitionary stage to the kind of movement that the human being represents to imaginative cognition. But, compared to the delicate, subtle movements of the human physical body observed by imaginative cognition, what occurs as blood circulation, as the movement of breathing, as other movements in the body, is relatively static.

In short, what is perceived with our ordinary consciousness and our object-based cognition as the human body is very different from what is perceived as the life of the soul—which is in a perpetual state of becoming, always inherently mobile, never resting. But if we observe the human body with imaginative consciousness, then it becomes inwardly mobile—that is to say, it becomes more like the life of the soul in its appearance. Imaginative cognition, therefore, gives us the possibility, one could say, of raising the appearance of the physical body to the level of the soul. Soul and body draw closer. The body, the physical body, becomes more soul-like to imaginative cognition.

But I have actually presented two things, which belong in completely different realms. I described how the physical body appears to imaginative cognition; I showed you that it is inherently mobile, always in a state of becoming. Then I pointed out that—even to our ordinary consciousness as it surveys the inner human being—the normal life of the soul is something that is forever becoming, never resting, always moving in time; that it is a life, in fact, that cannot be captured in definite contours, or drawn in fixed outlines.

But when we rise to imaginative cognition, the life of the soul changes also for this inner view, and it changes in an opposite direction to that of the life of the body. The remarkable thing here is that when we imbue ourselves with imaginative cognition, we no longer feel this free mobility in our thinking, this free mobility with respect to how one thought is combined with another thought. We also feel that, as we rise to imaginative cognition, our thoughts become something that subdues our soul life. In our ordinary consciousness we can add one thought to another. We can combine a subject with an object in complete inner freedom—or we can decide not to do so—and we feel free in this linking of one conception with another. This is not the case when we ascend to imaginative cognition. Then, we experience ourselves within the world of thinking as if we were in something that transpires entirely through its own forces. Then, we experience ourselves as if enmeshed in this web of thoughts in such a way that one thought is combined with another thought *not* through us but through the thoughts' own inherent forces. When we ascend to imaginative cognition, it becomes quite impossible to say, "I think." This is when we must begin to say, "It thinks." In fact, we are entwined in this "It thinks." We begin to perceive thinking as a real process. We feel it to be just as real a process within us as we feel, in ordinary everyday life, a pain taking hold of us and then leaving again, or something pleasant appearing and then withdrawing again. In ascending to imaginative cognition, we experience the reality of the world of thinking. We feel something in our world of thought that becomes similar to the experience we otherwise have in relation to the physical body.

From this you can see that through imaginative cognition, the conceptual life of the soul becomes even more similar to the life of the body than the soul-life is similar to the life of the body when inwardly surveyed and grasped by ordinary consciousness. In short, to imaginative cognition, the body becomes very soul-like while the soul becomes more like the body, or, strictly speaking, like those bodily processes which present themselves to imaginative cognition as being in a process of becoming. Thus, for imaginative cognition, the soul qualities approach those of the body and the bodily aspects those of the soul. We see, as it were, the soul-spiritual penetrating the bodily-physical, and the two becoming more alike as we ascend to imaginative cognition. One could say that, as we experience the realm of the soul, we are seized by a kind of materialism while our perception of the life of the body—of physical life in general—becomes spiritualized. This is an important fact that presents itself to imaginative cognition.

And as we advance further to inspirative cognition, another mystery about the human being is revealed to us. Having acquired the cognitive level of inspiration, we learn to better understand the material nature of our thinking, of our forming of mental images. We develop deeper insight into what actually happens when we think. I said before that we are getting away from the freedom in our life of thought; that "It thinks," and that we are enmeshed in this "It thinks." Depending on the circumstances, however, the same thoughts are involved—the thoughts which in our ordinary consciousness we combine or separate in freedom, and the thoughts which in our imaginative experience we perceive as occurring according to an inner necessity.

From this we can see that freedom and necessity are not based in our thought-life as such but, rather, in how we are placed and relate to the life of thought with our ordinary physical consciousness. We learn to recognize what the real reason is for our experiencing the "unreality" of thoughts—an experience that arises in our ordinary consciousness. We learn to understand why we experience the thoughts as unreal. For, what actually takes place is the following. The organic processes that occur in us proceed in such a way that our organism both takes in and also excretes substances. But it is not only a matter of substances being removed from the organic processes of our body and being discarded by the excretory organs; such substances are also constantly being deposited within us. They remain, to some extent, alongside our nerve tracts and in other places in our organism. They are emitted from the life processes.

What happens in our life processes is that lifeless matter is continuously separated out. Anyone able to follow the human life processes in detail will be able to see that inorganic substances are deposited everywhere in the organism. The coarser masses are excreted; but, in a more refined way, substances are deposited everywhere. Accordingly, we can say: The human organism lives in such a way that it initially carries within itself the organic process which I would like to illustrate for you in this diagram with white chalk (see diagram below, Plate 3 in the appendix). But everywhere within this organic process we see inorganic, lifeless matter, which is not excreted but is being deposited everywhere. I am indicating this in the diagram with red chalk. I drew these red dots rather heavily because it is mainly these non-excreting, lifeless substances that are separated off in the human head organism, where they then remain.

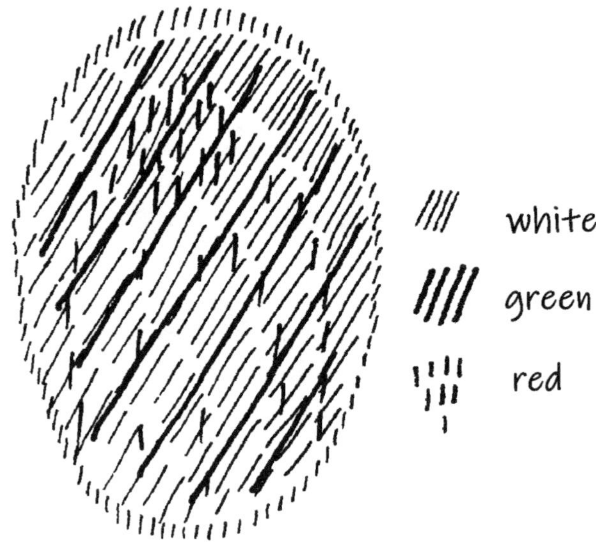

Now, the whole human organism is permeated by the I. This is indicated in the diagram with green chalk. Within our organism, the I encounters the lifeless substances that have been separated off, and permeates them. Accordingly, there is something in our organism which implies, on the one hand, that the I permeates the organic process (the process in which matter is incorporated as living substances), and, on the other, that the I also permeates the lifeless—or, shall we say, mineralized—substances in the organism.

When we think, what is taking place continuously is that, stimulated by outer sense-perceptions or also by memories, the I seizes these lifeless substances, and—by letting these substances oscillate in accordance with the stimuli of the senses or the memories—makes drawings with them in us (one can actually describe it thus). This is not a pictorial conception; rather, it is absolutely in keeping with reality to say that the I uses these inorganic substances in the same way as if, to use a comparison, I would pulverize this chalk, dip my finger in the chalk powder, and then draw all sorts of figures with this chalky finger. The fact is that the I actually lets these lifeless substances swing back and forth, takes possession of them, and then draws figures in us—although these figures do, of course, not look very much like those drawn in the outer world. But it is absolutely true that the I, with the help of these lifeless substances, draws and crystalizes within us—albeit not in the crystalline forms like those found in the mineral kingdom (see red in diagram, Plate 3).

What takes place in this way between the I and what has become mineralized in us—which has been separated off as refined, but solid, mineralized substances—this is what as material element forms the basis of our thinking. In other words, our thinking process, the process of forming mental images, actually presents itself to inspirative cognition as the handling of the mineralized substances in the human organism by the I. This is, in fact, a more precise depiction of what I have often abstractly characterized by saying: "Inasmuch as we think, we are perpetually dying." What is dying in us, what is isolating itself from life, what is becoming mineralized in us—this is the very thing with which the I draws in us, and with which the I actually draws the totality of our thoughts. What we have here is the I working and weaving in the mineral kingdom—the mineral kingdom which only comes into being within us and which we have as our faculty of thinking.

You see, what I am describing here is what dawned on the materialistic thinkers of the nineteenth century—albeit, one could say, more like an erroneous intimation. The foremost exponents of this materialism—and one of the best was Czolbe[†]—developed the notion that physical processes are taking place when thoughts are streaming through us. However, this materialistic opinion overlooked—and this is why the intimation was erroneous—that it is the purely spiritual I that makes inner drawings in us with the mineralized substances. What we recognize as the actual awakening of ordinary consciousness—this is precisely what depends on this process of drawing inwardly with the substances that have been mineralized in us.

Let us now consider the other side of the human being, the side of the will impulses. If you consider once more what I have just described, then you may perhaps think that the I becomes imprisoned by what has been mineralized within us. But the fact is that our I is able to utilize this mineralized substance, to draw inwardly with it. The I is able to immerse itself in what is mineralized in us. If, on the other hand, we consider the life processes, where the non-mineralized substances are—the substances involved in the living processes—then we come to what one might call the material aspect, the material basis, of the impulses of will. We know that during sleep, the I is outside the physical body. When the will is active, the I is outside certain regions of the organism. This is the case because at certain moments in time, nothing is being mineralized in such regions, and everything is alive. It is from these regions of the organism—where everything is alive and where at such moments nothing mineralized is becoming detached and separated off—that impulses of will unfold. But the I is driven out at such times; it is drawn into the mineral realm. The I can work with the mineralized substances but not with what is alive. The I is driven out of this living element, just as it is driven out of the whole physical body at night when we are asleep. But that is when the I is outside the body. Through the process of mineralization, the I is driven into the body. When the life-giving processes prevail, the I is driven out of certain parts of the body. It is then just as fully outside those parts of the body as it is outside the *whole* physical body during sleep. And we can therefore say that while one is engaged in an activity of the will, there are always parts of the I outside those areas of the physical body to which they are actually assigned.

Where, then, are these parts of the I that are outside the areas of the physical body that are assigned to them? They are outside in the surrounding space and are becoming one with the forces weaving through this space. When we engage our will, we are outside ourselves with part of our I, and we incorporate forces into ourselves that are coming from the cosmos. When I move an arm, I do not move it by something originating from within the organism but by a force that is outside my arm, and into which the I enters by virtue of the fact that it is driven out of certain parts of my arm. During an activity of will, I go out of my body and I make movements through forces that lie outside forces that are mine. I do not lift my leg by means of forces that are within, but through forces that are actually working from outside; it is the same with the arm.

In thinking, therefore, we are driven inward through the relationship of the I to the mineralized part of the human organism; whereas in willing, just as in sleep, we are driven outward. And one cannot understand the will unless one has a conception of the human being as a cosmic being, unless one moves beyond the limits of the human body, unless one knows that the human being integrates forces lying outside the body when engaged in an act of will. In our will, we immerse ourselves in the world, we surrender ourselves to the world. Accordingly, we can say: The material phenomenon associated with thinking is a mineral process in us; it is the drawing made by the I in the mineralized parts of the human organism. The will in us represents a vitalization, an expansion of the I, an integration of the I into the spiritual world outside, and a working upon the body by the I from out of the spiritual outer world.

If we want to draw the relationship between thinking and willing schematically, we must do it as follows (see diagram below, Plate 3 in the appendix). You see, it is quite possible to pass from the introspective view of the soul-life to the corresponding physical aspect of this life of the soul, without being tempted to fall into materialism in a one-sided way. We learn to recognize what takes place, in a material sense, in thinking and in willing. And we never let go of the I—inasmuch as we know how the I becomes inwardly active in relation to the inorganic aspect of thinking, and recognize, on the other hand, how the I is driven into the spirit through the organic vitalization processes in the body. When the I is driven out of the body it is brought together with forces of the cosmos; and from out of the spiritual part of the cosmos—that is, from the outside inward—the I unfolds the will.

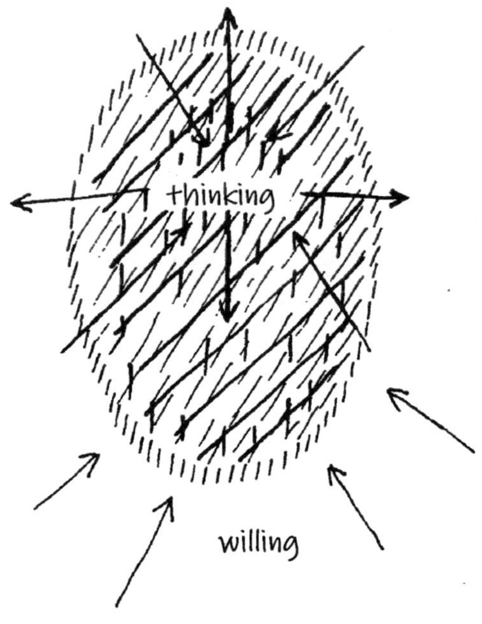

Materialism is therefore vindicated on the one hand, but is also simultaneously defeated. One will never get beyond dilettantism by merely attacking materialism. For what materialism has to say in a positive sense is entirely legitimate. It is at fault only when people want to make it into the be-all and end-all of our conception of the world. When we observe the world and everything occurring in it from an inner spiritual perspective, we will increasingly come to realize that, generally speaking, what individual people opine in a positive sense is justified and that these opinions only become unjustified when they express something negative. And in this respect, spiritualism is often as one-sided as materialism. To the extent that materialism has something positive to say, it is correct; to the extent that spiritualism has something positive to say, it is correct. It is only when they turn negative that they stray into what is unjustified and erroneous. And it is no small error when people who assume that they have attained a spiritual view of the world—without, however, having any understanding of material processes—look down on materialism in an amateurish manner.

The material world is permeated by spirit; but we must also get to know its material characteristics, not become one-sided, but know that one must look at reality from the most varied sides in order to arrive at the full significance of this reality. And this is what is taught in the best possible way by a worldview such as the one presented by anthroposophy.

IV

THE FESTIVAL OF THE APPEARANCE OF CHRIST

Lecture One

DORNACH, DECEMBER 24, 1921

IF PEOPLE ACCUSTOMED to present-day concepts hear that we are currently conducting a study course over the Christmas holidays,[†] then this may well seem strange to them because of the prevailing notion that work should stop during the great festival times of the year and that we should devote ourselves only to religious observations, especially at Christmas time. However, a deeper insight into present-day conditions will not fail to recognize that it is precisely during these festival times that something different is called for than what has been valid for a long time. We live in difficult times, and it really ought to seem frivolous today if—without considering these challenging times of great need—one simply wanted to continue with old customs, unaffected by what is happening, particularly at the present time, both in the visible and in the invisible world. We see how people give each other presents at these festival times, how they decorate the Christmas tree in the traditional manner, and how in various ways they do what people have become accustomed to do, according to tradition, for many centuries. But, especially today, we must become aware how these traditions and customs have almost become something superficial.

To those who were more profoundly involved in, and touched by, the experiences of the last few years it feels as if they had to live through centuries; and they can only look with a certain feeling of melancholy at that part of humanity that is still thinking in the more accustomed way, which was to some extent still justified until the beginning or the middle of the second decade of our century. To an unprejudiced mind, everything resulting from the events of the present time must appear loaded with questions, with questions that concern the archetypal aspects of all human life. Those of you, esteemed listeners, who have heard me speak on other occasions will know how little I am inclined to join in with the customary assertion that "we are living in a transitional period." This is, after all, something that can be said about any time period because there is always a transition from what happened in the past to what will happen in the future. The important thing, however, is what this transition consists of. And today we cannot fail to recognize that as human beings we are only conscious of our true nature when we take an active interest in the monumental things that are happening in the world.

One frequently hears the criticism that many people increasingly believe that being a Christian implies saying, "Lord, Lord" or uttering the name of Christ as often as possible. As a matter of fact, what is needed today is something essentially different. Our whole life needs to be Christianized through and through—a Christianization that calls for more than just uttering the name of Christ and, instead, requires us to connect intimately with the spirit of Christ. We see today how almost everywhere in the world major questions regarding human existence are raised. And we can already perceive that this region here, the European region, which has for many centuries been the actual arena of human civilization, can no longer be this arena in the future. We notice that the world problems now extend over larger territories, and we perceive above all—in view of certain symptomatic phenomena—that a great confrontation between the West and the East is foreshadowed in all areas of life.

The West has kindled a new spiritual life based on and derived from mechanical-naturalistic principles. One can only view this spiritual life correctly if one recognizes that it is merely at the beginning of its development. But we must look from this beginning spiritual life of the West to the East—with which we are becoming more and more connected geographically, historically, and culturally, and with which the West must come to terms.

In the East, there exists an ancient spiritual life that can be traced back thousands of years. And one can feel an enormous respect, an immeasurable reverence, for what is present in the East—albeit in a more dissipated form today—if one traces what still exists today back to the original source, from which it took its starting point as the primordial wisdom of humanity. When we consider the more spiritual aspects of life, a specific word is sounding across from the East, which, especially if we adopt the standpoint of the West, must sound peculiar to our hearts and minds. It is a word that is meant to express in the language of the East a characteristic feature of the physical world which we perceive all around us with our senses. The East, beginning with ancient India, had become accustomed—whether it be more clearly expressed or less so—to designate this physical, sensory world as *maya*, as the great illusion.

This is how the East—even if, as mentioned, these things are only present in a more dissipated form today—this is how the East encounters the external world; it views this world, which can be seen and heard by our eyes and ears, as the great illusion, as *maya*. Anyone becoming familiar with the characteristic features of this eastern way of looking at life will soon discover that this idea of *maya* was not originally part of the primordial wisdom of the Orient. And it is precisely with the help of anthroposophical spiritual science that we gain insight into the development of this eastern civilization, which spanned thousands of years. When we look back into a time that lies beyond the third millennium BC, and as we go further and further back into remote antiquity, we find less and less evidence of this concept of *maya*, of the great illusion of the external physical-sensory reality. If we want to give an approximate point in time, we can say that it was only around the transition from the fourth to the third millennium BC that this concept emerged as the prevailing conviction of the East—that the physical, sensory world surrounding human beings is not a reality, but a great illusion, a *maya*.

What is the cause of this tremendous change in the eastern view of life? This cause is deeply rooted in the soul development of humanity. If we look at the primeval wisdom of the East, and see how it later condensed into a poetical form in the Vedas, into a philosophical form in the Vedanta philosophy, and how it then developed into the yoga teachings, if we observe, for example, how the magnificence of this eastern teaching is contained in the *Bhagavad Gita*[†]—then we find that at one time the essence of this eastern wisdom had been such that human beings perceived not merely the outer sensory world, but that they perceived in this external physical world, in everything that they saw through their eyes, heard through their ears, or touched with their hands, a divine-spiritual reality.

These ancient human beings did not perceive trees as prosaically as we see trees today. In every tree, in every bush, in every cloud, in every well-spring there was something that revealed itself as a soul-spiritual cosmic world content. Wherever they looked, they saw the physical permeated by the spiritual. The well-spring did not only trickle in inarticulate sounds, but out of these trickling sounds of the spring people heard a soul-spiritual content. The forest did not only rustle in an inarticulate way, but out of these rustling sounds of the forest people heard the language of the eternal cosmic word, of a soul-spiritual being. Today's human beings can only form a miniscule idea of the tremendously living way in which people experienced the world in these remote, primeval times.

But this lively, spiritual alertness with which these people lived in their surroundings gradually abated as the third millennium BC approached. And if we place ourselves into the situation of the development of that era, then we become aware that humanity—seen as a whole, that is to say, as the humanity of the East—began to perceive the earthly manifestations with a certain feeling of melancholy; it was as if the gods were withdrawing, as if they were disappearing beneath the surface of things. And, undoubtedly, there were many who expressed this profoundly felt experience almost in the form of prayer by saying: "The old gods have disappeared behind the surface of the outer physical things. The world has become empty of the gods, and because it now appears as a world devoid of gods, it is *maya*, it is a great illusion."

Initially, people did not speak of the world as this great illusion; but it was because the world had become bereft of the gods that people experienced it as a great illusion, as *maya*. If we wanted to go back to a time when this view was still a living reality, then we must actually go as far back as the epoch before the Atlantean catastrophe, back to Atlantean humanity. For it was already shortly after the Atlantean catastrophe that civilization in general showed faint indications of regarding the whole realm of physical and sensory phenomena as something not real. Yet, until the end of the fourth millennium BC, this ability to perceive the gods in the physical-sensory world was still largely present. This ability was still there to the extent that people had not yet needed any real consolation for what had, up to that point, been experienced as the unreality of the physical world. But, starting from the end of the fourth millennium, some form of consolation was needed. And the initiates, teachers, and priests of the mysteries searched for this consolation on behalf of humanity; and it was sought in the language of the stars. "Here on earth," so they said, "there is no reality. But if we study the stars, then we can ascertain from the language of the stars how reality is poured down to the earth from distant parts of heavenly regions. The stars speak a language which, if we hear it, resounds in such a way that the *maya* of the world attains true meaning."

The star wisdom of the Chaldeans and the star wisdom of the ancient Egyptians made a strong impression on humanity; this star wisdom was perceived as something that gave *maya* a foundation of reality. "Here on this earth, we can only find what is not real," so people said; "we must look up to the eternal cosmic word that 'speaks' to receptive souls in the movements and positions of the stars. Then, reality will reveal itself in this *maya*." If people wanted to know something important, something significant for life, then they sought to investigate it from the stars and their language. And this remained the human soul condition until the time in which the Mystery of Golgotha took place.

From the language of the stars, the sages of the mysteries revealed to humanity what was real; for people did not believe that this reality could be found on earth. Anyone who understands the true essence of ancient Greek culture will certainly perceive—notwithstanding a certain superficial view, frequently heard, that life in Greece embraced a childlike joy about this reality—that there was something tragic weighing down this Greek culture, something that yearned for a kind of redemption within the life of human beings. This was, in fact, nothing but an echo of this oriental feeling, which I have described to you just now.

And as modern human beings we have reached the point where our present civilization regards it as a highest inner treasure to have developed the faculty of thinking, to have developed our thoughts in a most comprehensive way. But we have not reached the point of recognizing these thoughts as a reality. When we devote ourselves to our life of thought, we experience ourselves as if we were in a realm of unreality. Many people believe that the life of thought is nothing but an ideology. In using this term "ideology," many people actually want to indicate the same feeling, but now in relation to the inner life of the soul, as what the East experienced in relation to the external physical-sensory reality by calling it *maya*. We could also speak of *maya*, in the same way as we speak of ideology, but then we would have to mean it in relation to our inner soul life.

What was, during a certain time period, the most intense reality for the eastern people—the soul-spiritual—has for us become *maya*; and what was *maya* for the East—the outer physical-sensory world—has become our naturalistic reality. And so, this is how we live today, inasmuch as we call the thoughts that are developing within us an ideology (or *maya*). The eastern people once perceived gods in the external, sense-perceptible world of nature. But these gods vanished from their sight. The East did not have the faculty of thinking as we have it today. It is the special characteristic of the West that it attained the faculty of thought as the purest, most light-filled configuration of the life of the soul. But what has not yet dawned for us is the divine element in our thoughts. We are waiting for the divine in our thinking to arise for us. What had disappeared from the external physical world for the eastern people, and had thus become *maya* for them, does not as yet exist with respect to our world of ideas, our thoughts, our inner thought-filled world. In the course of the historical development, the external world of the senses has, for the eastern people, gradually become empty of gods. Our thoughts are still empty of gods, of the divine element. We can only understand our thinking in this way if we experience it as a kind of prophecy that, one day, the *maya* of our thinking will be filled with an inner reality.

The history of human evolution is thus divided into two meaningful segments. One segment develops from a life filled with the divine to one being devoid of the gods; the other segment—and we are now at the beginning of it—develops from a life bereft of the gods toward a life anticipating to be filled with the divine. And in the middle between these two evolutionary streams stands the cross erected on Golgotha. But how does this cross on Golgotha stand within the consciousness of humanity? If we look back to a time some six centuries before the Mystery of Golgotha, then we see the Buddha, revered by an ever-increasing congregation. We see this Buddha leaving home, going out into the world, and observing a corpse—one of the manifold things he encountered. The sight of this corpse affected his soul in such a way that he withdrew from the *maya* of the external world. The corpse had a deterring, frightening effect on Buddha. And because he had to see death, the corpse, he felt compelled to turn his gaze away from the physical world to another sphere, to the divine-spiritual that cannot be found on the earth. The sight of the dead human being became the point of departure for Buddha to withdraw from the world and take refuge in an extra-earthly sphere of reality.

And now we turn to a point in time some six hundred years after the Mystery of Golgotha. There, we see many people looking upon that great symbol—the crucifix, the cross with the corpse hanging on it. They were looking at the lifeless human being. Yet they looked upon this dead human being not in order to flee, not in order to leave him and seek another reality; rather, in this dead human being they saw the very entity in whom they were meant to find refuge. In just twelve centuries humanity had changed in such a way that it learned to love death on the cross, the very death from which Buddha fled. Nothing can indicate more profoundly, more intimately, the great change that took place through the Mystery of Golgotha, which lies right in the middle between these two points in time. And as we turn our thoughts in this way to the Mystery of Golgotha, we must reflect on what was actually revered there in the sense of early Christianity.

Paul, an initiate in the mysteries of his time, was not able to believe in the living Jesus; he disputed the living Jesus. But when, on his way to Damascus, he became aware that Christ lives, that Christ reveals himself from out of the world's darkness, Paul was able to believe, not in the living Jesus but in the risen Christ; and he began to value the living Jesus because he is the bearer of the risen Christ. As a result of this special insight into the world's interrelationships, Paul gained certainty as regards the divine-spiritual life, a certainty that sprang from death.

What had thus taken place in the development of humanity was that at one time people had found comfort by looking up from the earth to the stars, out of which the eternal word spoke to them, whereas now they looked upon the historical event of Golgotha and upon a human body that contained the mystery of existence. This mystery of existence is what the apostle John wanted to express in the words, "In the beginning was the Word" (John 1:1).

Indeed, in the primordial beginning the Word spoke out of the movements and the positions of the stars! The Word sounded down from the cosmos. This Word could not be found on the earth. This Word penetrated the earth below from heavenly expanses, from the home of the Father. And the writer of the Gospel of John ventured to say the words, "And the Word became flesh and dwelt among us" (John 1:14)! This meant to express the following. What once lived out there in the stars had lived in the body that hung on the cross; what formerly had been sought outside in the cosmic expanses now had to be seen in a human being; what previously had streamed down to earth only in the splendor of light had now come down to human beings. This view of life had been guided from a cosmology encompassing the whole universe to a conception of a central human being, who was permeated by what had once shone down from the stars, who was imbued with the living cosmic Word.

That it is also possible to view the origin of earthly existence by looking into the inner life of the human being Jesus and establishing an intimate connection between one's own inner being and the human inner being of Jesus—just as a relationship had previously been established between human beings living on earth and the eternal cosmic Word speaking from the stars—*this* is the essential meaning that is to be revealed to humanity through the Mystery of Golgotha. This Mystery of Golgotha is indeed the most important, decisive moment in the evolution of the earth; and this is what is indicated through the New Testament.

It is wonderfully profound, and immeasurably poignant, how people are told, through the Gospels—sometimes by one Gospel, sometimes by another Gospel—about the coming of Christ Jesus. From the one side, we are told of the three wise men, the magi from the Orient, the bearers of an ancient star wisdom, who gleaned the cosmic Word from the star-scripture of the universe; they were endowed with the highest wisdom then accessible to human beings. And the Gospels intimate that this highest wisdom could, at that historical point in time, say nothing more than, "Christ Jesus has appeared, for the stars tell us so." The eternal cosmic Word, which came down from the stars, which lives in the star constellations, is what revealed to humanity that Christ Jesus would appear.

The ancient schools, the schools of wisdom, proclaimed: Since the emergence of present humanity on earth, Jupiter has completed its planetary orbit 354 times. A Jupiter year, a great Jupiter year, has been completed since that point in time which had been regarded—for example, by the ancient Hebrews—as the beginning of human existence on earth. In accordance with the world conception of that time, an ordinary year had 354 days. 354 Jupiter days had elapsed and these 354 Jupiter days constitute something that "speaks" out of the cosmic wisdom; it speaks a sentence, as it were, a sublime sentence, in which the individual words indicate the orbits of Mercury. A Mercury day had elapsed seven-times-seven, that is forty-nine, times—the same length of time as it takes for one Jupiter day to elapse. These were the relationships that the ancient sages looked for in the scripture of the stars. And what they received as inspirations into their souls by deciphering the star-scripture was interpreted in such a way that they could clothe it in the words: "Christ Jesus has appeared, for the time is fulfilled. The Jupiter time, the Mercury time is fulfilled. The great universal 'chronometer,' which is located in the stars, indicates that the time is fulfilled."

This is what the Gospels relate from the one side. From the other side they bear witness to what was revealed to the poor shepherds in the fields; how, from a dream springing up from their simple hearts—without any wisdom, merely by listening to the simple, pious voice of the human soul—the poor shepherds received this revelation from the depths of the human breast. And it is the same message: Christ has appeared.

Highest wisdom and the greatest human soul-simplicity are sounding together in the words: Christ has appeared. At that time, the highest human wisdom was already in decadence; the highest human wisdom was losing its glow. But what was intensifying its glow was a capacity that comes from the inner human being. And ever since, the faculty of thinking—the thought—has developed from within the human being. We cannot yet raise it to the stage of reality; it is still a *maya* for us. But we are faced with the need today to increasingly develop insight into how our thoughts can become a reality. In pre-Christian times, people looked up to the stars in order to experience reality. We must look to Christ in order to have reality for our inner being. "Not I, but Christ in me"[†]—these are the words that will give inner weight and inner reality to our thoughts.

The theology of the nineteenth century has progressively changed Christ Jesus into a mere human figure, who can also be recognized by external history—Jesus, the simple, albeit highly developed, man of Nazareth. But Christ has been lost. He will only emerge in his true form through the revivification of a worldview that includes the supersensible, a view of life that turns its gaze from the sense-perceptible to the supersensible. To the extent that humanity has lost the spiritual in the sense-perceptible, to that same extent must it find the inner reality in human thought—which has, in fact, advanced to the stage of being filled with light, but has done so in an abstract way.

Humanity can attain this inner reality by recognizing something in the events taking place on the earth itself, as a result of the Mystery of Golgotha—something that can only arise for the human soul through supersensible concepts. To the extent that humanity resolves to gain an understanding of the Mystery of Golgotha through supersensible knowledge, to that same extent will Christ be born anew within the evolution of human civilization. By taking in supersensible knowledge, human beings may hope for a real, perennial Bethlehem. A profound meaning lies in the perceptive words of someone like Angelus Silesius:[†] "If Christ were born in Bethlehem a thousand times, but not in thee, thy soul would still be lost eternally."

But it is not only in empty phrases that Christ must be born, but in every form of cognition and knowledge. We must reach the point of considering what can be gained by simply observing the world, just as Paul considered what the outer world could reveal to him before he was confronted by the event of Damascus, before he perceived the earth permeated by the forces of the living Christ. We must carry these forces of the living Christ into all forms of cognition. We must fill with warmth all the cold, abstract knowledge that has led us into the distress of the present time. We must permeate this knowledge with the living power of Christ.

This is something that stands before us as a significant task of the present time. We must feel that we should first find our way to Christ. We must develop a deep inner sense of the concept of Christ. We must be clear about the fact that the present destitution is too great to simply cling to outer Christmas customs. We must rise to the conviction that clinging to these customs is a falsehood in the face of other prevailing views in the present time. We must realize that the great confrontation between the East and the West must also take place in the spiritual realm, that the *maya* of the East and the *maya* of the West—the *maya* of the outer sensory world and the *maya* of thought—must come to a harmonious, common understanding.

We should not believe that we already "have" the Christ in our present time. We should imagine ourselves to be like the poor shepherds who were aware of their destitution. We must seek Christ in the innermost realm of the human being, just as the shepherds sought Christ in the stable in Bethlehem. We must bring sacrifices for this Christ who transforms the *maya* of our thoughts into realities. We must be humble enough to realize that we should first rise to an understanding of Christ's birth. We must realize that we should first gain an understanding of the Christmas idea before we will be able to appreciate Christmas in the right way. We must penetrate every single sphere of life with the living power of Christ. We must strive—and we can celebrate the festivals best if we strive in this way in these difficult times—to achieve in a spiritual sense what meets us historically in the form of a symbol, but a symbol of a reality, from the "place of skulls" of Golgotha.[†]

In this way, we should understand that the most important thought we can have about Christmas is that we can bring about a world Christmas by understanding Christianity in the right way. This inner voice, this inner longing, can lead us beyond the actual Christmas night in a way that corresponds to the needs of today. The festival of the end of the year, of the holy nights, can only acquire life if we experience the desire to look at these Christmas nights as an invitation to gain insight into what humanity needs for its development. The festive feeling that we experience at this time of the year can then emit something of the fact that, by making an effort to understand the inner reality that is still a *maya* for us, we can bring about a resurrection of the divine-spiritual reality that had lost its glow in earlier times and therefore had led to the conception of *maya*.

Humanity has arrived in *maya*, in an outer *maya*, and it must now evolve from an inner *maya* into a true soul-spiritual reality. If we understand this, then all our thoughts about Christmas during the festive season will be filled with a feeling for the world, which we need today if we are to experience true human value and true human dignity. Then something will stream into us from what we feel in connection with any of the yearly festivals, and this will encourage us to acknowledge: In times of need we must celebrate in such a way that we gradually see the new Christmas lights of a new spiritual life. We must learn to celebrate not just a single Christmas time; we must learn to celebrate a universal world Christmas.

Lecture Two

DORNACH, DECEMBER 25, 1921

ANYONE WHO LOOKS at the historical development of humanity only in terms of cause and effect, as is customary today, will not be able to gain from history itself what it could actually reveal in its own way to the individual human being—through its forces and impulses—if one tried to penetrate into the true essence of this historical process of becoming. The process of historical development can really only reveal itself to someone who is able to perceive a wisdom-filled activity in the historical sequence of events. We have almost reached the point today where people are of the opinion that anyone who sees a wisdom-filled event, either in the broader world context in general or in the historical development of humanity in particular, must have surrendered to superstitious ideas and have introduced something self-fabricated into the events. And it is true, of course, that one should not project onto historical events whatever one may have thought up. We should not forcefully alter things to fit our own way of thinking, but instead try to let them speak to us through what they really are. And in the case of the historical process of becoming, provided we are sufficiently unbiased, we will be able to perceive something like an active wisdom everywhere, and especially at important turning points in human evolution.

One of the things that has come about as a result of historical development is, above all, the timing of the individual festival days of the year, especially the days related to the important festivals. We cannot fail to notice, once we become aware that Christmas is a so-called immovable festival, that, each year, it falls near the winter solstice, on December 24 and 25. In contrast, we have the Easter festival, which is a so-called movable festival with its dates being determined according to the constellation of the sun and the moon, meaning that these dates are "brought down" from the extra-earthly universe, as it were. And it is certainly the case that if we take these festival days of the year in earnest, they have meaning for our life, they have a decisive impact on our life. And this is what they are meant to have. Meaningful, intense thoughts should arise in us on such festival days. Deeply felt perceptions and feelings should spring up from our heart and soul. Human beings should, precisely because of what they can experience inwardly during such festival times, feel connected to the passage of time and to what is actively at work in the passage of time.

Now, for certain historical reasons, this way of determining the festival times has been fixed, and we should give some thought to this fact that Christmas is an immovable festival, whereas Easter is a movable festival; that Christmas occurs at a time when the earth is most closed off, as it were, from the influences of the extra-earthly universe. When the sun has the least effect upon the earth, when the earth uses its own forces, which it has retained from the time of summer and autumn, to call up its special garment for the shortest days, that is to say, when the earth becomes what it can inherently be through its own forces, with the least influence from the cosmos—that is when we celebrate Christmas. When the time then arrives again during which the earth experiences the most significant influences from the extra-earthly cosmos, when the warmth of the sun, the light of the sun, calls forth the vegetation from the soil, that is, when heaven is working together with the earth to weave the garment of the earth, as it were—that is when we celebrate Easter.

And because this way of determining the festival dates has arisen from human thoughts that were not arbitrarily and abstractly conceived by any one person, but rather from thoughts that have, as it were, permeated humanity throughout long epochs, thoughts that have evolved innately—because of this, something has flowed into the development of history, something which, if understood, will create at the same time the possibility of inwardly venerating it, the possibility of looking back into the times of our forefathers with reverence, with devotion, with love. And when our attention is drawn to something like this, we can even come to realize that, if we can see this wisdom at work in the development of history, then we will also be able to see arising from this history those forces and impulses that can then enter the human soul in the right way and work within the human soul in the right way.

Christmas, as we celebrate it today during the shortest days of the year, on December 24 and 25, has only been celebrated in the Christian church since the year AD 354. People do not usually think very deeply about the fact that even in Christian-Catholic Rome in the year AD 353, the Christmas festival, the festival of the birth of Christ, was not celebrated on this day. It could be said that it is one of the most interesting things in the study of history to see how, out of an instinctive sense of the historical process and out of deeper sources of wisdom—although perhaps working unconsciously for the most part—the date of this Christmas festival was instituted.

Something similar, and yet fundamentally different, had been celebrated in earlier times—January 6, which was the festival of the appearance of Christ. And this festival of the appearance of Christ signified the remembrance of the baptism by John in the Jordan. This festival of the baptism by John in the Jordan had been celebrated as the decisive festival of Christianity during the earliest centuries. And it is only from the above-mentioned point in time that the festival of the appearance of Christ—the festival of the commemoration of the baptism by John in the Jordan—migrated back through the twelve holy nights to December 25, and was replaced by the festival of the birthday of Christ Jesus. This has to do with deep, meaningful, inner processes of the development of Christianity throughout history.

What is indicated by the fact that during the first centuries of the Christian worldview it was the remembrance of the baptism in the Jordan that was celebrated? What does this baptism by John in the Jordan mean? This baptism by John in the Jordan signifies that, for extra-earthly, cosmic reasons, the being of Christ descended from heavenly heights and united with the being of the man Jesus of Nazareth. Accordingly, this baptism by John in the Jordan implies a fertilization of the earth out of cosmic expanses. This baptism by John in the Jordan means an interaction and collaboration between heaven and earth. And inasmuch as this was a celebration of the festival of the appearance of Christ, it was a festival of a supersensible birth—the festival of the birth of Christ in the thirty-year-old human being Jesus.

In the first centuries of the development of Christianity, people turned their attention above all to the appearance of Christ on the earth; and, next to this view of the appearance of the extra-earthly being of Christ in the earthly realm, less significance was assigned to the earthly birth of the human being Jesus of Nazareth, who received Christ into his own bodily nature only in his thirtieth year. This is how it was pictured in the early Christian centuries. In these centuries, therefore, it was the descent of the extra-earthly Christ that was celebrated. And people had tried to understand what it was that had actually taken place in the course of earthly existence.

If we allow ourselves to get a sense of the historical development up to the time of the Mystery of Golgotha, then it appears that in primordial times humanity had been endowed with a primal wisdom of a supersensible nature, a primal wisdom for which we should have the deepest reverence, if we are able to fully perceive its inward qualities and its real essence. In these initial wisdom treasures of humanity, which appear childlike only when seen from an outer point of view, an infinite number of things are revealed, not only about the earthly but especially also about the extra-earthly aspects and how this extra-earthly element works on the earth. Then we see how, in the course of human evolution, this light of a primordial wisdom shone less and less within human souls, and how human beings gradually lost their connection with this primordial wisdom. And it was precisely at the time when the Mystery of Golgotha was approaching that this primal wisdom had lost its shine and had faded from human minds and souls. All aspects of the historical development in Greek and especially in Roman culture show in a variety of ways that humanity's most advanced were aware that a new heavenly element had to make its mark on earthly life, so that earth and humanity would be able to continue their essential development.

To an unbiased observer, the entire earthly evolution of humanity reveals a separation into two parts. The first part is the era during which people were awaiting the Mystery of Golgotha—with a sense of waiting that lived not only in simple, childlike human souls but also in those imbued with the highest wisdom. The second part is the era following the Mystery of Golgotha, the time in which we stand at present. With respect to this era, there is an expectation of an ongoing, far-reaching fulfillment of the supersensible world, for a renewed influence of the extra-earthly cosmic reality upon the earthly events occurring in world evolution. This is how the Mystery of Golgotha stands in the middle point of earth evolution and how it gives this evolution its real meaning.

I have often tried to illustrate this pictorially for my listeners by saying that one could look at something like the important painting of the Last Supper, made by Leonardo da Vinci,[†] in Milan—although it no longer exists in its former artistic perfection—and observe how the redeemer is pictured among his twelve disciples, how John's relationship to Christ is contrasted with Judas' relationship to Christ, and how we have the whole picture in front of us in all its color nuances. These events are depicted in a most characteristic way in this painting and, seen from the perspective of the Mystery of Golgotha, one could actually say that if any being were to come down to earth from a foreign celestial body, it would be amazed at what it encounters of external reality—for we must assume that such a being from another planet would be accustomed to completely different surroundings—and it would be amazed at all the things created by human beings on the earth. But if this being were then led in front of this painting, in which the Mystery of Golgotha has been uniquely presented in a most characteristic way, then it would immediately and intuitively sense something of the meaning of earthly existence from this picture, simply through the way in which Christ Jesus has been placed among his twelve disciples—who, in turn, are the representatives of the whole human race.

One can indeed, based on a variety of perspectives, sense that the Mystery of Golgotha gives the earth-evolution its actual meaning. But the reality of this fact can only be fully experienced if one endeavors to understand that through the baptism by John in the Jordan a supersensible being—Christ—entered a human being. This is how the

Gnostics† understood it—albeit not in the sense of the worldview that we are trying to regain through anthroposophy today. They understood it in the sense of their worldview, which represented the last remnant of the ancient primordial wisdom of humanity. One could say that there was just enough left of the instinctive primal wisdom of humanity in the first Christian centuries, after Christ had appeared, to allow for the possibility that a number of people would still be able to understand what actually took place with the appearance of Christ on the earth. The kind of wisdom that the Gnostics had can no longer be ours. Because humanity must be in a continual state of progress, we must advance toward a much more conscious, less instinctive, understanding—also of the supersensible. Nevertheless, we can still look with reverence at the wisdom of the Gnostics, who had retained enough of the original, instinctive, primal wisdom of human beings to be able to grasp the full meaning of the Mystery of Golgotha.

And it was this understanding of the meaning of the Mystery of Golgotha and of the essential, central occurrence—the baptism by John in the Jordan—that led to the resolve to celebrate this first great festival. But the development of the history of humanity had been structured in such a way that the old primordial wisdom had to fade away and dwindle. And it was precisely in the fourth century AD that people no longer knew how to interpret this primal wisdom. Yesterday, I described from a different point of view how this primordial wisdom was gradually becoming obscure. In a certain sense, the fourth century denotes the first time that human beings were placed in the situation of having to rely completely on themselves, of having nothing around them for their forming of conceptions other than what the senses can perceive and what the rational intellect can make out of these sense perceptions. One could say that, in order to attain freedom, humanity had to lose the old primordial wisdom; that humanity could never have attained freedom as long as it depended on extra-earthly things and as long as the primordial wisdom had not dwindled; that, therefore, in order to attain freedom, humanity had to lose the old primordial wisdom and be "thrown out" into the materialistic view of the world. This materialistic view emerged, in its first beginnings, during the fourth century AD and grew stronger and stronger until it reached its culmination point in the nineteenth century.

But even materialism has its positive aspects in the history of human development. Because human beings no longer had a supersensible light shining into their minds and souls, because they had to rely on what they observed around them with their senses, an independent force, predisposed toward freedom, had been awakened in them. There is wisdom even in the fact that materialism made its appearance in the history of human evolution. But it was precisely at the time when materialism took possession of the earthly nature of human beings that it was no longer possible to understand that the influence of an extra-earthly, heavenly reality had been placed before humanity in the symbol of the baptism by John in the Jordan. That is when people lost, in a way, the meaning of the festival of January 6, the festival of the appearance of Christ, and when they began to take refuge in other things. Everything that people experienced as impressions, as depths of feeling regarding the Mystery of Golgotha—all this was now no longer experienced in relation to the extra-earthly Christ but, rather, in relation to the earthly Jesus of Nazareth. And the festival of the appearance of Christ became the festival of the appearance of the child Jesus. At the present time, however, evolution has once again reached a pivotal point, a point where new essentialities are called for with respect to our human endeavors, in accordance with our current understanding of the world.

We can see that, as early as the fourth century, it was no longer possible for human beings to grasp the appearance of Christ with a wisdom-filled understanding. But, in the course of history, human perception, human will, and human feeling develop at a slower pace than human thinking. When thoughts had long since ceased to focus on the appearance of Christ, hearts still turned to this appearance of Christ. Deep inner feelings lived in Christianity and, for many centuries, these inner feelings formed the content of historical development. These deep inner feelings were an expression—albeit more like instinctive impulses—of the real meaning of what had taken place with the appearance of Christ, and of its significance for the evolution of the earth.

The festival of the birth of Jesus of Nazareth had been linked with the Adam-and-Eve Day, the festival of humanity's beginning on earth. Adam-and-Eve Day is on December 24, the festival of Jesus' birthday on December 25. In Adam and Eve, people saw the human beings with whom earthly evolution began, the human beings who descended from spiritual heights, who sinned on earth, who became entangled in material things on earth, who lost their connection with the supersensible worlds. People spoke of the first Adam in the Pauline sense,[†] and of the second Adam as of Christ himself, meaning that in the Christian era, we can only be complete human beings if we unite the powers that had fallen away from God through Adam with the powers that lead the human being back to God through Christ—if we unite these two powers within ourselves. This is what was meant to be expressed by moving the Adam-and-Eve festival closely together with the festival of Jesus' birthday. The perception of this connection, which gives life on earth its real meaning, has been preserved in a most intimate way for centuries.

One example of this is the emergence of the deeply intimate paradise and nativity plays, such as the ones that have been performed here on the stage[†]; they stem from the later medieval times, from the very beginning of our modern age, and were brought to regions further east by certain German tribes who had originally lived in more western regions. These tribes had settled in present-day Hungary. We can find such tribes north of the Danube in the Pressburg area; we find them south of the Carpathians in the so-called Zipser area[†]; and we see them settled in Transylvania. In these regions we find primarily Alemannic-Saxon tribes; and in the Banat[†] we find Swabian tribes. All these German tribes brought with them, from their original homeland, their treasured folklore that had assimilated what humanity, out of deepest heartfelt feelings, had experienced over the centuries in relation to the most important event on earth.

But this wisdom of humanity increasingly evolved to a stage where even the Christ-event became entwined in the materialistic conception of the world. In the nineteenth century, we see a theology emerging which itself was becoming materialistic. This is the time when Bible criticism began. People were losing the possibility of being able to sense—as ought to be the case in relation to supersensible descriptions—that what is presented as an imagination of the supersensible appears differently, depending on whether it is seen from one viewpoint or another. People no longer have a concept of the fact that the sages of earlier centuries must also have seen the so-called contradictions in the gospels, but that these were not denounced by them in a critical way. People become engrossed in these contradictions in the gospels in a dogmatic manner. The contradictions are resolved, and everything supersensible is removed from the gospels. The Christ of the gospels is lost. People then attempt to make something like an ordinary profane story out of the gospel story. It reaches a point where one can no longer distinguish what the theological historians say from what a secular historian such as Ranke† says about the Mystery of Golgotha.

If we look at the Jesus figure as described by the famous historian Ranke and see how he depicts Jesus as the simple human being—albeit the most excellent who has ever walked the earth—if we read all the lovingly described features of Ranke's secular story about Jesus, then, in an inner sense, this description can hardly be distinguished from what the materialistically inclined theologians of the nineteenth century have to say about the Jesus figure. Theology has become materialistic. It is especially in the "enlightened" theology that Christ disappears from humanity's understanding. To those who undertake to describe the nature of Christianity, the "simple man from Nazareth" gradually becomes the one and only thing to be considered. And it is particularly Adolf Harnack's description of the nature of Christianity that has become famous.

There are two passages in this book by Adolf Harnack,† *The Essence of Christianity*, that can really be quite shattering for anyone who has a sense of the real essence of Christianity. The one thing is that this theologian, who aspires to be a Christian theologian, said that Christ does not really belong in the gospels, that the Son does not belong in the gospels; that the Father alone belongs in the gospels. Consequently, Christ Jesus, who walked on the soil of Palestine at the beginning of our era, this Christ Jesus simply becomes the human being proclaiming the teachings of the Father. "The Father alone belongs in the gospels"—so says Adolf Harnack and, in doing so, considers himself to be a Christian theologian! It must be said that the essence of Christianity has completely disappeared from this "Essence of Christianity"—I am referring to what Adolf Harnack describes—and that, in reality, such an opinion should no longer be considered Christian.

Another passage in this book, *The Essence of Christianity*, that can have a devastating effect came to my attention once when I attended a lecture given in a society that called itself the Giordano Bruno Society.[†] As a consequence of what was said there by a certain speaker, I had to come to the conclusion that the most important thing about the essence of Christianity has disappeared from modern theology. I had to point to a comment by Harnack in this book, *The Essence of Christianity*, where he says: "Whatever may have happened in the garden of Gethsemane, the idea of the resurrection, the Easter belief, arose from this event; and we want to adhere to this belief." This means that, to present-day Christian theologians, the resurrection itself has become a matter of indifference. They do not want to concern themselves with the actual resurrection as a factual reality. "Whatever may have happened in the garden of Gethsemane," people began to believe that the resurrection occurred there, and that it is not the resurrection itself that they want to abide by but rather "this belief."

At that time, I pointed out that the essence of Christianity was articulated by Paul, who, as a direct result of what he experienced before Damascus, said: "And if Christ had not risen, we would all be lost."[†] It is not the human being Jesus that is the essence in Christianity but, rather, the supersensible being who entered the human being Jesus through the baptism by John in the Jordan—who rose from the grave in Gethsemane, and who became visible to those who had the ability to perceive this visibleness. Paul had most recently developed such abilities and was able to see it; and Paul called upon the risen Christ.

And so, in those days I had to point out that the observations of one of the most famous so-called Christian theologians of that time failed to notice what is the essence of Christianity—namely, its supersensible nature. The chairman of this society then replied to me in a very peculiar manner. He said that these remarks could not possibly be in Harnack's book, because Harnack was a protestant, an evangelical theologian and if Harnack had said something like that, it would be tantamount to statements that could only come from the Catholic side, such as the one about the holy tunic in Trier.[†] He said that, to a Catholic, it is not important whether one can prove that this holy tunic in Trier really comes from Jerusalem but what matters, rather, is that faith is tied to this holy robe. The chairman of this society was so prejudiced that he could not even admit that these remarks are actually in Harnack's book. I even offered to write the applicable page number on a postcard for the next day, since I did not have the book at hand.

Incidentally, this is also characteristic of the "thoroughness" with which such undeniably important books are read these days. People read a book, believe that it has a significant impact on life, but then do not even notice one of the most important observations in it and, instead, actually believe that these remarks are not even in the book! But they are in the book! In any case, all this shows us how the supersensible Christ has been cast out of human evolution by a theology that is becoming more and more materialistic, and how people are clinging only to the external physical appearance of the human being, Jesus.

However, the festival customs and ceremonies of the simple, unpretentious souls who took hold of the Christmas plays were beautiful; they arose from holy feelings. Even if people were no longer able to understand the full meaning of the Mystery of Golgotha, it still existed in their feelings, also when they adhered to the physical appearance of the child Jesus in an outer sense. And presented in this way, the celebration of Christ's birth is beautiful and intimate.

The intellectual reasoning that eradicates Christ in the human being Jesus is not beautiful, and—seen from the highest perspective, also of the Christian worldview—is not true either. It is as if the wisdom-filled guidance of humanity had first taken stock of what needed to happen, so that the materialistic view—and with it, the development of humanity toward freedom—could have its start and then advance from there. Just as materialism had to occur at all, for the sake of humanity's freedom, so it was necessary that the festival of the appearance of Christ, which can only be understood through supersensible perception, be moved back from January 6 to the festival of Jesus' birthday on December 25.

And in between these two dates lie the twelve holy nights. One could say that humanity underwent a reverse journey through the entire zodiac by experiencing, at least in a symbolic sense, a twelvefold quality in moving this festival. Today, by combining everything that, through the human being Jesus, is associated with Christ, we can indeed unfold a sense of intimacy and a profundity of inner feelings at the festival of Christmas. And in yesterday's contemplation about Christmas, I attempted to express in words what is appropriate for our present time in this regard. However, now that materialism has found its greatest triumphs in theology, now that Christ Jesus has become merely the "simple man Jesus" to an enlightened theology, we must find our way back again to developing a sense of the supersensible, extra-earthly Christ-being. But if one presents this viewpoint, then it is precisely the materialistically inclined theology of the present time that feels offended.

Just as the sun sends its physical light down from extra-earthly, cosmic expanses, so Christ descended to humanity as the spirit-sun and united with Jesus of Nazareth. Just as we can see a manifestation of the soul-spiritual in a person's outer physiognomy, in the facial features and in the gestures, so we can see an outer physiognomy in what is taking place in the cosmos, that is to say, in those gestures that are sketched into the cosmos by the passage of the stars, in what is displayed externally as the inner soul-warmth of the universe through the rays of the sun—in all this we can see the outer physiognomy of the soul-spiritual that permeates the entire cosmos. And, in what is concentrated spiritually in the descent of Christ to the earth we can see the inner aspect of what is streaming down to the earth externally in the concentrated rays of the sun. And then you will understand the following statement in the right way: The sun-being of Christ descended to the earth.

We must find our way again to this supersensible understanding of Christ. And, even though we want to preserve the inner reverence for the festival of Jesus' birth, for what Christmas has become exclusively, we must nevertheless learn again to develop a sense of the other birth, which is an extra-earthly birth that came to pass through the baptism by John in the Jordan. We want to learn to understand what arises before our souls—as a significant historical symbol—through the baptism by John in the Jordan, just as we understand what happened in the stable of Bethlehem or Nazareth. We want to learn to understand, in the right way, the words that are communicated in the gospel of Luke: "This is my son; today I have begotten him."[†] We want to learn to understand the mystery of Christmas in such a way that it again becomes the source of our understanding of Christ's appearance on the earth. We want to augment our remembrance of the physical birth with learning to understand the spirit-birth.

Such an awareness can only emerge gradually, as the result of a largely spiritual understanding of the mysteries of the universe. We must gradually aspire again to a spiritual conception of the Mystery of Golgotha. For this, however, we need insight into the origin of the kind of impulses that were present in the earthly development of humanity, such as the one that arose in the fourth century AD, when, out of the innermost needs of a developing humanity, the festival of Christ's appearance was moved from January 6 to December 25, the festival of Jesus' birth. We must learn to observe how the wisdom-filled guidance of the history of humanity works. We must learn to immerse ourselves in this historical development with our whole being. Then we will recognize the wisdom-filled guidance in the history of humanity, without bringing superstition or self-made fantasies into it. We must learn to deepen our understanding of history, not just with abstract notions or from the perspective of cause and effect, but we must learn to devote ourselves to this historical development with our whole being. Only then will we understand what makes our time truly a period of transition, a time in which a spiritual worldview must be wrested from the materialistic view, a time in which we should strive to ascend to the supersensible in a natural way. And one expression of such an ascent to the supersensible will be a new understanding of the appearance of Christ on earth, of the Mystery of Golgotha.

And so, to those who are really able today to immerse themselves in the spirit of the time, the Christmas festival is something twofold. It is what has arisen in our most recent history since the fourth century AD; what has produced such wonderful loveliness especially in the simple, unpretentious folklore; what still elicits an inner delight from us today when we see these folk plays again in a renewed production—as we are attempting to do here out of our anthroposophical knowledge. It also is everything that people have poured into life in the way of heartfelt warmth throughout the centuries, during which the concept of Christianity assumed ever more materialistic forms, until it reached a point in the nineteenth century where this concept's own absurdity made it necessary to turn around and come back to the spiritual again. And this is what has led us as human beings of the present time to the second aspect concerning Christmas. It is the awareness that—along with the feelings we bring toward the traditional Christmas festival (which first emerged in the fourth Christian century) and the warmth of heart with which we want to accompany this festival—a new Christmas must be born out of a time-appropriate understanding, a second Christmas to join the old Christmas.

Christ must be reborn through human beings today. In keeping with remembrance, Christmas should be the festival of Jesus' birth; in keeping with the spirit, it should become the festival of the birth of a new conception of Christ—new, not as compared with the earliest centuries, but new as compared with the centuries since the fourth century AD. And in this way, the Christmas festival itself should not be only a festival of the remembrance of a birth, but it should become—inasmuch as it will be experienced year after year in the near future—a festival of an immediately present birth, a festival of a currently occurring event. This birth of the new Christ-concept must be fulfilled. And the Christmas festival should attain the kind of inner intensity that makes it possible—each year again, and especially at that time of the year—for people to particularly reflect on the fact that a new conception of Christ must be born.

From a festival of remembrance, the Christmas festival must become a festival of the present time, a festival of what human beings experience as a birth in the immediate present time. Then it will truly find its way into our more current historical process of becoming; then it will gradually gain strength within this historical development of humanity—also into the future, where it will be so very much needed. Then it will become a world Christmas.

Lecture Three

BASEL, DECEMBER 26, 1921

For centuries, Christmas was a festival that celebrated the most important remembrance for all of Christendom. And if we understand this festival of Christmas as a festival of remembrance, then we have to think of everything that has been associated with this festival in people's feelings and perceptions over the centuries. We must think of the fact that this festival of December 25 did not exist as such within the development of Christianity until the fourth century; and that in this fourth century—in fact, for the first time in the year AD 354, in Rome—the festival of Jesus' birth was introduced to the Christian world as a meaningful tribute to that particular time period. The fact that such a contribution had to be made to this time in the fourth century undeniably has its roots in the deep Christian instincts of the evolution of humanity.

The peoples of the North collided with what was developing in the southern regions of Europe. Many of the old pagan customs were still present and alive in the wider vicinity of the southern regions of Europe, in the Roman and Greek regions. Many of these pagan customs were also prevalent in northern Africa and in Asia Minor, in short, in those places that had gradually assimilated Christian thoughts, feelings, and perceptions. But, by its very nature, Christianity had never been intended to be a sectarian stream, meant for one or another group of people; instead, regardless of how many different factors had opposed it, either from within or from outside its own sphere, Christianity had been intended from the outset to nourish the souls and hearts of *all* people.

A religious consciousness was still alive in the pagan peoples of the northern and the southern regions, a consciousness that connected the divine powers to the stars, and the mightiest of these godly powers to the sun. And what still existed as a living thought within this pagan view was the idea that the time when the earth experiences its darkest days, at the winter solstice, is also the moment when the victorious power of the sun begins to unfold once again for the benefit of all earthly fertility. This perception of the earth having to rely on itself, of the earth being isolated from the cosmic-divine powers, of the earth being alone, as it were, within the cosmic world—this perception was replaced with a feeling of hope at this time of the winter solstice, hope that the beneficial effects of light and love from the realm of the sun would indeed be coming again and reawaken everything fruitful on the earth.

There was an intimate connection between such a perception and the way people experienced their own soul-being. Especially within the old pagan religions, people felt themselves to be inwardly connected with the earth. In a certain sense, they felt themselves to be part of the earth; they felt the life of the earth continuing on into their own life. And so, when the earth received its most significant influences of warmth and light from the heavenly sphere of the sun in summer, human beings felt as if they had surrendered themselves to the very sphere from which the radiant and warming rays of the sun come down to earth. During the height of summer, they felt themselves unfurled into cosmic expanses. At the time of the winter solstice, they felt intimately connected with the earth, with everything that the earth had preserved from the warm, luminous summer. Initially, human beings felt somewhat alone with their earth within the whole universe, and the return of the divine-spiritual to the earthly realm at this time of the winter solstice was a deeply felt reality for them.

Accordingly, human beings had introduced[†] into their concept of this festival all those things which—in their feelings, in their whole life of soul and spirit—had brought them so intimately together with the universal essence of the cosmos. And, because Christianity had come upon something most precious with this festival of the winter solstice, there was no other course possible than for Christianity to bestow this most precious treasure of the winter solstice festival even onto those peoples who had opposed Christianity. And what had become the most precious, the most important, treasure to Christendom—in the sense of the turning point that had come to pass between the Old and the New Testament—was undoubtedly the memory of the birth of Jesus.

The peoples of the Old Testament articulated the whole mystery of human life and its connection with human death by saying: "When the soul passes through the gate of death, it embarks on a path that will reunite it with the ancestral fathers." What did this imply? It implied a longing for a return to the fathers; this was the treasured feeling experienced in accord with the concepts of the Old Testament. And, in the course of the first four centuries of Christianity, this longing for community with the fathers was transformed into a vision of the birth of the being who is the uniting force of Christianity. The experience associated with the Old Testament was transformed into a vision of Nazareth or Bethlehem, into the vision of the birth of the Jesus child.

And so, one could say that, by establishing the date of the Christmas festival in the fourth century AD, Christianity has made a tribute to the unification of human beings all over the earth and has also associated a most precious feeling with this Christmas festival. And if we pursue these things further and see how the Christmas festival has been celebrated throughout the ages, then we see everywhere within Christendom how, as the time of this festival approaches, human souls are filled with a loving devotion for the Jesus child. This loving devotion can be seen as something very special manifesting in the course of the Christian centuries that came after the fourth century AD.

It is important to have an inner understanding of the fact that the Christmas festival was instituted on December 25—around the time of the winter solstice. For, as late as AD 353, even in Rome itself, Christmas was neither celebrated on December 25 nor as the birthday of Jesus of Nazareth or Bethlehem; instead, it was customary to celebrate the festival of January 6. This festival was meant to be the commemoration of the baptism by John in the Jordan, the festival of the remembrance of Christ. And this remembrance was linked to the idea that, through the baptism by John in the Jordan, the extra-earthly Christ-being—coming from realms beyond the earth, from heavenly realms—had entered into and united with the human being Jesus of Nazareth.

It was not an ordinary birth that was celebrated but, rather, the descent of the Christ-being into earthly existence so that life on earth could be fructified anew with quickening forces. By celebrating the day of Christ's appearance, people wanted to develop an awareness of the mystery that a heavenly being had united with the earth, that humanity had received a new impulse for its development through this heavenly intervention. The mystery of this descent of something extra-earthly, something heavenly, into earthly existence was still understood at the time of the Mystery of Golgotha, and for some time afterwards. Some remnants of the ancient primordial wisdom were still present at that time and could contribute to insight into a reality such as this, which is perceptible only in the realm of the supersensible. The old instinctive knowledge, the primordial wisdom which, as a gift from the gods, had been bestowed on humanity at the time of its earthly beginnings—this primordial wisdom was gradually lost. It became weaker and weaker over the centuries. But at the time of the Mystery of Golgotha there was just enough left of it for people to be able to recognize the immenseness of what had unfolded in this Mystery of Golgotha.

And so, during the earliest centuries, the Mystery of Golgotha was taken up in wisdom. This wisdom had almost entirely dwindled by the fourth century AD. People had to rely on other things, on what the pagans brought to them from many sides, and they could no longer develop a true comprehension of the deeply mysterious nature of the union of Christ with the human being Jesus. One could say that the possibility of comprehending the real Mystery of Golgotha was lost to the human soul's faculty of perception. And this is how things remained for the following centuries. The primordial wisdom was lost to humanity. This needed to happen because human beings could never have gained their freedom and their state of self-dependence from this ancient wisdom. One could say that human beings had to enter into the darkness for a while in order to gain out of this darkness—in freedom—their innate forces of selfhood. But the Christian instinct has substituted something else for this wisdom—the wisdom through which the Mystery of Golgotha had been accepted by the Christian world, the wisdom used to some extent in discussions about the Mystery of Golgotha, until it was no longer understood. The Christian instinct has replaced this wisdom with something else.

Today's Christianity has little understanding of the profound discussions that took place in the early Christian centuries among the wise church fathers of Christendom regarding the two natures—the divine and the human—and how they were united in the personality of Jesus of Nazareth. This was something that "spoke" to a wisdom that was still alive in the first Christian centuries, something that later devolved into empty abstractions. Very little remains today, in western Christendom, of the holy zeal with which people sought to understand how the divine and the human were united in the Mystery of Golgotha. But the Christian impulse is powerful; the Christian impulse is formidable. And so, what took the place of this wisdom that had greeted the Mystery of Golgotha when it shone across the earth, was *love*. And it is wonderful to see the abundance of love that, over the course of centuries of Christian development, has been directed toward the baby Jesus lying in the manger. It is wonderful how this love continues to be reflected in the Christmas plays that shine forth to us in such a delightful way from earlier Christian centuries.

If we let all this work on our souls, then we will understand to what extent the Christmas festival was a festival of remembrance. If we let all this work on us, then we understand that, just as the people of the Old Testament longed to be gathered with their ancestral fathers in wisdom, so did the people living on earth during the early Christian centuries long to be gathered around the manger at Christmas time, while offering their best and their devoted love to that innocent child. But who could deny that this love—which streamed out of so many hearts toward this original source of Christianity—that this love has gradually become more or less a habit, right down to our own time? Who would want to deny that we live in a time when Christmas no longer has the living quality it once had? But, from the love that was bestowed upon the Christmas festival, something significant has arisen—even in these modern times. The people of the Old Testament sought to return to their origins, declaring that they wanted to be gathered with their ancestral fathers. Christians want to look at the source of the essential human being by observing the festival of the birth of Jesus. And it was out of this Christian instinct that people linked the festival of Christmas to the earthly origins of humanity, by letting the Adam-and-Eve Day—December 24—precede the actual birthday of Jesus. And finally, out of this deep instinct, the tree of paradise was linked to the Christmas festival, as a symbol.

We first turn our gaze to the stable in Bethlehem, to the child lying between the animals in front of the blessed mother. We look to this heavenly token of the primal origin of humanity. And humanity was impelled, as a result of the feelings it experienced, to look simultaneously to the earthly origin of the human being, to the tree of paradise; and then it associated the manger with the tree of paradise, just as a sacred legend[†] had already pointed to a connection between humanity's earthly origin and the Mystery on Golgotha. This legend describes how the wood of the tree of paradise was passed down in a miraculous way from generation to generation, down to the time of the Mystery of Golgotha, and how the cross on the "place of skulls"—Golgotha—on which Christ Jesus hung, had been made of the very wood of the tree of paradise. Here we see how, in this legend, the heavenly origin of the human being is inescapably linked with the earthly origin of human beings.

But in another sense, all this has in turn also blurred the true fundamental Christian experience. Who can fail to recognize that humanity today does not seem to have a sense of how, on the one hand, the godhead is revered as something fatherly, and how at the same time the godhead can be regarded as the Son-principle? Humanity has more or less lost its ability to distinguish its perception of the Father-God from that of the Son-God—a loss that stretches even into modern theology. And because this ability to distinguish such perceptions has been lost, we see respected theologians today taking the view that the Son does not really belong in the gospels at all, but only the Father; and that Jesus of Nazareth was only the great teacher, the herald of the Father-God. People speak of Christ today, and they still have some recollection of everything that is connected with the sacred history of Christ; but they no longer have a clearly distinguishable sense of the Son-God on the one hand and of the Father-God on the other.

When the Mystery of Golgotha impacted earthly evolution, this perceptive ability was definitely still very much present and alive. Over in Asia, at a place that was little noticed by Rome at that time, Christ appeared in Jesus of Nazareth, and the early Christians viewed him as the divinity who had permeated the soul of a human being in a way that had not occurred on earth before and was never to occur again on earth. Accordingly, this unique event on Golgotha, this soul-permeation of a human being with a divine being—with Christ—imparts meaning to the whole earth evolution. All previous earth evolution should be understood as a preparation, an expectation, of this event of Golgotha and everything that comes later as the fulfillment of what must arise from the Mystery of Golgotha.

This is what took place over in Asia. And in Rome, Caesar Augustus was sitting on his throne. Today, people no longer realize what it signified that Caesar Augustus occupied the Roman throne—that he sat there as the embodied godhead. The Roman Caesar himself was viewed as a god in human form. A differently envisaged god on the Roman throne, and now a differently envisaged god over there on the "place of skulls" of Golgotha—a mighty contrast! What contrast? Let us consider Caesar Augustus, this "god" embodied in a human being. According to the view of his followers, according to the edicts of the Roman state, he had descended to the earth as a divine being. Divine forces had united with the forces of birth, with the blood; and in this blood lives, weaves, and surges the divine power that has descended into the earthly realm—this is approximately how the notion of a divine being dwelling on earth had been envisioned throughout the world, albeit in a variety of different forms. It was only among the Jewish people that it was not pictured in that way, since they experienced their god as remaining forever in yonder world. The other people all around experienced God as joined with the forces of the blood. They experienced God in such a way that they could express this divineness in the words: *Ex deo nascimur* [from God we are born]. However, people still felt related, even as they lived in their own lowly domain, to the entity that dwelled on the highest pinnacle of humanity in a personality such as Caesar Augustus. But it was always a fatherly-divine principle that was revered in this way, for it lived in the blood, which is given to human beings as they are born into the earthly world.

In the Mystery of Golgotha, the divine Christ-being united with the human being Jesus of Nazareth—but this time not with the blood but, rather, with the best forces of the human soul, forces that are striving for the highest. Now a god has united with a human being in such a way that humanity is saved from succumbing to mere earthly-material powers.

The Father-God lives in the blood. The Son-God lives in the soul and spirit of human beings. The Father-God leads human beings into material life: *Ex deo nascimur.* The Son-God in turn leads human beings out of material life. The Father-God leads human beings from the supersensible into the sense-perceptible, the Son-God from the sense-perceptible into the supersensible: *In Christo morimur* [In Christ we die]. These were two distinctly different types of perception. The perception of the Father-God had been supplemented with the perception of the Son-God. However, as a result of other underlying root causes, this distinction between God the Father and God the Son was lost in the course of human evolution. And these root causes have remained connected with humanity, also with Christianity, to this day. When we look at the primordial wisdom of human beings, we see everywhere that people—insofar as they had absorbed what this ancient wisdom offered—were convinced of the fact that they had descended from divine-spiritual heights into the physical-sensory world. The existence of a life before birth was a certain and universally known fact to human beings. People looked back beyond birth, or even conception, up into the divine-spiritual world from which the soul descends by entering physical-sensory existence through birth.

In our language we have only the word "immortality." We no longer have a word in our language for the other side of eternity. We do not have the word "unbornness" in our modern languages.

But if eternity is something that is all-encompassing, then the word "unbornness" must be there, just as we have the word "immortality." What potentially is implied with the word "unbornness" is even more significant for human beings than what can be implied with the word "immortality." As true as it is that human beings go through the gate of death into a life in the spiritual world, it is no less true that nowadays this life in the spiritual world after death is often promoted to people in an exceedingly egotistical sense.

Human beings live here on earth. They long for immortality. They do not want to sink into nothingness with death. Consequently, one only has to stir people's egotistic instincts when speaking to them of immortality. Just listen carefully to many sermons and note how they speculate on human egotistic sentiments in order to bring the idea of immortality to the human soul. It is not possible to speculate in the same way on the egotistic sentiments of human beings when speaking of unbornness. People do not yearn in the same egotistical sense for an existence in the spiritual world before birth, before conception, as they yearn for a life in the spiritual world after death. Once they are here, they are content with that. Why should they be bothered about where they came from? However, guided by a certain egotism, they are concerned about where they are going. But, if we find our way again to an unselfish wisdom, then *unbornness* will become as important to human beings as *immortality* is important to them today.

In ancient times, however, these two viewpoints were linked together. In those times, people knew that they had lived in divine-spiritual worlds; that they descended through birth; that what had been in their surroundings in this purely spiritual world was joined with the human blood; and that it then lived on in the human blood. This view gave rise to the concept: *Ex deo nascimur*. The God who lives in the blood, the God whom the physical human being here represents in the flesh—this is the fatherly God.

The other pole of life—death—demands a different impulse of the life of the soul. There has to be something in the human being that does not come to an end with death. The only concept in consonance with this thought is the idea of a divinity through whom the earthly-physical passes over into the supersensible, the superphysical.

And this is precisely what took place in the Mystery of Golgotha. The divine Father-principle has always been viewed as the transition from the supersensible to the sense-perceptible, while the divine Son-principle is seen as the transition from the sense-perceptible to the supersensible. This is why the idea of resurrection is necessarily connected with the Mystery of Golgotha. Hence, an integral part of Christianity is what Paul expressed† by saying that it is only because Christ is the risen one that he became for humanity what he has become, and now is.

In the course of the centuries, people have increasingly lost a real understanding of the risen one, the one who overcame death; and the "enlightened" theology of more recent times has only recognized the man Jesus of Nazareth. But the human being Jesus of Nazareth cannot be a second principle next to the Father-principle. He could proclaim the Father, but he could not stand next to the Father in the sense of the discussions of early Christianity. However, what *is* standing side-by-side in equal value is the divine Father, who brings about the transition from the supersensible to the physical—*Ex deo nascimur*—and the divine Son, who brings about the transition from the physical to the supersensible—*In Christo morimur*. And majestically above these two principles—of being born and of dying—is a third principle, which emanates from both, is of equal value, and is equally connected with both the divine Father and the divine Son. This principle is the Spirit, the Holy Spirit. This means that within the human being we are to see the transition from the supersensible to the sensory: *Ex deo nascimur*; the transition from the sensory to the supersensible: *In Christo morimur*; and the union of both, the joining with that principle in whom neither birth nor death have their being—the revivification though the Spirit: *Per spiritum sanctum reviviscimus* [through the Holy Spirit we live again].

Christmas has been celebrated as a festival of remembrance for centuries. The extent to which this memory has been lost is shown by the fact that what remained of Christ Jesus for the enlightened theology is only Jesus of Nazareth. This also illustrates that the Christmas festival needs to be transformed for us today from a mere festival of remembrance into a festival that becomes an invitation to something new. A new being must be born. Christianity is in need of an impulse of renewal because, having lost a full understanding of the Christ in Jesus of Nazareth, it has actually lost its meaning. But this meaning needs to be found again. Humanity must recognize again that the Mystery of Golgotha can only be understood through knowledge of the supersensible.

But something else has occurred as well, besides this failure to understand the Mystery of Golgotha. We can look to the manger with love, but no longer with a full, wisdom-filled understanding of the union of Christ with the human being Jesus of Nazareth. Nor are we able to look up to the heavenly heights with the kind of feelings with which people had still looked heavenward around the time of the Mystery of Golgotha. At that time, people had looked up to the starry worlds and saw in the planetary orbits, in the star constellations, something like a physiognomic expression of the divine, soul-spiritual forces holding sway in the cosmos. And in the sun, they saw something like the heart of this divine-spiritual cosmic order. At that time, people were able to see in Christ the spiritual aspect of what they perceived as the sense-perceptible, external beauty of the world of the stars.

To modern human beings, the starry world and everything that can be seen in outer space has more or less become the equivalent of an arithmetic model—a cosmic mechanism. This world has become empty of gods, empty of the divine. And it is obvious that from this god-empty world, which is explored today by means of astronomy and astrophysics, Christ could not have descended. But, in terms of the primordial human wisdom, this world was something entirely different; it was the body of the divine world-spirit and of the divine world-soul. And from this spiritualized cosmos, Christ could descend to earth and unite with a human being in Jesus of Nazareth.

In a profound way, this comes to expression in human evolution itself. Throughout all ancient times before the Mystery of Golgotha, there were mystery centers all over the earth, sacred places that were schools as well, schools of the highest order in which religious life was cultivated at the same time. In all these mystery centers, attention was drawn to what was to come. Everywhere, it was pointed out that human beings carry a power within them that is victorious over death. And this victory over death is what the initiates in the mysteries underwent in the form of mighty experiences. Those wanting to become initiates had to inwardly cultivate a profound experience, an experience that brought them to the conviction: Yes, you have awakened in you the force that is victorious over death. Those initiated into the mysteries experienced in pictures what would actually only take place in the future as part of the whole plan of world history. Everywhere among peoples near and far, a sacred secret was proclaimed within the mysteries: The human being can conquer death. But at the same time, it was pointed out that all the things that could only be presented in pictures in the mysteries would one day stand before world history as a unique event. The Mystery of Golgotha was foretold, also by the pagan mysteries of antiquity. It was the fulfillment of what had been foretold everywhere, especially in these sacred places.

Those to be initiated had to go through initial preparations in the mysteries and then through more difficult exercises—the kind of exercises that brought about initiation in olden times. Then, when their soul had become sufficiently free of the body so that, in this state of detachment, it could unite with the spiritual worlds and be able to perceive in the spiritual worlds—in order to develop its own conviction that life always triumphs over death within human nature—when those to be initiated had reached that point, they were led toward the most profound experience associated with the mysteries of antiquity. And this deepest experience was brought about when the obstacle of the earth, the material obstacle, was removed and no longer stood before the human being's spiritual gaze, when that which is spiritual and material at the same time was meant to become visible—the sun. And those to be initiated were then led to the mysterious phenomenon, which is well known to every initiate, of being able to see the sun through the earth—that is, on the other side of the earth—at the midnight hour.[†]

All throughout history, human beings actually still had instinctive perceptions of what is most holy and sublime. Some of these feelings weakened over time, but the original meaning is still discernible to those who try to be impartial. And even today, we can still infer something from the fact that on Christmas Eve the midnight mass is celebrated in Christian churches at the midnight hour of December 24 into December 25. In some ways, the mass is nothing other than a consolidation of the mystery rituals that guided the initiates to seeing the sun at midnight. In this celebrating of the midnight mass, we can still witness an echo of the old initiation, which enabled those to be initiated to see the sun on the opposite side of the earth at midnight. It also enabled them to perceive the universe as something spiritual, and, simultaneously, to hear the cosmic word sounding through the cosmos, the word that announced—out of the orbits of the planets, out of the constellations of the stars—the cosmic being.

Blood divides human beings. Blood binds that which descends from heavenly heights as the human element to the material, to the earthly element. Especially in our century, people have really sinned against the Christian principle by turning again to the principle of the blood. But they must find the way back to Christ Jesus, who does not speak to the blood, who has shed his blood and linked it to the earth, who instead speaks to the soul and the spirit and unites all people and does not divide them. And so, with his help, people will be able to gain an understanding of the cosmic word, "peace among human beings," which can then enter the earthly realm.

Through this new understanding of the Christmas festival—and through supersensible knowledge—the material universe can then be transformed into spirit before the eye of the soul. The sun can become visible again at midnight—that is, it can be recognized in its spiritual aspects. In this way, an understanding can be gained of the extra-earthly Christ-being, the sun-being, who has united with the human being Jesus of Nazareth. And a renewed understanding can then also be achieved of what should be present among the peoples of the earth as a unifying peace-oriented disposition: "May the divine beings in the heights be revealed, and through these revelations, may peace ring forth from the hearts of human beings who are of good will."

These are the true Christmas words—the sounding-in-unison of "peace on earth" with the divine light that shines onto the earth. We need not only the remembrance of Jesus' birth. We need an understanding of the concept that a new Christmas festival must come; that something must be born; that a festival of birth must emerge out of the present and lead on into the immediate future; that a new Christ-impulse must be born; that Christ must be known again through this new Christ-impulse. We need a renewed understanding of the fact that the divine-spiritual, heavenly worlds and the physical, sense-perceptible earthly world are bound to one another, and that the Mystery of Golgotha is the most significant expression of this connection.

We must understand again why, in the midnight hour of Christmas, we hear, as it were, a reminder to reflect on the divine-spiritual origin of human beings; why, at this time, we hear this reminder to think of the heavenly revelation as being linked to "peace on earth." We can only do this if we become convinced of the reality of this cosmic Christmas, if we are no longer content with the old, customary way of giving each other presents at Christmas, just because that is the custom—once those warm feelings, which throughout the centuries have enlivened Christianity, have been lost. What we need is a new Christmas, a Christmas which not only reminds us of the fact that the birth of Jesus of Nazareth took place but also brings a new birth—the birth of a new Christ-impulse.

We must learn to understand again, in full consciousness, that a supersensible reality is expressed in the Mystery of Golgotha—which then becomes manifest in the sense-perceptible realm on earth. We must understand again in full consciousness what had resounded in the old mysteries. There, it had sounded forth instinctively; now we want to take it up in full consciousness. We want to learn to understand again that, if Christmas becomes a reality for human beings, they will be able to perceive the sun at midnight and experience the wonderful midnight union between the heavenly revelation and *peace on earth*—sounding together through the harmony of the spheres.

It is in this sense that the following words, meant to be dedicated to Christmas, were written down, based on these underlying considerations. They summarize what I wanted to convey to your souls and hearts at this time. Out of an awareness of the anthroposophical understanding of Christ, these words intend to express how we can find our way again to what had lived—albeit instinctively—as human primal wisdom and was still present at the time of the Mystery of Golgotha to the extent that people were able to celebrate the appearance of Christ.

And we do want to find our way again to this understanding of Christ as a cosmic being who has united with the earth. When a large segment of human beings on earth will have regained this understanding—that will be the time of a world Christmas, a time whose approach we are awaiting. Then, a feeling will come alive in us, which, I hope, will have been expressed in the following words:

Behold the sun
At the midnight hour!
Build with stones
In the lifeless ground,

Thus, in decay
And in the night of death
Find the creation's new beginning,
Young morning's strength;

Glory in the heights
The eternal word of Gods;
Shelter in the depths
The powers of peace.

In darkness dwelling,
Create a sun.
In matter weaving,
Know the joy of spirit![†]

V

COSMIC NEW YEAR

New Year's Eve Lecture

DORNACH, DECEMBER 31, 1921

I BELIEVE THAT on this day, the turning point between the old and the new year, it is also appropriate to speak about a turning point in the history of humanity's development, and I will speak today about a particular turning point—the change in human cognition that occurred in the time of transition between the oldest period that humanity can look back on in a historical sense, and our own time. It was especially in these earliest times that people were quite aware that any knowledge of the human being's actual, deeper essential nature can only be attained when those forces of cognition that are concealed in the human being are brought to the surface. It had always been said that perceptions of the external world can only lead to knowledge regarding the external nature of the human being. But, within the special proceedings in the mystery centers, the possibility had been provided—for those aspiring to do so—to achieve a higher knowledge of the real human being, through forces otherwise hidden in the depths of human essential nature. People were quite aware, especially in those earlier times when a certain instinctive wisdom prevailed, that the true nature of the human being is different from what can be found in the everyday surroundings experienced in ordinary life. This is why mention was often made of initiation as the only means through which the deeper secrets of life, related to human essential nature, could become accessible to human beings.

Even today it is necessary to speak of an initiation in this regard, and anthroposophical spiritual science is able to show this. People can say, of course, that today's human consciousness—which has developed under very specific, egotistically driven conditions—resists the idea that real insight into the human being and the world can only arise through such special preparations and developments within the human soul; that modern human beings would like to make decisions regarding the most far-reaching questions of life strictly based on what ordinary life exposes them to—without resorting to such methods of inner development. And when people have a sense that they cannot decide about these highest questions of life with the usual powers of knowledge, then they claim that the human faculty of cognition has limitations anyway and that it would be absurd to try to go beyond these general limits of human cognition. People also demonstrate prejudice toward the principle of initiation by questioning whether the things presented by this science of initiation have any merit for those who cannot yet achieve such initiation in their present incarnation, and how such people could become convinced of a truth that is the result of a specially prepared faculty of cognition?

But this is not how these things transpire. And the latter objection in particular is quite unwarranted. For, what does actually happen when a human being encounters the findings of the science of initiation?

Let us assume that someone first enters a dark room. While walking around, that person distinguishes objects through their shapes, by touching them. Suppose this room is suddenly lit up by a lamp placed somewhere in such a way that it is not even noticeable in the room itself. All objects will now appear different to the usual faculties of the person who previously had walked around the dark room, had only touched things, and, in doing so, had formed a picture of the shapes of the objects in the dark room. With the light shining on them, all objects will now appear different, without anything having been added, without anything now becoming inaccessible to the person who is standing in the illuminated room; they will now reveal their nature and at the same time the nature of the light. In the same way, when we encounter the science of initiation, all we need to do is to cautiously acknowledge what this science offers—regardless of whether we can directly attain it ourselves or not—and look at it in such a way that we allow this initiation science to shine its light on the things we know, on the world that is accessible to us.

This science of initiation does not in any way attempt to bring something else to the world than what this world already is. But just as little as we can recognize what is in a dark room in the darkness—but are able to immediately recognize it in the light—just as little can the objects around us that exist for our ordinary consciousness reveal their inherent nature, unless they are illuminated by perceptions derived from the science of initiation. The real human being stands before us in the ordinary world. And this human being holds an immortal soul within, just as a picture hanging on the wall in a dark room perhaps contains something that cannot be seen in the dark room. But once the room is illuminated, one can see it immediately. It is not as if the initiate had added the immortal soul to the human being; this soul becomes discernible to anyone once the essential nature of the human being is illuminated by the science of initiation. And only a prejudiced science can deny that the world in which we continuously exist with our earthly consciousness between birth and death—that this world itself, which can be accessed through ordinary healthy reasoning, confirms the truth of everything presented by initiation science.

However, the science of initiation has itself undergone a transformation. It was something quite different in the ancient epochs of humanity, and is now appearing again in a changed form for today's human beings. Admittedly, between these two epochs lies a time of world evolution for humanity, a time that began around the fifteenth century and is now coming to an end, a time that was dark with respect to the spiritual light that initiation science aspires to be—although its darkness is at the same time deeply ingrained in the nature of the entire evolution of earth and humanity.

If we look back to older times—whose traditions were still preserved in the Christian era, but began to fade away in the fifteenth century and eventually became incomprehensible during this time period—if we look back to these olden times, then we find that when human beings perceived the world with their instinctive forces of cognition, they did not merely see what can be perceived by human beings today through sense-perception and intellect. In everything perceived with the senses, people saw something spiritual at the same time, not in an abstractly spiritual way, but in a concretely spiritual way; they saw real spiritual beings. Even in the time of ancient Greece, people still saw these concrete spiritual beings. And one can trace this right down to the transformation of sense-perception itself, and follow how it was that people were able to see such spiritual beings. Today, people believe that the tapestry of the senses, which is spread out in front of us, has always been the way it is today. But even external science can demonstrate that this is not the case.

The Greeks, for example, did not see the blue sky in the same way as we see blue today.† The Greeks had no concept of the blue in the sky. For them, this blue was shaded. On the other hand, they saw the so-called light colors more vividly and even more brightly than we see them. This can actually be inferred from the related literature. Furthermore, to a sense-perception that perceives things in this way, the spiritual element lies directly spread out over the sense-tapestry itself. It is only when the world begins to appear in a blue coloring, when it takes on a blue tinting, as it were, that this coloring lets the spiritual aspect of the external realm recede. But, during that very time when human instinctive consciousness perceived something quite elementary in all outer things, human beings also perceived something elementary in their own soul-spiritual inner being.

Today, we speak of our conscience telling us one thing or another. The Greeks spoke of the Erinyes.† This was mostly the case when a particularly striking event occurred; then, the Greeks became aware that something like an elementary spiritual power was approaching them in the form of an objective entity. But in more ancient times, this was experienced in relation to all things—things which we now assume to simply arise from within the human being; people felt that this was brought about by something like an unknown spiritual force approaching the human being. However, what is absolutely normal in one era of human evolution should not occur in the same way in another time period. If someone today were to become conscious of a moral voice in the same way as was still the case in the earlier period of Greek development, when Aeschylus was writing his tragedies, then this would point to a mental illness today, and people might well explain it by saying—although this expression no longer feels quite right today—that the person in question is possessed by an external power. Being "possessed" in this sense was absolutely the normal condition in earlier Greek times. Today, we must sense that what was felt to have come from an unknown power in earlier times now comes from within us, from our conscience.

In the past, when a human being—having perceived out of an innate, instinctive awareness that elementary spiritual beings were working in the outer world, and also that elementary spiritual beings were working in one's own inner being—when that person was accepted as a pupil into the mysteries, then these elementary spiritual beings would be illuminated, as it were, by higher spiritual beings through the light of a new cognition. With an instinctive consciousness, people perceived nature spirits as well as certain demonic forces working in human nature. Through initiation, one descended deeper into nature and also deeper into one's own human essential nature. And the most meaningful, the supremely significant thing that occurred in someone who underwent the first stage of initiation in ancient times was that, as a direct result of the initiation, one ceased to perceive both the elemental beings in outer nature and the demonic entities within one's own being.

One could say that what is normal for us today, what we bear within us as our normal, natural view of the outer and inner realms—this is what the pupils of the ancient mysteries first had to acquire. Humanity advances in such a way that certain things that become natural at a later time have to be acquired through the science of initiation in earlier times. When, through initiation, someone had developed a perception both of nature and of the human being, as was available only to the mystery-pupils at that time, then such a person could in an individual way approach the spiritual beings who governed both the essence of the inner human being and the essence of outer nature. This is why the principle of these older initiations was expressed in the following way. It was said that the pupil ascended from the ordinary view of life to the elements of earth, water, fire, and air. With the ordinary view at that time, what people saw was the elementary-spiritual aspect of air, the elementary-spiritual aspect of fire, the elementary-spiritual aspect of water, and the elementary-spiritual aspect of earth. It was only through the first stage of initiation-science that earth, water, fire, and air could be perceived purely as such.

The essential thing is that, as humanity progresses, what takes the place of this perceiving of soul-spiritual elemental beings, both in the external world and in the inner human being, is what can be called a soul-less nature and—if I may use this expression—a translucid human being, when inwardly observed. Today, when we look at the inner human being, we only see reminiscences of the outer world in the form of mental memory images. Everything else remains invisible to us, just as a completely translucid body remains invisible. But, when people in ancient times looked into their inner being, it was not in that sense spiritually translucid to them. They saw soul-spiritual beings within their inner being.

If things had remained like this, then human beings would never have been able to attain a full awareness of freedom; for this full freedom-consciousness has only penetrated all of the human soul-spiritual forces since this particular time period during which the old instinctive way of perceiving the spiritual had been receding. Within the world of spiritual beings, necessity reigns. In that world, the activity of the spiritual beings prevails; in that world, the course of events is determined by what results from the activity of these spiritual beings. There, if one is engaged in soul in this world of spiritual beings, then one is interwoven into a realm of necessity. There, one is bound to explore the longings, the intentions, the thoughts of the spiritual beings in whose sphere one is interwoven, and to act in the sense of the intentions and impulses of these spiritual beings. There, one has no intention of realizing one's own impulses. In that world, there is no reason for freedom at all. It is only when we stand before a soul-less nature, when we do not find imprints of spiritual beings in nature, that we develop a cognitive knowledge in relation to the outer world which no longer holds any reality, which only contains mental thought images. And the cognitive knowledge that has come down to us since the fifteenth century consists entirely of mental thought images.

And, just as little as images seen in a mirror imply anything compelling to us, just as little as, for example, the reflection of a person standing behind me—unseen by me—can attack me, just as little can thoughts indicate any real action, any real power. The thoughts that we carry within us—and humanity has attained the ability to grasp such purely pictorial thoughts, which do not reflect reality, only in the course of its development, that is, from the fifteenth century onward—these thought-images cannot exert any kind of compulsion, any kind of determinations onto us. Inasmuch as they permeate our cognitive powers, we do not have to comply with them. Just as a mirror image cannot push me, so a thought cannot rule me. But, just as I can make a determination concerning myself as the result of looking at an image in the mirror, so can purely pictorial thoughts determine my conduct. This is why pure thinking—the kind of pure thinking that has essentially become a human property since the fifteenth century—is the foundation for the human experience of freedom. This is what I wanted to address in my *Philosophy of Freedom*[†] at the beginning of the 1890s—that pure thinking is the basis of freedom. And spiritual science shows which place this pure thinking has in the overall development and the overall essential nature of the human being—how this pure thinking entered the historical development of humanity.

This impulse of freedom has now, since the middle of the fifteenth century, entered humanity. It is here. It had to be gained through this perception of a nature devoid of soul, of an inner human being free of spirit. It had to be gained at a time when supersensible realms were mentioned only in the traditional religious confessions and in the traditional philosophical worldviews—which no longer offer anything that can be directly experienced. If human beings were to persist much longer with this perception of a soul-less nature, of a spirit-free human being, then they would have to lose their connection with their own origin.

The time is here, and a time will have to come, when people turn their attention again to their soul-spiritual origins, meaning that they will again become aware that in this world, the world in which we live, there is not just a soul-less nature; that we are not just participants in a soul-less nature; rather, that we live in a world that is filled with concrete spiritual beings. With the hard-won awareness of freedom, we will be able once again to immerse ourselves in the world of necessity. For, within this world, we will then be the very beings who have been summoned to freedom, inasmuch as we have, in our physical incarnations, gone through the state in which we were left to ourselves with our physical bodies. We can begin to explore the divine origin of the voice of conscience again—now that we have come to know the feeling of responsibility that arises from developing this freedom-consciousness during the time when conscience only manifested as an inner voice in the human being, that is, as an image.

It is not as if the development of humanity took its course in such a way—as so many supercilious modern minds believe—that people remained in a state of childlike comprehension of the external world for the longest time, and that they then finally reached the point where everything that now exists as knowledge, even with its limitations, must now remain as it is. No, this is not how evolution unfolds. Someone observing human evolution with an unbiased mind will find that this development of humanity has progressed from one stage to another stage; that the kind of knowledge we have at present also represents such a stage; and that human beings in future times will experience nature differently from how we experience nature today.

As we look back at Thales[†] today, and if we then say in a supercilious manner: "Thales childishly sought the origin of all things in water, but today we know better"—and there are many who indeed believe that presently we know everything there is to know, and will ever be able to know, from what we investigate in chemistry and physics laboratories—if we adopt this supercilious view, then we would actually have to expect that there will come a time in future centuries when people, if they have that same attitude, would look back at our era and say: "These people of the twentieth century still had such childish notions, derived from their tests in chemistry and physics laboratories"! But this is simply not how it is. These ideas—which seem so childish to today's supercilious minds and which, according to this way of thinking, should at best only be considered historically—represent important developmental impulses which humanity had to go through in the past, just as it has to go through today's developmental impulses. And, just as humanity has moved beyond Thales, so it will move beyond Lavoisier,† will surpass Newton,† will surpass what today is regarded as definitive knowledge, will surpass even Einstein.† The world must indeed be thought of as "in flux," also in a soul-spiritual sense, and we must think of ourselves as part of this living flow.

But the fact remains that in the world of external manifestations there is, to begin with, nothing that guides human beings to their own origins; that, instead, it has always been necessary to develop forces hidden within the human being in order to find the way to the realm of our human origins. Today, if we simply look at outer nature with our ordinary consciousness, with our ordinary sense-capacities, then we do not readily find elemental beings, and, as we look within ourselves, we do not readily find demonic entities. What we find outside are the laws of nature, and what we find inside ourselves is something like conscience and equivalent qualities. But if we actually develop what can be developed in terms of our ability to form concepts, in terms of our ability to think in relation to the outside world, if we bring our faculty of thinking to the level where it comes alive—in the same way as otherwise only sensory perceptions come alive—then we will find the possibility again to perceive spiritual beings in outer nature.

What had existed for the old, instinctive consciousness—but in a way that is no longer useful for us—becomes visible to us again, visible to supersensible perception, if we solidify our thinking. With the kind of thinking that has become thin and pictorial, we no longer penetrate through to the spirit of nature. But, if we condense our thinking, if we strengthen it—in the same way as we ordinarily have the strength of our senses—then we penetrate through the external tapestry of the senses to the spirituality that underlies the outer world, and we surpass the correctly presumed limits of the cognitive knowledge of our ordinary consciousness.

We have to cultivate this self-education to the extent that we learn to look at ourselves, with respect to these will-impulses, in the same way as we look at other people. And if we learn not only to look at ourselves but also to form will-impulses out of our consciousness in the same way as these will-impulses normally only form passively in life, if, in other words, we do this not just out of an inner necessity, but out of insight into the world—insight that solidifies into love, into love for whatever impulse is entrusted to us not only through our freedom but also by the wisdom-filled world order—if, in this way, we make ourselves into the executors of the impulses that are needed in this world for world-guidance, then this love will solidify within us. Then we will develop a loving devotion to purely spiritual impulses. And when this devotion has undergone the necessary schooling, then we will be able to find the spiritual within us again and we will find the harmony between the spiritual in outer nature and the spiritual within. For, wherever the search for the spirit has been carried through far enough, people have arrived at the same results. When the initiates of the ancient mysteries searched in the outer world and found, as they called them, the higher gods, then they turned their gaze back into the inner realm of the human being and found there, as they called them, the lower gods. But in the end, they arrived at a stage of development where the world of the higher gods and the world of the lower gods were one, where the above became the below and the below became the above, where the kind of definitions that were derived strictly from the spatial realm, were no longer applicable or essential.

And this is also the case with respect to initiation today. We penetrate into the soul-spiritual aspect of nature. What is then revealed to us is not a world of atoms bumping into one another but, rather, the spiritual powers of the spiritual beings behind our sense-perceptions, and what is revealed to us when we look inward, beyond the limitations of memory, is the soul-spiritual beings within the human inner being. But these two worlds, the outer world of spirituality and the inner world of spirituality, eventually merge into one. Pictorially, we are already able to view this one spiritual world.

Take human beings with their ordinary consciousness. We look out into outer nature; we perceive color, light. We direct our other senses toward outer nature; we perceive sounds, differences in warmth, and other sensory qualities in external nature. We then look at our own body; we perceive our own body in its sensory qualities. We look at nature; it reveals itself to us in sensory qualities. We look at our own body; it reveals itself in sensory qualities. When we begin to activate our will, when we wander through the world, we become aware that these forces of will work into and affect the movements of our eyes; that, even already for our sensory perception, the same thing flows into the essential nature of our eyes as what directs the movements of our legs. If we immerse ourselves deeply enough, even externally, into the sense-perceptible, then we become aware of the same thing as what transpires when we connect to the outer world through the unfolding of our will. What actually happens is that the sense-perceptible world merges into a unitary world for us. This flowing-together into a unity, this merging of the sensory world is superficial, but is nonetheless a reflection of the merging of the world of outer spirituality and the world of inner spirituality.

By uncovering these two worlds, which are one unitary world, human beings become aware again of their soul-spiritual origins. And so, one could say that today we stand at the end of an ancient time, a time that shows an earlier epoch during which human beings were able to see into the spiritual worlds, both when looking out into nature, and when looking inward. Then came a time when it became dark, when the greatest triumphs were celebrated, particularly in this domain of darkness—without initiation science.

But the cosmic year has ended; the cosmic New Year's Eve is here. A new cosmic year must begin. What we were able to say about Christmas is what we also want to experience in relation to a symbolic festival such as the one that is approaching us at this moment; we want to experience it in the same way; we want, through such a festival, to experience symbolically the turning point in time—which must, even today, already be perceived as a *cosmic* turning point in time. Times have become serious; they have become so serious today that we must of necessity look upward from the narrowly defined events occurring within the limited horizon—which the majority of humanity prefers to recognize as the only legitimate one—to the cosmic expanses, also to the cosmic expanses of human soul-spiritual experiences. This is where we witness the cosmic turning point in time.

If we become aware of this cosmic turning point in time, then we become aware that a cosmic New Year of the spirit must begin for humanity. Only if we learn to recognize such things will we be able to feel true humanity in our present era. For true humanity is experienced only when the human being, who goes through repeated lives on earth, finds the possibility in each single earthly life not only to feel as a human being in general, but as a human being with specific tasks related to the specific epoch during which one of these lives is taking shape.

Human beings can live with eternity only if they find the possibility of living in time in the right way. For the eternal should not only be revealed to the human being in time; rather, through the human being and through time, the eternal should become something that can be experienced by the human being. The eternal holds sway in timeless duration; it also holds sway in timeless duration through all human existence. But its pulsations are seen in the events of each single epoch, and in how they impact the human experience. And it is only when we experience these pulse beats and are able to unite them into a comprehensive rhythm that we will experience the eternal through time. Duration belongs to our true human nature. We can only experience duration if we lovingly, and with inner strength, let the individual pulsations of the eternal cosmic essence become our own experience.

This is what I wanted to place into your hearts, into your souls today, at this turn of the year. May the near future bring all of us the opportunity to use the impulses in our thinking, feeling, and willing—those we are capable of developing as our best impulses within our inner being—may we use them in this sense in the smallest and, if granted to us, also in a larger context.

EDITORIAL AND REFERENCE NOTES

This volume consists of lectures given by Rudolf Steiner to members of the Anthroposophical Society in various places in November/December 1921. The first three lectures (in Kristiania, now Oslo) were given between a series of public lectures which Rudolf Steiner gave at the request of various public associations at the time. See *Self-consciousness: The Spiritual Human Being* (CW 79).

Textual basis: The lectures were all stenographically recorded by the professional stenographer Helene Finckh.

The *title of the volume* and the table of contents were provided by the editors.

The following *single editions* of lectures were previously published:

Dornach, December 18, 1921, *Das verlorengegangene Urwort. Das Alphabet, ein Ausdruck des Menschengeheimnisses* [The lost primordial word. The alphabet, an expression of the mystery of man], Dornach, 1938.

Basel, December 26, 1921, *Fest der Erscheinung Christi* [Festival of the appearance of Christ], Dornach, 1939.

Dornach, December 24 and 25, 1921, Basel, December 26, 1921, *Das Fest der Erscheinung Christi* [The festival of the appearance of Christ], Dornach, 1958, 1982.

The following lectures were published in *journals*:

November 24, 27, and December 4, 1921, in *Das Goetheanum*, 1928, year 7, nos. 31–41, and in *Gegenwart* 1964/65, year 26, nos. 4–11.

December 12, 1921, in *Was in der Anthroposophischen Gesellschaft vorgeht. Nachrichten für deren Mitglieder*, 1931, year 8, nos. 21–24, and in *Gegenwart* 1945/46, year 7, no. 11.

December 18, 1921, in *Gegenwart* 1965/66, no. 1.

December 23, 1921, in *Das Goetheanum*, 1939, year 18, nos. 1–2.

December 24, 1921, in *Das Goetheanum*, 1937, year 16, no. 52, and in *Blätter für Anthroposophie* 1952, year 4, no. 12.

December 25, 1921, in *Das Goetheanum*, 1934, year 13, no. 51–52, and in *Die Menschenschule*, 1952, year 26, no. 12.

December 26, 1921, in *Blätter für Anthroposophie*, 1956, year 8, no. 12.

December 31, 1921, in *Die Menschenschule*, 1938, year 12, no. 1, and in *Gegenwart*, 1960/61, year 22, nos. 9–10.

Blackboard drawings: Beginning in 1919, Rudolf Steiner's blackboard drawings, which he often made during his lectures, were recorded using sheets of black paper that were then rolled up and saved. Roughly 1,100 such drawings were preserved in this way. The three relevant blackboard drawings from the lectures of December 18 and 23, 1921, have been reproduced at the end of the present volume.

Notes on the text

Works by Rudolf Steiner within the Collected Works (CW) are indicated in the notes with the bibliographic number. See also the overview at the end of the volume.

I. Cosmic Influences and the Spiritual Task of Northern Europe

Lecture One
Kristiania (Oslo), November 24, 1921

1 **such a long time**
Rudolf Steiner had been in Kristiania (Oslo) in October 1913.

difficult times
This refers to World War I, which had ended in 1918—only three years before these lectures were held.

of the European peoples
Ten lectures given in June, 1910, in Kristiania (Oslo): Rudolf Steiner, *The Mission of Folk Souls* (CW 121).

with a personality
Prince Max von Baden, who in October 1918, for a short time, became the Imperial Chancellor (*Reichskanzler*) of Germany.

2 **a certain remark**
For example, in *The Mission of Folk Souls* (CW 121), particularly in the last lecture.

3 **this anthroposophical branch**
This branch was called *Vidar Branch*, after the god of the future, as described in Norse mythology.

4 **a South-African statesman**
Jan Christiaan Smuts (1870–1950), South African statesman, military leader, and philosopher. He was one of the leaders during the Second Boer War (1899–1902) against the English. He was prime minister from 1919–1924 and 1939–1948 and advocated for the union and reconciliation of the races.

in Washington
This refers to the disarmament treaty taking place from November 11, 1921, to February 6, 1922.

5 **in the wonderful Vedanta philosophy**
The *Vedas*, meaning "sacred knowledge," are four collections of sacred hymns and oblational verses composed in ancient Sanskrit: Rig Veda, Sama Veda, Yajur Veda, and Atharva Veda. *Vedanta*, meaning "end of the Vedas," consists primarily of the Upanishads, the Brahmasutras (commentaries on the Upanishads), and the *Bhagavad Gita* (part of the epic poem, the *Mahabharata*).

8 **for the teachers**
Rudolf Steiner held two lectures for the "Pedagogical Society" in Kristiania (Oslo) on November 23 and 24, 1921; see *Waldorf Education and Anthroposophy, 1* (CW 304).

11 cultural epoch
The post-Atlantean era will, according to Rudolf Steiner, comprise seven cultural epochs. The first of these is the ancient Indian (c. 7200–5050 BC), followed by the ancient Persian (c. 5050–2900 BC), the Chaldean-Egyptian (c. 2900–750 BC), the Greco-Roman (c. 750 BC–AD 1400), and our own fifth epoch, which will continue until approximately AD 3500. In the future, there will be two more cultural epochs, each one also lasting about 2,160 years. See, for example, Rudolf Steiner, *An Outline of Esoteric Science* (CW 13).

13 fish-tail
Rudolf Steiner does not elaborate on this here but, traditionally, Capricorn, which is now viewed as a goat, was seen as a sea-goat, a hybrid animal with the front portion of a goat and the hind quarters of a fish's tail. Rudolf Steiner explains this a bit further in some of the lectures given just before this lecture cycle, in *Cosmosophy, Volume II* (CW 208).

from the cosmos
In this section, the stenography is at times incomplete or illegible.

14 life-levels
In this lecture Rudolf Steiner does not elaborate on the "life-levels," but he had spoken of these life-levels in a lecture given a month earlier, in Dornach; see *Cosmosophy, Volume II* (CW 208), lecture 5. There, these seven levels are identified as: life of the senses, nerves, breathing, circulation, metabolism, movement, reproduction.

15 same way as the stomach
See also Rudolf Steiner and Ita Wegman, *Fundamentals of Therapy*, chapter 1.

16 seven levels of life
See note to page 14.

Lecture Two
Kristiania (Oslo), November 27, 1921

22 imagination, inspiration, intuition
Rudolf Steiner refers to imagination, inspiration, and intuition as three progressive stages of higher spiritual consciousness that can be achieved by following the path described in *Knowledge of the Higher Worlds* (CW 10) and in the fifth chapter of *An Outline of Esoteric Science* (CW 13).

world of the hierarchies
Dionysius the Areopagite, a disciple of Paul, describes in his book, *Celestial Hierarchies*, nine hierarchies of angels, in descending order: the Seraphim (Spirits of Love), Cherubim (Spirits of Harmony), Thrones (Spirits of Will), Kyriotetes (Spirits of Wisdom), Dynamis (Spirits of Movement), Exusiai (Spirits of Form), Archai (Spirits of Personality), Archangeloi (Spirits of Fire/archangels), and Angeloi (Sons of Life/angels). Rudolf Steiner sometimes uses these Greek and Hebrew names and at other times the designations here given in parentheses.

23 can be known and seen
Rudolf Steiner mentions elsewhere that one can learn to know and see this tableau already during life by following the path of inner development, but that it can also occur spontaneously when death is immanent. In *An Outline of Esoteric Science* (chapter 3), he cites an autobiographical account of someone who almost drowns and then experiences this instantaneous life-tableau.

in the public lectures of the last few days
This refers to two lectures given in Kristiania (Oslo) on November 25 and 26, 1921, which are included in *Self-consciousness: The Spiritual Human Being* (CW 79).

24 Vienna in 1914
Rudolf Steiner, *The Inner Nature of Man and Our Life between Death and Rebirth* (CW 153), course of eight lectures given in Vienna.

25 the *midnight hour* of existence
In *The Soul's Awakening*, the fourth drama in *Four Mystery Dramas* (CW 14).

32 yesterday's lecture
Lecture of November 26, 1921, "Paths Leading to a Knowledge of Higher Worlds," included in *Self-consciousness: The Spiritual Human Being* (CW 79).

Lecture Three
Kristiania (Oslo), December 4, 1921

39 Thirty Years' War
The Thirty Years' War was one of the longest and most destructive conflicts in European history, lasting from 1618 to 1648, and was caused by complex religious and political rivalries. Its destructive campaigns and battles occurred over most of Europe.

40 so-called Gnosis
Gnosticism developed in the late first century AD among Jewish and early Christian sects. According to Rudolf Steiner, the Gnostics viewed Christ as a cosmic being and could not conceive of the Christ-being incarnating in the physical body of Jesus.

writer like Origen
Origen (182–254), founder of Christian Gnosis.

Julian, the so-called Apostate
Julian (331–363), Roman emperor since AD 361, called Apostate, the "renegade," by the Christians because he wanted to renew the pagan mysteries. He was murdered.

the deed of Constantine
Constantin I, "the Great," (286–337), Roman emperor who made Christianity into a state religion in AD 313.

40 European folk souls
Rudolf Steiner, *The Mission of Folk Souls* (CW 121), eleven lectures given in Kristiania (Oslo) from June 7 to 17, 1910.

41 philosophical schools of Athens were closed
This happened under Justinian I, in AD 529.

Academy of Gondishapur
The Academy of Gondishapur was founded in the third century AD in Persia. It was home to the oldest known teaching hospital, a library, and an academy where various sciences were taught. It was especially active between the sixth and the tenth centuries AD and had a major impact on world history. For more on Gondishapur, see Rudolf Steiner, *Eternal and Transient Elements in Human Life* (CW 184).

43 turned to the Varangians
This happened around AD 860. The Varangians were Viking conquerors, traders, and settlers, mostly from present-day Sweden. The Varangians invaded and settled parts of Russia and Ukraine from the eighth to the eleventh centuries.

48 your physical senses
Halfway through this sentence, and then throughout most of the following paragraph, Rudolf Steiner addresses the Norwegian audience sitting in front of him directly—that is, he switches to "your" spirit-body-existence, "your" physical senses, and so on.

50 *The Decline of the West*
Oswald Spengler (1880–1936), German historian and cultural philosopher, one of the most profound pessimists of modern times. *The Decline of the West* was published in 1918 and reissued in 1922.

II. Father-Consciousness and Christ-Consciousness

A Lecture
Berlin, December 7, 1921

59 Waldorf pedagogy
The first Waldorf school had started two years earlier, in 1919, in Stuttgart, Germany. Rudolf Steiner gave lectures for the teachers, some of which can be found in *Study of Man: General Education Course* (CW 293), *Practical Advice to Teachers* (CW 294), and *Discussions with Teachers* (CW 295).

60 Stuttgart Congress
This conference took place from August 28 to September 7, 1921, in Stuttgart, Germany. See Rudolf Steiner, *Anthroposophie, ihre Erkenntniswurzeln und Lebensfrüchte* [Anthroposophy, its roots of knowledge and fruits for life] (GA 78).

Aarau, Switzerland
This lecture was given on November 11, 1921. See Rudolf Steiner, *Waldorf Education and Anthroposophy, 1* (CW 304).

67 particularly Solovyov
Vladimir Solovyov (1853–1900), Russian philosopher, theologian, poet, and literary critic.

about the Father
This quote is by Adolf von Harnack (1851–1930), German protestant theologian, from *The Essence of Christianity* (1899). The whole quote states: “It is neither a paradox nor ‘rationalism,’ but simply an expression of the facts as they are presented in the Gospels: ‘Not the Son, but only the Father belongs in the Gospels as they were preached by Jesus.’”

69 Vedanta philosophy
See note to page 5 regarding the Vedas and Vedanta.

70 infused with the breath of life
Rudolf Steiner uses the word *eingebildet*, so, “the breath of life was (literally) ‘built into, created within’ the human being.” Compare Genesis 2:7, “And the Lord God formed man of the dust of the ground, and breathed into his nostrils the breath of life; and man became a living soul” (Updated King James Version).

71 Spirit of Music
Friedrich Wilhelm Nietzsche (1844–1900), German philosopher, prose poet, cultural critic, and philologist. The *Birth of Tragedy Out of the Spirit of Music* was written in 1872. It was reissued in 1886 as *The Birth of Tragedy: Hellenism and Pessimism.*

The Therapeutae, the Essenes
The Essenes were members of a Jewish religious order, related to the Therapeutae. They lived from the second century BC to the first century AD in communal life, dedicated to asceticism. Early accounts of the Essenes can be found in the writings of Josephus, Philo, and Pliny the Elder.

72 Savior
The German word *Heiland* means “the healer.”

73 such as Ranke
Leopold von Ranke (1795–1886), German historian and founder of modern source-based history. As a researcher, he focused on the importance of primary sources and narrative history.

76 Washington conferences
See second note to page 4.

78 last few days
This refers to what happened in Kristiania (Oslo) a few days earlier. Rudolf Steiner presumably had referred to these events before he began with this lecture in Berlin.

last time I was here
This refers to a public lecture given in Berlin on November 19, 1921, contained in *Das Wesen der Anthroposophie* [The being of anthroposophy] (GA 80a).

III. The Human Being as an Earthly and Cosmic Being

Lecture One
Dornach, December 12, 1921

84 Jean Paul
Jean Paul (1763–1825), one of the most prolific and prominent German writers of his generation. The quote is from *Levana, or the Doctrine of Education.*

86 tantamount to experiencing
The German word here is *miterleben.* There is no direct word for this in English, but it means something like "co-experiencing," or "experiencing together with."

87 progressive firebrand
This reference could not be ascertained.

90 that became Paul's
Paul (born Saul of Tarsus, c. AD 5–65) was a diaspora Jew, a member of the Pharisees, who experienced a spiritual revelation of the risen Christ at the gates of Damascus (Acts of the Apostles 9:1–9). After this experience, he traveled widely throughout the eastern Roman Empire, spreading the gospel to the gentiles and founding Christian communities.

93 Ranke
See note to page 73.

Lecture Two
Dornach, December 18, 1921

97 breathed into him
See note to page 70.

100 evil in human beings
Rudolf Steiner is here referring to the lecture of September 23, 1921, in *Cosmosophy, Volume I* (CW 207).

music of the spheres
Music (or harmony) of the spheres, the idea, originating in ancient Greece, that celestial proportions and movements express sounds which, although imperceptible to the human ear, can be perceived with a higher level of consciousness. See also *The Mysteries of Initiation* (CW 144), lecture 3.

as you will also remember
This was discussed in lectures given in Dornach in October/November, 1921, just prior to the present set of lectures; see *Cosmosophy*, vols. 1 and 2 (CW 207 and 208).

107 music, and astronomy
The Seven Liberal Arts in the Middle Ages were divided into the so-called Trivium (Grammar, Logic, and Rhetoric) and the Quadrivium (Arithmetic, Geometry, Music, and Astronomy). These were studied, for instance, in the

mediaeval cathedral school of Chartres, France, where they can still be seen today, depicted in the cathedral's sculptures at the western portal and in its stained-glass windows.

109 *An Outline of Esoteric Science*
Rudolf Steiner, *An Outline of Esoteric Science* (CW 13).

Lecture Three
Dornach, December 23, 1921

112 imaginative cognition
Rudolf Steiner refers to imagination, inspiration, and intuition as three progressive stages of higher spiritual consciousness that can be achieved by following the path described in *Knowledge of the Higher Worlds* (CW 10), and *An Outline of Esoteric Science* (CW 13), chapter 5.

120 Czolbe
Heinrich Czolbe (1819–1873), German physician and materialist philosopher. See also Rudolf Steiner, *Riddles of Philosophy* (CW 18), chapter on "The Struggle for the Spirit."

IV. The Festival of the Appearance of Christ

Lecture One
Dornach, December 24, 1921

127 Christmas holidays
This refers to the course for teachers taking place concurrently in Dornach, from December 23, 1921, to January 7, 1922; see *Soul Economy: Body, Soul, and Spirit in Waldorf Education* (CW 303).

129 *Bhagavad Gita*
The *Bhagavad Gita* is a 700-verse Hindu scripture that is part of the epic *Mahabharata*, dated to the second half of the first millennium BC.

136 Not I, but Christ in me
For this important quote, Rudolf Steiner always uses a more concentrated version of the passage from Galatians 2:20: "I am crucified with Christ: nevertheless, I live; yet not I, but Christ lives in me: and the life which I now live in the flesh I live by the faith of the Son of God, who loved me, and gave himself for me."

Silesius
Angelus Silesius, also known as Johannes Scheffler (1624–1677), German mystic and poet. The quote is from *The Cherubinic Wanderer*.

137 place of skulls of Golgotha
The term "place of skulls" for the location of Christ's crucifixion on Golgotha is mentioned in all four Gospels (Matthew 27:33, Mark 15:22, Luke 23:33, and John 19:17); in some Christian traditions it is also sometimes called Calvary (from Latin *calva*: "bald head" or "skull").

Lecture Two
Dornach, December 25, 1921

143 Leonardo da Vinci
Leonardo da Vinci (1452–1519), Italian Renaissance painter, architect, draftsman, sculptor, engineer, inventor. *The Last Supper* was painted, probably between 1495 and 1498, on the wall of the refectory of the Dominican monastery Santa Maria delle Grazie in Milan, Italy.

144 the Gnostics
See first note to page 40.

146 in the Pauline sense
See I Corinthians 15.

on the stage
This refers to the Oberufer plays, collected by Karl Julius Schröer, Rudolf Steiner's literature professor in Vienna.

Zipser area
A region in central-eastern Europe.

in the Banat
A region bordered by Romania, Hungary, and Serbia.

147 such as Ranke
See note to page 73.

this book by Adolf Harnack
Regarding the first passage, see second note to page 67. The second passage (discussed in the next few paragraphs of the lecture) reads literally: "Whatever may have taken place at the grave and in the appearances, one thing is certain: It is from this grave that the incorruptible belief in the overcoming of death and in an eternal life originates."

148 Giordano Bruno Society
The Giordano Bruno Society in Berlin. See Rudolf Steiner, *Autobiography* (CW 28) and *On History, Philosophy, and Literature* (CW 51), especially the appendix. The name of the speaker mentioned could not be ascertained.

would all be lost
Freely quoted from I Cor 15:14: "And if Christ be not risen, then is our preaching vain, and your faith is also vain" (Updated King James Version).

149 holy tunic in Trier
This refers to a "holy tunic" stored in the cathedral of Trier, Germany, which is said to be the robe that Christ wore on his way to the crucifixion.

151 today I have begotten him
Luke 3:22. See also Luke 9:35; Math 3:17 and 17:5; Mark 1:11 and 9:7. These passages all read "This is my beloved Son, in whom I am well pleased" or something similar. Rudolf Steiner frequently pointed out that this passage should be translated as it appears in this lecture. Compare also Psalm 2, verse 7: "I will declare the decree: the Lord has said unto me, You are my Son; this day have I begotten you."

Lecture Three
Basel, December 26, 1921

154 had introduced
Rudolf Steiner uses a strong word here (*hineingedrängt*), which would literally translate as: "Human beings had 'forced/pushed/pressed' into their concept."

158 a sacred legend
Rudolf Steiner mentions this legend in the lecture of May 29, 1905, in *The Temple Legend* (CW 93) and in the lecture of May 21, 1907, in *Rosicrucianism Renewed* (CW 284). See also Jacobus de Voragine, *The Golden Legend: Readings on the Saints* (Princeton, NJ: Princeton University Press, 2012).

162 what Paul expressed
I Cor 15:17: "And if Christ be not raised, your faith is vain; all of you are yet in your sins."

164 at the midnight hour
See also the lecture of December 21, 1909, in *Deeper Secrets of Human Evolution in Light of the Gospels* (CW 117).

167 the joy of spirit
Translation of this verse is by D. S. Osmond from the lecture "Signs and Symbols of the Christmas Festival" in *The Festivals and their Meaning* (London: Rudolf Steiner Press, 1981), with a few minor changes by the present translator.

Below is the original German:

Die Sonne schaue
Um mitternächtige Stunde.
Mit Steinen baue
Im leblosen Grunde.

So finde im Niedergang
Und in des Todes Nacht,
Der Schöpfung neuen Anfang,
Des Morgens junge Macht.

Die Höhen lass offenbaren
Der Götter ewiges Wort;
Die Tiefen sollen bewahren
Den friedevollen Hort.

Im Dunkel lebend
Erschaffe eine Sonne.
Im Stoffe webend
Erkenne Geistes Wonne.

V. Cosmic New Year
New Year's Eve Lecture
Dornach, December 31, 1921

174 as we see blue today

Rudolf Steiner also refers to this in the lecture of March 24, 1920, in *Fachwissenschaften und Anthroposophie* [Specialized fields of knowledge and anthroposophy] (GA 73a).

spoke of the Erinyes

For example, in the *Oresteia* by Aeschylus (525–456 BC), the main character, Orestes, is pursued by the Erinyes, or furies.

177 *Philosophy of Freedom*

Rudolf Steiner, *The Philosophy of Freedom* (CW 4).

178 look back at Thales

Thales of Miletus (*c.* 624–547 BC), pre-Socratic Greek philosopher, regarded as the first representative of Western philosophy; credited with the saying "know thyself," which was inscribed on the Temple of Apollo at Delphi. See also Rudolf Steiner, *Riddles of Philosophy* (CW 18).

179 Lavoisier

Antoine Laurent Lavoisier (1743–1794), French chemist, known today as the father of modern chemistry. He established the law of conservation of mass and helped systematize chemical nomenclature.

Newton

Isaac Newton (1642–1727), English mathematician, physicist, astronomer, alchemist, theologian, and author. He formulated the laws of motion and of universal gravity.

Einstein

Albert Einstein (1879–1955), German-born theoretical physicist. Best known for developing the theory of relativity, but he also made important contributions to the development of the theory of quantum mechanics.

RUDOLF STEINER'S COLLECTED WORKS

The German Edition of Rudolf Steiner's Collected Works (the *Gesamtausgabe* [GA], published by Rudolf Steiner Verlag, Dornach, Switzerland) will be completed in the year 2025. The works are organized either by type of work (written, spoken, artistic creations), chronology, audience (public or other), or subject (education, art, etc.). For ease of comparison, the Collected Works in English (CW), listed below, follows the German organization and numbering.

The volumes that have so far been published in the English Collected Works edition appear *in italics with their published titles*; all other volumes, including those that have appeared in editions other than the CW, are set in Roman type with *literal translations* of the German titles. Published English titles are not necessarily the same as the German.

This list is current as of the date of this volume's publication.

A. Written Works

I. Writings 1884–1925

CW 1	Introductions and Selected Commentary on Goethe's Natural-scientific Writings
CW 1a–e	Goethe's Natural-scientific Writings
CW 1f	Editorial Afterwords to Goethe's Natural-scientific Writings in the Weimar Edition (1891–1896)
CW 2	*Goethe's Theory of Knowledge: An Outline of the Epistemology of His Worldview*
CW 3	Truth and Science
CW 4	The Philosophy of Freedom
CW 4a	Documents to "The Philosophy of Freedom"
CW 5	Friedrich Nietzsche, A Fighter against His Own Time
CW 6	Goethe's Worldview
CW 7	Mysticism at the Dawn of Modern Spiritual Life and Its Relationship with Modern Worldviews
CW 8	*Christianity as Mystical Fact and the Mysteries of Antiquity*
CW 9	Theosophy: An Introduction into Supersensible World Knowledge and Human Purpose
CW 10	How Does One Attain Knowledge of Higher Worlds?
CW 11	From the Akasha-Chronicle
CW 12	Levels of Higher Knowledge
CW 13	Occult Science in Outline
CW 14	*Four Modern Mystery Dramas*
CW 15	The Spiritual Guidance of the Individual and Humanity
CW 16/17	*A Way of Self-Knowledge & The Threshold of the Spiritual World*
CW 18	The Riddles of Philosophy in Their History, Presented as an Outline
CW 18a	Views of the World and of Life in the Nineteenth Century
CW 19	Thoughts during the Time of War (1915) and Further Texts on the Events of the World War (1917–1921)
CW 20	The Riddles of the Human Being: Articulated and Unarticulated in the Thinking, Views and Opinions of a Series of German and Austrian Personalities
CW 21	The Riddles of the Soul

CW 22 Goethe's Spiritual Nature and Its Revelation in "Faust" and through the "Fairy Tale of the Snake and the Lily"
CW 23 The Central Points of the Social Question in the Necessities of Life in the Present and the Future
CW 24 Essays Concerning the Threefold Division of the Social Organism and the Period 1915–1921
CW 25 Three Steps of Anthroposophy. Philosophy – Cosmology – Religion
CW 26 Anthroposophical Leading Thoughts
CW 27 Fundamentals for Expansion of the Art of Healing according to Spiritual-Scientific Insights
CW 28 *Autobiography: Chapters in the Course of My Life: 1861–1907*

II. Collected Essays

CW 29 Collected Essays on Dramaturgy, 1889–1900
CW 30 Methodical Foundations of Anthroposophy: Collected Essays on Philosophy, Natural Science, Aesthetics and Psychology, 1884–1901
CW 31 Collected Essays on Culture and Current Events, 1887–1901
CW 32 Collected Essays on Literature, 1884–1902
CW 33 Biographies and Biographical Sketches, 1894–1905
CW 34 Lucifer-Gnosis: Foundational Essays on Anthroposophy and Reports from the Periodicals "Luzifer" and "Lucifer-Gnosis," 1903–1908
CW 35 Philosophy and Anthroposophy: Collected Essays, 1904–1923
CW 36 The Goetheanum-Idea in the Middle of the Cultural Crisis of the Present: Collected Essays from the Periodical "Das Goetheanum," 1921–1925
CW 37 Writings on the History of the Anthroposophical Movement and Society 1902–1925

III. Publications from the Literary Estate

CW 38/1 Complete Letters, Vol. 1: Weimar Period 1879–1890
CW 38/2 Complete Letters, Vol. 2: Weimar Period 1890–1897
CW 38/3 Complete Letters, Vol. 3: Early Berlin Period 1897–1905 [forthcoming]
CW 38/4 Complete Letters, Vol. 4: Activity within the Theosophical Society 1905–1912 [forthcoming]
CW 38/5 Complete Letters, Vol. 5: From the Founding of the Anthroposophical Society to the Opening of the Goetheanum 1913–1920 [forthcoming]
CW 38/6 Compelte Letters, Vol. 6: The Last Years 1920–1925 [forthcoming]
CW 40 Truth-Wrought Words
CW 40a Sayings, Poems and Mantras; Supplementary Volume
CW 41a Translations and Free Renderings from the Old and New Testaments
CW 41b Translations and Free Renderings of Various Works
CW 42 Stage Adaptations I: Dramas by Edouard Schuré
CW 43 Stage Adaptations II: The Oberufer Christmas Plays
CW 44 Sketches, Fragments and Paralipomena on the Four Mystery Dramas
CW 45 Anthroposophy: A Fragment from the Year 1910
CW 46 Posthumous Essays and Fragments 1879–1924
CW 47/48 Notebooks and Notepads (digital edition)

CW 49	Notes for and about Helmuth and Eliza von Moltke and Relatives, 1904–1924 [forthcoming]
CW 50	[Blank number]

B. Lectures

I. Public Lectures

CW 51	*On Philosophy, History, and Literature: Lectures at the Worker Education School and the Independent College, Berlin, 1901–1905*
CW 52	Spiritual Teachings Concerning the Soul and Observation of the World
CW 53	The Origin and Goal of the Human Being
CW 54	The Riddles of the World and Anthroposophy
CW 55	Knowledge of the Supersensible in Our Times and Its Meaning for Life Today
CW 56	Knowledge of the Soul and of the Spirit
CW 57	Where and How Does One Find the Spirit?
CW 58	The Metamorphoses of the Soul Life. Paths of Soul Experiences: Part One
CW 59	The Metamorphoses of the Soul Life. Paths of Soul Experiences: Part Two
CW 60	The Answers of Spiritual Science to the Biggest Questions of Existence
CW 61	Human History in the Light of Spiritual Research
CW 62	*Results of Spiritual Research*
CW 63	Spiritual Science as a Treasure for Life
CW 64	Out of Destiny-Burdened Times
CW 65	Out of Central European Spiritual Life
CW 66	Spirit and Matter, Life and Death
CW 67	The Eternal in the Human Soul. Immortality and Freedom
CW 68a	On the Being of Christianity
CW 68b	The Cycle of the Human Being within the Sense-, Soul-, and Spirit-World
CW 68c	Goethe and the Present
CW 68d	The Being of Man in the Light of Spiritual Science
CW 69a	Truths and Errors of Spiritual Research. Spiritual Science and the Future of Mankind
CW 69b	Knowledge and Immortality
CW 69c	New Christ-Experience
CW 69d	Death and Immortality in the Light of Spiritual Science
CW 69e	Spiritual Science and the Spiritual Goals of Our Time
CW 70a	Human Soul, Destiny and Death
CW 70b	Paths to the Knowledge of the Eternal Powers of the Human Soul
CW 71a	Soul Immortality [forthcoming]
CW 71b	The Human Being as a Soul and Spirit Being
CW 72	Freedom – Immortality – Social Life
CW 73	The Supplementing of the Modern Sciences through Anthroposophy
CW 73a	Specialized Fields of Knowledge and Anthroposophy
CW 74	The Philosophy of Thomas Aquinas
CW 75	*Anthroposophy and the Natural Sciences: Foundations and Methods*
CW 76	The Fructifying Effect of Anthroposophy on Specialized Fields

CW 77a The Task of Anthroposophy in Relation to Science and Life: The Darmstadt College Course
CW 77b Art and Anthroposophy. The Goetheanum-Impulse
CW 78 Anthroposophy, Its Roots of Knowledge and Fruits for Life
CW 79 The Reality of the Higher Worlds
CW 80a The Being of Anthroposophy
CW 80b The Inner Realm of Nature and the Being of the Human Soul
CW 80c Anthroposophical Spiritual Science and the Great Civilizational Questions of the Present
CW 81 *Reimagining Academic Studies: Science, Philosophy, Education, Social Science, Theology, Theory of Language*
CW 82 *Becoming Fully Human: The Significance of Anthroposophy in Contemporary Spiritual Life*
CW 83 *The Tension between East and West*
CW 84 *The Aims of Anthroposophy and the Purpose of the Goetheanum*
CW 85 Supplementary Volume: Individual Public Lectures I [forthcoming]
CW 86 Supplementary Volume: Individual Public Lectures II [forthcoming]

II. Lectures to the Members of the Anthroposophical Society

CW 87 Ancient Mysteries and Christianity
CW 88 *Concerning the Astral World and Devachan*
CW 89 Consciousness–Life–Form. Fundamental Principles of a Spiritual-Scientific Cosmology
CW 90a Self-knowledge and Knowledge of the Divine, Vol. I. Theosophy, Christology, and Mythology
CW 90b Self-knowledge and Knowledge of the Divine, Vol. II. Theosophy, Christology, and Mythology
CW 90c Theosophy and Occultism
CW 91 Cosmology and Human Evolution. Introduction to Theosophy – Theory of Colors
CW 92 *The Occult Truths of Myths and Legends: Greek and Germanic Mythology: Richard Wagner in the Light of Spiritual Science*
CW 93 The Temple Legend and the Golden Legend as a Symbolic Expression of Past and Future Secrets of Human Development. From the Contents of the Esoteric School
CW 93a Fundamentals of Esotericism
CW 94 Cosmogony. Popular Occultism. The Gospel of John. Theosophy Based on the Gospel of John
The Theosophy in the Gospel of John
CW 95 At the Gates of Theosophy
CW 96 Origin-Impulses of Spiritual Science. Christian Esotericism in the Light of New Spirit-knowledge
CW 97 The Christian Mystery
CW 98 *Nature Beings and Spirit Beings: Their Activity in Our Visible World*
CW 99 The Theosophy of the Rosicrucians
CW 100 *True Knowledge of the Christ: Theosophy and Rosicucianism—The Gospel of John*
CW 101 Myths and Legends. Occult Signs and Symbols

CW 102 *Good and Evil Spirits and Their Influence on Humanity*
CW 103 *The Gospel of John*
CW 104 The Apocalypse of John
CW 104a From the Picture-Script of the Apocalypse of John
CW 105 *Universe, Earth, Human Being: Their Relationship to Egyptian Myths and Modern Civilization*
CW 106 Egyptian Myths and Mysteries in Relation to the Active Spiritual Forces of the Present
CW 107 *Disease, Karma, and Healing: Spiritual-scientific Enquiries into the Nature of the Human Being*
CW 108 Answering the Questions of Life and the World through Anthroposophy
CW 109 The Principle of Spiritual Economy in Connection with the Question of Reincarnation. An Aspect of the Spiritual Guidance of Humanity
CW 110 *The Spiritual Hierarchies and the Physical World: Zodiac, Planets, and Cosmos*
CW 111 Introduction to the Foundations of Theosophy
CW 112 The Gospel of John in Relation to the Three Other Gospels, Especially the Gospel of Luke
CW 113 The Orient in the Light of the Occident. The Children of Lucifer and the Brothers of Christ
CW 114 The Gospel of Luke
CW 115 Anthroposophy – Psychosophy – Pneumatosophy
CW 116 *The Christ-Impulse and the Development of Ego-Consciousness*
CW 117 *Deeper Secrets of Human Evolution in Light of the Gospels*
CW 117a The Gospel of John and the Three Other Gospels
CW 118 The Event of the Christ-Appearance in the Etheric World
CW 119 *Macrocosm and Microcosm: The Greater and the Lesser World: Questions Concerning the Soul, Life and the Spirit*
CW 120 The Revelations of Karma
CW 121 *The Mission of Folk Souls*
CW 122 The Secrets of the Biblical Creation-Story. The Six-Day Work in the First Book of Moses
CW 123 The Gospel of Matthew
CW 124 *Background to the Gospel of St. Mark*
CW 125 *Paths and Goals of the Spiritual Human Being: Life Questions in the Light of Spiritual Science*
CW 126 Occult History. Esoteric Observations of the Karmic Relationships of Personalities and Events of World History
CW 127 *The Mission of the New Spiritual Revelation: The Pivotal Nature of the Christ Event in Earth Evolution*
CW 128 An Occult Physiology
CW 129 *Wonders of the World: Trials of the Soul, Revelations of the Spirit*
CW 130 Esoteric Christianity and the Spiritual Guidance of Humanity
CW 131 From Jesus to Christ
CW 132 *Inner Experiences of Evolution*
CW 133 The Earthly and the Cosmic Human Being
CW 134 *The World of the Senses and the World of the Spirit*
CW 135 Reincarnation and Karma and Their Meaning for the Culture of the Present

CW 136 *Spiritual Beings in the Heavenly Bodies and in the Kingdoms of Nature*
CW 137 The Human Being in the Light of Occultism, Theosophy and Philosophy
CW 138 On Initiation. On Eternity and the Passing Moment. On the Light of the Spirit and the Darkness of Life
CW 139 The Gospel of Mark
CW 140 Occult Investigation into the Life between Death and New Birth. The Living Interaction between Life and Death
CW 141 *Between Death and Rebirth: In Relation to Cosmic Facts*
CW 142/46 *The Bhagavad Gita and the West: The Esoteric Significance of the Bhagavad Gita and Its Relation to the Epistles of Paul*
CW 143 *Three Paths to Christ: Experiencing the Supersensible*
CW 144 *The Mysteries of Initiation: From Isis to the Holy Grail*
CW 145 What Significance Does Occult Development of the Human Being Have for the Sheaths – Physical Body, Etheric Body, Astral Body, and Self?
CW 146 [See CW 142/46]
CW 147 The Secrets of the Threshold
CW 148 The Fifth Gospel
CW 149 *Christ and the Spiritual World: The Quest for the Holy Grail*
CW 150 *How the Spiritual World Projects into Physical Existence: The Influence of the Dead*
CW 151 *Human and Cosmic Thought*
CW 152 *Approaching the Mystery of Golgotha*
CW 153 The Inner Being of Man and Life Between Death and New Birth
CW 154 How does One Gain an Understanding of the Spiritual World? The Flowing in of Spiritual Impulses from out of the World of the Deceased
CW 155 *Christ and the Human Soul: The Meaning of Life – The Spiritual Foundation of Morality – Anthroposophy and Christianity*
CW 156 *Inner Reading and Inner Hearing: And How to Achieve Existence in the World of Ideas*
CW 157 Human Destinies and the Destiny of Peoples
CW 157a The Formation of Destiny and the Life after Death
CW 158 *Our Connection with the Elemental World: Kalevala – Olaf Åsteson – the Russian People: The World as the Result of Balancing Influences*
CW 159 *The Mystery of Death: The Nature and Significance of Central Europe and the European Folk-Spirits*
CW 160 [Blank number]
CW 161 *Artistic Sensitivity as a Spiritual Approach to Knowing Life and the World*
CW 162 Questions of Art and Life in Light of Spiritual Science
CW 163 Coincidence, Necessity and Providence. Imaginative Knowledge and the Processes after Death
CW 164 *The Value of Thinking for a Cognition that Satisfies the Human Being: The Relationship between Spiritual Science and Natural Science*
CW 165 *Unifying Humanity Spiritually through the Christ Impulse*
CW 166 Necessity and Freedom in World Events and in Human Action
CW 167 *The Human Spirit Past and Present: Occult Fraternities and the Mystery of Golgotha*
CW 168 *The Connection between the Living and the Dead*

CW 169 World-being and Selfhood
CW 170 The Riddle of the Human Being. The Spiritual Background of Human History
CW 171 Inner Development-Impulses of Humanity. Goethe and the Crisis of the 19th Century.
CW 172 The Karma of the Vocation of the Human Being in Connection with Goethe's Life.
CW 173a Observations of Modern History, Vol. I: Paths to an Objective Judgment;
CW 173b Observations of Modern History, Vol. II: The Karma of Untruthfulness
CW 173c Observations of Modern History, Vol. III: The Reality of Occult Impulses
CW 174a *Europe Between East and West in Cosmic and Human History*
CW 174b *The Spiritual Background to the First World War*
CW 175 *Building Stones for an Understanding of the Mystery of Golgotha: Human Life in a Cosmic Context*
CW 176 *The Karma of Materialism: Aspects of Human Evolution*
CW 177 *The Fall of the Spirits of Darkness: The Spiritual Background to the Outer World: Spiritual Beings and Their Effects*
CW 178 Individual Spiritual Beings and Their Influence in the Soul of the Human Being
CW 179 *The Influence of the Dead on Destiny*
CW 180 Mystery Truths and Christmas Impulses. Ancient Myths and their Meaning.
CW 181 *Dying Earth and Living Cosmos: The Living Gifts of Anthroposophy: The Need for New Forms of Consciousness*
CW 182 Death as Transformation of Life
CW 183 *Human Evolution: A Spiritual-Scientific Quest*
CW 184 *Eternal and Transient Elements in Human Life: The Cosmic Past of Humanity and the Mystery of Evil*
CW 185 Historical Symptomology
CW 185a Historical-Developmental Foundations for Forming a Social Judgment
CW 186 The Fundamental Social Demands of Our Time. In Changed Times
CW 187 How Can Humanity Find the Christ Again? The Threefold Shadow-Existence of our Time and the New Christ-Light
CW 188 Goetheanism, a Transformation-Impulse and Resurrection-Thought. Science of the Human Being and Science of Sociology
CW 189 *Conscious Society: Anthroposophy and the Social Question*
CW 190 *Past and Future Impulses in Societal Events*
CW 191 *Understanding Society through Spiritual-Scientific Knowledge: Social Threefolding, Christ, Lucifer, and Ahriman*
CW 192 Spiritual-Scientific Treatment of Social and Pedagogical Questions
CW 193 *Problems of Society: An Esoteric View, from Luciferic Past to Ahrimanic Future*
CW 194 *Michael's Mission: Revealing the Essential Secrets of Human Nature*
CW 195 *Cosmic New Year: Thoughts for New Year 1920*
CW 196 *What Is Necessary in These Urgent Times*
CW 197 *Polarities in the Evolution of Humanity: West and East – Materialism and Mysticism – Knowledge and Belief*
CW 198 Healing Factors for the Social Organism

CW 199 Spiritual Science as Knowledge of the Foundational Impulses of Social Formation
CW 200 The New Spirituality and the Christ-Experience of the 20th Century
CW 201 The Correspondences Between Microcosm and Macrocosm. The Human Being – A Hieroglyph of the Universe.
CW 202 *Universal Spirituality and Human Physicality: Bridging the Divide: The Search for the New Isis and the Divine Sophia*
CW 203 The Responsibility of Human Beings for the Development of the World through their Spiritual Connection with the Planet Earth and the World of the Stars.
CW 204 Perspectives of the Development of Humanity. The Materialistic Knowledge-Impulse and the Task of Anthroposophy.
CW 205 Human Development, World-Soul, and World-Spirit. Part One: The Human Being as a Being of Body and Soul in Relationship to the World.
CW 206 Human Development, World-Soul, and World-Spirit. Part Two: The Human Being as a Spiritual Being in the Process of Historical Development
CW 207 Anthroposophy as Cosmosophy. Part One: Characteristic Features of the Human Being in the Earthly and the Cosmic Realms.
CW 208 Anthroposophy as Cosmosophy. Part Two: The Forming of the Human Being as the Result of Cosmic Influence.
CW 209 *The Language of the Cosmos: Cosmic Influences and the Spiritual Task of Northern Europe*
CW 210 Old and New Methods of Initiation. Drama and Poetry in the Change of Consciousness in the Modern Age
CW 211 *The Sun Mystery and the Mystery of Death and Resurrection: Exoteric and Esoteric Christianity*
CW 212 *Life of the Human Soul: And Its Relation to World Evolution*
CW 213 Human Questions and World Answers
CW 214 The Mystery of the Trinity: The Human Being in Relationship with the Spiritual World in the Course of Time
CW 215 Philosophy, Cosmology, and Religion in Anthroposophy
CW 216 *Supersensible Impulses in the Historical Development of Humanity*
CW 217 *Becoming the Archangel Michael's Companions: Rudolf Steiner's Challenge to the Younger Generation*
CW 217a *Youth and the Etheric Heart: Rudolf Steiner Speaks to the Younger Generation*
CW 218 *Spirit as Sculptor of the Human Organism*
CW 219 The Relationship of the World of the Stars to the Human Being, and of the Human Being to the World of the Stars. The Spiritual Communion of Humanity
CW 220 *Awake! For the Sake of the Future*
CW 221 Earth-Knowing and Heaven-Insight
CW 222 *The Driving Force of Spiritual Powers in World History*
CW 223 The Cycle of the Year as Breathing Process of the Earth and the Four Great Festival-Seasons. Anthroposophy and the Human Heart (*Gemüt*)
CW 224 The Human Soul and its Connection with Divine-Spiritual Individualities. The Internalization of the Festivals of the Year
CW 225 *Three Perspectives of Anthroposophy: Cultural Phenomena from the Point of View of Spiritual Science*
CW 226 Human Being, Human Destiny, and World Development

CW 227 Initiation-Knowledge
CW 228 *Initiation Science: And the Development of the Human Mind*
CW 229 The Experiencing of the Course of the Year in Four Cosmic Imaginations
CW 230 The Human Being as Harmony of the Creative, Building, and Formative World-Word
CW 231 The Supersensible Human Being, Understood Anthroposophically
CW 232 The Forming of the Mysteries
CW 233 *World History and the Mysteries in the Light of Anthroposophy*
CW 233a *Rosicrucianism and Modern Initiation: Mystery Centres of the Middle Ages: The Easter Festival and the History of the Mysteries*
CW 234 Anthroposophy. A Summary after 21 Years
CW 235 Esoteric Observations of Karmic Relationships in 6 Volumes, Vol. 1
CW 236 Esoteric Observations of Karmic Relationships in 6 Volumes, Vol. 2
CW 237 Esoteric Observations of Karmic Relationships in 6 Volumes, Vol. 3: The Karmic Relationships of the Anthroposophical Movement
CW 238 Esoteric Observations of Karmic Relationships in 6 Volumes, Vol. 4: The Spiritual Life of the Present in Relationship to the Anthroposophical Movement
CW 239 Esoteric Observations of Karmic Relationships in 6 Volumes, Vol. 5
CW 240 Esoteric Observations of Karmic Relationships in 6 Volumes, Vol. 6
CW 241 [Blank number]
CW 242 [Blank number]
CW 243 *True and False Paths of Spiritual Research*
CW 244 Answers to Questions, and Interviews
CW 245 [Blank number]
CW 246 Supplementary Volume I: Individual Members Lectures
CW 247 Supplementary Volume II: Individual Members Lectures
CW 248 [Blank number]
CW 249 [Blank number]
CW 250 On the History of the German Section of the Theosophical Society 1902–1913. Lectures, Speeches, Reports, and Minutes
CW 251 On the History of the Anthroposophical Society 1913–1922
CW 252 On the History of the Building Association and the Goetheanum Association 1911–1924
CW 253 *Sexuality, Inner Development, and Community Life: Ethical and Spiritual Dimensions of the Crisis in the Anthroposophical Society in Dornach, 1915*
CW 254 The Occult Movement in the 19th Century and Its Relationship to World Culture. Significant Points from the Exoteric Cultural Life around the Middle of the 19th Century
CW 255b Anthroposophy and Its Opponents
CW 256 [Blank number]
CW 257 Anthroposophical Community-Building
CW 258 *The Anthroposophic Movement: The History and Conditions of the Anthroposophical Movement in Relation to the Anthroposophical Society: An Encouragement for Self-Examination*
CW 259 The Year of Destiny 1923 in the History of the Anthroposophical Society. From the Burning of the Goetheanum to the Christmas Conference

CW 260 The Christmas Conference for the Founding of the General Anthroposophical Society 1923/24

CW 260a The Constitution of the General Anthroposophical Society and the School for Spiritual Science. The Rebuilding of the Goetheanum

CW 261 *Our Dead: Memorial, Funeral, and Cremation Addresses 1906–1924*

CW 262 Rudolf Steiner and Marie Steiner-von Sivers: Correspondence and Documents, 1901–1925

CW 263/1 Rudolf Steiner and Edith Maryon: Correspondence: Letters, Verses, Sketches, 1912–1924

CW 264 *From the History and Contents of the First Section of the Esoteric School: Letters, Documents, and Lectures: 1904–1914*

CW 265 *Freemasonry and Ritual Work: The Misraim Service*

CW 265a Teaching and Instruction Lessons for Members of the Knowledge-Cultic Section of the Esoteric School 1904–1914 [forthcoming]

CW 266/1 *From the Esoteric School: Esoteric Lessons 1904–1909*

CW 266/2 *From the Esoteric School: Esoteric Lessons 1910–1912*

CW 266/3 *From the Esoteric School: Esoteric Lessons 1913–1923*

CW 267 *Soul Exercises: Word and Symbol Meditations*

CW 268 *Mantric Sayings: Meditations 1903–1925*

CW 269 Ritual Texts for the Celebration of the Free Christian Religious Instruction. The Collected Verses for Teachers and Students of the Waldorf School

CW 270 Esoteric Instructions for the First Class of the School for Spiritual Science at the Goetheanum 1924, 4 Volumes

III. Lectures and Courses on Specific Realms of Life

Lectures on Art

CW 271 *Art and Theory of Art: Foundations of a New Aesthetics*

CW 272 *Anthroposophy in the Light of Goethe's* Faust*: Volume One of Spiritual-Scientific Commentaries on Goethe's* Faust

CW 273 *Goethe's* Faust *in the Light of Anthroposophy: Volume Two of Spiritual-Scientific Commentaries on Goethe's* Faust

CW 274 Addresses for the Christmas Plays from the Old Folk Traditions

CW 275 Art in the Light of Mystery Wisdom

CW 276 *The Arts and Their Mission*

CW 277a The Origin and Development of Eurythmy 1912–1918

CW 277b The Origin and Development of Eurythmy 1918–1920

CW 277c The Origin and Development of Eurythmy 1920–1922 [forthcoming]

CW 277d The Origin and Development of Eurythmy 1923–1924 [forthcoming]

CW 278 Eurythmy as Visible Song

CW 279 *Eurythmy as Speech Made Visible: Speech Eurythmy Course*

CW 280 The Method and Nature of Speech Formation

CW 281 The Art of Recitation and Declamation

CW 282 Speech Formation and Dramatic Art

CW 283 The Nature of the Musical Element and the Experience of Tone in the Human Being

CW 284 *Rosicrucianism Renewed: The Unity of Art, Science & Religion: The Theosophical Congress of Whitsun 1907*

CW 285 [Blank number]
CW 286 Paths to a New Style of Architecture. "And the Building Becomes Man"
CW 287 *Architecture as Peacework: The First Goetheanum, Dornach, 1914*
CW 288 *Architecture, Sculpture, and Painting of the First Goetheanum*
CW 289 The Building-Idea of the Goetheanum: Lectures with Slides from the Years 1920–1921
CW 290 *Toward a New Theory of Architecture: The First Goetheanum in Pictures* [no longer in the German GA]
CW 291 The Being of Colors
CW 291a Knowledge of Colors. Supplementary Volume to "The Being of Colors"
CW 292 *Art History as a Reflection of Inner Spiritual Impulses*

Lectures on Education

CW 293 General Knowledge of the Human Being as the Foundation of Pedagogy
CW 294 The Art of Education: Methodology and Didactics
CW 295 The Art of Education: Seminar Discussions and Lectures on Lesson Planning
CW 296 The Question of Education as a Social Question
CW 297 The Idea and Practice of the Waldorf School
CW 297a Education for Life: Self-Education and the Practice of Pedagogy
CW 298 Rudolf Steiner in the Waldorf School
CW 299 Spiritual-Scientific Observations on Speech
CW 300a Conferences with the Teachers of the Free Waldorf School in Stuttgart, 1919 to 1924, in 3 Volumes, Vol. 1
CW 300b Conferences with the Teachers of the Free Waldorf School in Stuttgart, 1919 to 1924, in 3 Volumes, Vol. 2
CW 300c Conferences with the Teachers of the Free Waldorf School in Stuttgart, 1919 to 1924, in 3 Volumes, Vol. 3
CW 301 The Renewal of Pedagogical-Didactical Art through Spiritual Science
CW 302 Knowledge of the Human Being and the Forming of Class Lessons
CW 302a Education and Teaching from a Knowledge of the Human Being
CW 303 The Healthy Development of the Human Being
CW 304 Methods of Education and Teaching Based on Anthroposophy
CW 304a Anthroposophical Knowledge of the Human Being and Pedagogy
CW 305 The Soul-Spiritual Foundational Forces of the Art of Education. Spiritual Values in Education and Social Life
CW 306 Pedagogical Praxis from the Viewpoint of a Spiritual-Scientific Knowledge of the Human Being. The Education of the Child and Young Human Beings
CW 307 The Spiritual Life of the Present and Education
CW 308 The Method of Teaching and the Life-Requirements for Teaching
CW 309 Anthroposophical Pedagogy and Its Prerequisites
CW 310 The Pedagogical Value of a Knowledge of the Human Being and the Cultural Value of Pedagogy
CW 311 The Art of Education from an Understanding of the Being of Humanity

Lectures on Medicine

CW 312 *Introducing Anthroposophical Medicine*
CW 313 *Illness and Therapy: Spiritual-Scientific Aspects of Healing*
CW 314 *Physiology and Healing: Treatment, Therapy, and Hygiene*
CW 315 Curative Eurythmy
CW 316 *Understanding Healing: Meditative Reflections on Deepening Medicine through Spiritual Science*
CW 317 *Education for Special Needs: The Curative Education Course*
CW 318 The Working Together of Doctors and Pastors
CW 319 *The Healing Process: Spirit, Nature & Our Bodies*

Lectures on Natural Science

CW 320 Spiritual-Scientific Impulses for the Development of Physics 1: The First Natural-Scientific Course: Light, Color, Tone, Mass, Electricity, Magnetism
CW 321 Spiritual-Scientific Impulses for the Development of Physics 2: The Second Natural-Scientific Course: Warmth at the Border of Positive and Negative Materiality
CW 322 The Borders of the Knowledge of Nature
CW 323 *Interdisciplinary Astronomy: Third Scientific Course*
CW 324 Nature Observation, Mathematics, and Scientific Experimentation and Results from the Viewpoint of Anthroposophy
CW 324a The Fourth Dimension in Mathematics and Reality
CW 325 Natural Science and the World-Historical Development of Humanity since Ancient Times
CW 326 The Moment of the Coming Into Being of Natural Science in World History and Its Development Since Then
CW 327 Spiritual-Scientific Foundations for Success in Farming. The Agricultural Course

Lectures on Social Life and the Threefold Arrangement of the Social Organism

CW 328 The Social Question
CW 329 The Liberation of the Human Being as the Foundation for a New Social Form
CW 330 The Renewal of the Social Organism
CW 331 Work-Council and Socialization
CW 332a The Social Future
CW 332b Lectures and Speeches on Social and Economic Issues
CW 333 *Freedom of Thought and Societal Forces: Implementing the Demands of Modern Society*
CW 334 From the Unified State to the Threefold Social Organism
CW 335 The Crisis of the Present and the Path to Healthy Thinking
CW 336 The Great Questions of the Times and Anthroposophical Spiritual Knowledge
CW 337a Social Ideas, Social Realities, Social Practice, Vol. 1: Question-and-Answer Evenings and Study Evenings of the Alliance for the Threefold Social Organism in Stuttgart, 1919–1920

CW 337b Social Ideas, Social Realities, Social Practice, Vol. 2: Discussion Evenings of the Swiss Alliance for the Threefold Social Organism

CW 338 *Communicating Anthroposophy: The Course for Speakers to Promote the Idea of Threefolding*

CW 339 Anthroposophy, Threefold Social Organism, and the Art of Public Speaking

CW 340/41 *Rethinking Economics: Lectures and Seminars on World Economics*

Lectures and Courses on Christian Religious Work

CW 342 *First Steps in Christian Religious Renewal: Preparing the Ground for The Christian Community*

CW 343 Lectures and Courses on Christian Religious Work, Vol. 2: Spiritual Knowledge – Religious Feeling – Cultic Doing

CW 344 Lectures and Courses on Christian Religious Work, Vol. 3: Lectures at the Founding of the Christian Community

CW 345 Lectures and Courses on Christian Religious Work, Vol. 4: Concerning the Nature of the Working Word

CW 346 Lectures and Courses on Christian Religious Work, Vol. 5: The Apocalypse and the Work of the Priest

Lectures for Workers at the Goetheanum

CW 347 The Knowledge of the Nature of the Human Being According to Body, Soul and Spirit. On Earlier Conditions of the Earth

CW 348 On Health and Illness. Foundations of a Spiritual-Scientific Doctrine of the Senses

CW 349 On the Life of the Human Being and of the Earth. On the Nature of Christianity

CW 350 Rhythms in the Cosmos and in the Human Being. How Does One Come To See the Spiritual World?

CW 351 The Human Being and the World. The Influence of the Spirit in Nature. On the Nature of Bees

CW 352 Nature and the Human Being Observed Spiritual-Scientifically

CW 353 The History of Humanity and the World-Views of the Folk Cultures

CW 354 The Creation of the World and the Human Being. Life on Earth and the Influence of the Stars

C. Artistic Works

CW A 1–10; 57 The Architectural Work I: The Goetheanum and Its Predecessors

CW A 11 The Sculptural Work

CW A 12 The Goetheanum Windows. The Speech of Light. Sketches and Studies

CW A 13–16; 52–56 The Painting Work

CW A 14 Sketches for the Painting of the Small Dome of the First Goetheanum

CW A 27–43 The Architectural Work II: Commercial and Residential Buildings in Dornach and Other Places [forthcoming]

CW A 45 The Graphic Work

CW A 48 The Drawing Work

CW A 51 The Art of Jewelry as a Goethean Language of Form

CW A 54.0 A Path of Training in Painting. Pastel Sketches and Watercolors

CW A 54.1 Nature Moods. Nine Training Sketches for Painters

Eurythmy Figures

CW A 26 Skectches of the Eurythmy Figures
CW A 26a The Eurythmy Figures of Rudolf Steiner, Artistically Executed by Annemarie Bäschlin
CW A 26b Eurythmy Figures from the Time When They Were Created

Eurythmy Forms

CW A 23/1 Volume I: Eurythmy Forms for Poems by Rudolf Steiner
CW A 23/2 Volume II: Eurythmy Forms for the Calender of the Soul by Rudolf Steiner
CW A 23/3 Volume III: Euythmy Forms for Poems by J. W. von Goethe
CW A 23/4 Volume IV: Eurythmy Forms for Poems by Christian Morgenstern
CW A 23/5 Volume V: Eurythmy Forms for Poems by Albert Steffen
CW A 23/6 Volume VI: Eurythmy Forms for German Poems by Fercher von Steinwand, Hamerling, Hebbel, C. F. Meyer, Nietzsche, among others
CW A 23/7 Volume VII: Eurythmy Forms for English Poems
CW A 23/8 Volume VIII: Eurythmy Forms for French and Russian Poems
CW A 24 Volume IX: Eurythmy Forms for Tone Eurythmy

Blackboard Drawings from Lectures

CW A 58/1 Volume I: 20 Plates from Public Lectures 1920–1924 in CWs 73a, 74, 76, and 84
CW A 58/2 Volume II: 38 Plates from Lectures in 1919 in CWs 191 and 194
CW A 58/3 Volume III: 34 Plates from Lectures in 1920 in CWs 196 and 198
CW A 58/4 Volume IV: 33 Plates from Lectures in 1920 in CWs 199 and 200
CW A 58/5 Volume V: 31 Plates from Lectures in 1920 in CW 201
CW A 58/6 Volume VI: 46 Plates from Lectures 1920–1921 in CWs 202–204
CW A 58/7 Volume VII: 38 Plates from Lectures in 1921 in CWs 205 and 206
CW A 58/8 Volume VIII: 42 Plates from Lectures in 1921 in CWs 207–209
CW A 58/9 Volume IX: 40 Plates from Lectures in 1922 in CWs 210–212
CW A 58/10 Volume X: 35 Plates from Lectures in 1922 in CWs 213–215
CW A 58/11 Volume XI: 41 Plates from Lectures 1922–1923 in CWs 216, 218–220
CW A 58/12 Volume XII: 37 Plates from Lectures in 1923 in CWs 221–225
CW A 58/13 Volume XIII: 38 Plates from Lectures in 1923 in CWs 227–230
CW A 58/14 Volume XIV: 36 Plates from Lectures in 1923 in CWs 232 and 233
CW A 58/15 Volume XV: 37 Plates from Lectures in 1924 in CWs 233a, 234, and 243
CW A 58/16 Volume XVI: 56 Plates from the "Karma Lectures" in CWs 235–238 and 240
CW A 58/17 Volume XVII: 21 Plates from Lectures on the History of the Anthroposophical Society in CWs 257, 258, 260, and 260a
CW A 58/18 Volume XVIII: 33 Plates from Lectures on Art in CWs 271, 276, 283, 288–290, and 291
CW A 58/19 Volume XIX: 41 Plates from Lectures on Eurythmy in CWs 278, 279, and 315
CW A 58/20 Volume XX: 27 Plates from Lectures on Speech Formation in CWs 281 and 282

CW A 58/21 Volume XXI: 42 Plates from Lectures on Education in CWs 296, 303, 304, 306, and 311

CW A 58/22 Volume XXII: 46 Plates from Lectures on Medicine in CWs 312–315

CW A 58/23 Volume XXIII: 48 Plates from Lectures in 1924 in CWs 316–318

CW A 58/24 Volume XXIV: 39 Plates from Lectures on Natural Science and the Social Question in CWs 322, 326, 327, 339, and 340

CW A 58/25 Volume XXV: 33 Plates from the "Workers Lectures" (Volumes 1 and 2) in CWs 347 and 348

CW A 58/26 Volume XXVI: 51 Plates from the "Workers Lectures" (Volumes 3 and 4) in CWs 349 and 350

CW A 58/27 Volume XXVII: 35 Plates from the "Workers Lectures" (Volumes 5 and 6) in CWs 351 and 352

CW A 58/28 Volume XXVIII: 42 Plates from the "Workers Lectures" (Volumes 7 and 8) in CWs 353 and 354

CW A 58/29 Volume XXIX: 43 Plates from Lectures and Courses on Christian Religious Activity in CWs 342–344 and 346

CW A 58/30 Volume XXX: 27 Plates from CWs 255b, 324a, 337b, and 340, Corrigenda, Plates without CW Assignment, Copies

SIGNIFICANT EVENTS IN THE LIFE OF RUDOLF STEINER

1829: June 23: birth of Johann Steiner (1829–1910)—Rudolf Steiner's father—in Geras, Lower Austria.

1834: May 8: birth of Franciska Blie (1834–1918)—Rudolf Steiner's mother—in Horn, Lower Austria. "My father and mother were both children of the glorious Lower Austrian forest district north of the Danube."

1860: May 16: marriage of Johann Steiner and Franciska Blie.

1861: February 25: birth of *Rudolf Joseph Lorenz Steiner* in Kraljevec, Croatia, near the border with Hungary, where Johann Steiner works as a telegrapher for the South Austria Railroad. Rudolf Steiner is baptized two days later, February 27, the date usually given as his birthday.

1862: Summer: the family moves to Mödling, Lower Austria.

1863: The family moves to Pottschach, Lower Austria, near the Styrian border, where Johann Steiner becomes stationmaster. "The view stretched to the mountains...majestic peaks in the distance and the sweet charm of nature in the immediate surroundings."

1864: November 15: birth of Rudolf Steiner's sister, Leopoldine (d. November 1, 1927). She will become a seamstress and live with her parents for the rest of her life.

1866: July 28: birth of Rudolf Steiner's deaf-mute brother, Gustav (d. May 1, 1941).

1867: Rudolf Steiner enters the village school. Following a disagreement between his father and the schoolmaster, whose wife falsely accused the boy of causing a commotion, Rudolf Steiner is taken out of school and taught at home.

1868: A critical experience. Unknown to the family, an aunt dies in a distant town. Sitting in the station waiting room, Rudolf Steiner sees her "form," which speaks to him, asking for help. "Beginning with this experience, a new soul life began in the boy, one in which not only the outer trees and mountains spoke to him, but also the worlds that lay behind them. From this moment on, the boy began to live with the spirits of nature...."

1869: The family moves to the peaceful, rural village of Neudorfl, near Wiener-Neustadt in present-day Austria. Rudolf Steiner attends the village school. Because of the "unorthodoxy" of his writing and spelling, he has to do "extra lessons."

1870: Through a book lent to him by his tutor, he discovers geometry: "To grasp something purely in the spirit brought me inner happiness. I know that I first learned happiness through geometry." The same tutor allows him to draw, while other students still struggle with their reading and writing. "An artistic element" thus enters his education.

1871: Though his parents are not religious, Rudolf Steiner becomes a "church child," a favorite of the priest, who was "an exceptional character." "Up to the age of ten or eleven, among those I came to know, he was far and away the most significant." Among other things, he introduces Steiner to Copernican, heliocentric cosmology. As an altar boy, Rudolf Steiner serves at Masses, funerals, and Corpus Christi processions. At year's end, after an incident in which he escapes a thrashing, his father forbids him to go to church.

1872: Rudolf Steiner transfers to grammar school in Wiener-Neustadt, a five-mile walk from home, which must be done in all weathers.

1873–75: Through his teachers and on his own, Rudolf Steiner has many wonderful experiences with science and mathematics. Outside school, he teaches himself analytic geometry, trigonometry, differential equations, and calculus.

1876: Rudolf Steiner begins tutoring other students. He learns bookbinding from his father. He also teaches himself stenography.

1877: Rudolf Steiner discovers Kant's *Critique of Pure Reason*, which he reads and rereads. He also discovers and reads von Rotteck's *World History*.

1878: He studies extensively in contemporary psychology and philosophy.

1879: Rudolf Steiner graduates from high school with honors. His father is transferred to Inzersdorf, near Vienna. He uses his first visit to Vienna "to purchase a great number of philosophy books"—Kant, Fichte, Schelling, and Hegel, as well as numerous histories of philosophy. His aim: to find a path from the "I" to nature.

October 1879–1883: Rudolf Steiner attends the Technical College in Vienna—to study mathematics, chemistry, physics, mineralogy, botany, zoology, biology, geology, and mechanics—with a scholarship. He also attends lectures in history and literature, while avidly reading philosophy on his own. His two favorite professors are Karl Julius Schröer (German language and literature) and Edmund Reitlinger (physics). He also audits lectures by Robert Zimmerman on aesthetics and Franz Brentano on philosophy. During this year he begins his friendship with Moritz Zitter (1861–1921), who will help support him financially when he is in Berlin.

1880: Rudolf Steiner attends lectures on Schiller and Goethe by Karl Julius Schröer, who becomes his mentor. Also "through a remarkable combination of circumstances," he meets Felix Koguzki, an "herb gatherer" and healer, who could "see deeply into the secrets of nature." Rudolf Steiner will meet and study with this "emissary of the Master" throughout his time in Vienna.

1881: January: "... I didn't sleep a wink. I was busy with philosophical problems until about 12:30 a.m. Then, finally, I threw myself down on my couch. All my striving during the previous year had been to research whether the following statement by Schelling was true or not: *Within everyone dwells a secret, marvelous capacity to draw back from the stream of time—out of the self clothed in all that comes to us from outside—into our innermost being and there, in the immutable form of the Eternal, to look into ourselves.* I believe, and I am still quite certain of it, that I discovered this capacity in myself; I had long had an inkling of it. Now the whole of idealist philosophy stood before me in modified form. What's a sleepless night compared to that!"

Rudolf Steiner begins communicating with leading thinkers of the day, who send him books in return, which he reads eagerly.

July: "I am not one of those who dives into the day like an animal in human form. I pursue a quite specific goal, an idealistic aim—knowledge of the truth! This cannot be done offhandedly. It requires the greatest striving in the world, free of all egotism, and equally of all resignation."

August: Steiner puts down on paper for the first time thoughts for a "Philosophy of Freedom." "The striving for the absolute: this human yearning is freedom." He also seeks to outline a "peasant philosophy," describing what the worldview of a "peasant"—one who lives close to the earth and the old ways—really is.

1881–1882: Felix Koguzki, the herb gatherer, reveals himself to be the envoy of another, higher initiatory personality, who instructs Rudolf Steiner to penetrate Fichte's philosophy and to master modern scientific thinking as a preparation for right entry into the spirit. This "Master" also teaches him the double (evolutionary and involutionary) nature of time.

1882: Through the offices of Karl Julius Schröer, Rudolf Steiner is asked by Joseph Kurschner to edit Goethe's scientific writings for the *Deutschen National-Literatur* edition. He writes "A Possible Critique of Atomistic Concepts" and sends it to Friedrich Theodor Vischer.

1883: Rudolf Steiner completes his college studies and begins work on the Goethe project.

1884: First volume of Goethe's *Scientific Writings* (CW 1) appears (March). He lectures on Goethe and Lessing, and Goethe's approach to science. In July, he enters the household of Ladislaus and Pauline Specht as tutor to the four Specht boys. He will live there until 1890. At this time, he meets Josef Breuer (1842–1925), the coauthor with Sigmund Freud of *Studies in Hysteria*, who is the Specht family doctor.

1885: While continuing to edit Goethe's writings, Rudolf Steiner reads deeply in contemporary philosophy (Edouard von Hartmann, Johannes Volkelt, and Richard Wahle, among others).

1886: May: Rudolf Steiner sends Kurschner the manuscript of *Outlines of Goethe's Theory of Knowledge* (CW 2), which appears in October, and which he sends out widely. He also meets the poet Marie Eugenie Delle Grazie and writes "Nature and Our Ideals" for her. He attends her salon, where he meets many priests, theologians, and philosophers, who will become his friends. Meanwhile, the director of the Goethe Archive in Weimar requests his collaboration with the *Sophien* edition of Goethe's works, particularly the writings on color.

1887: At the beginning of the year, Rudolf Steiner is very sick. As the year progresses and his health improves, he becomes increasingly "a man of letters," lecturing, writing essays, and taking part in Austrian cultural life. In August–September, the second volume of Goethe's *Scientific Writings* appears.

1888: January–July: Rudolf Steiner assumes editorship of the "German Weekly" (*Deutsche Wochenschrift*). He begins lecturing more intensively, giving, for example, a lecture titled "Goethe as Father of a New Aesthetics." He meets and becomes soul friends with Friedrich Eckstein (1861–1939), a vegetarian, philosopher of symbolism, alchemist, and musician, who will introduce him to various spiritual currents (including Theosophy) and with whom he will meditate and interpret esoteric and alchemical texts.

1889: Rudolf Steiner first reads Nietzsche (*Beyond Good and Evil*). He encounters Theosophy again and learns of Madame Blavatsky in the Theosophical circle around Marie Lang (1858–1934). Here he also meets well-known figures of Austrian life, as well as esoteric figures like the occultist Franz Hartman and Karl Leinigen-Billigen (translator of C.G. Harrison's *The Transcendental Universe*). During this period, Steiner first reads A.P. Sinnett's *Esoteric Buddhism* and Mabel Collins's *Light on the Path*. He also begins traveling, visiting Budapest, Weimar, and Berlin (where he meets philosopher Edouard von Hartman).

1890: Rudolf Steiner finishes volume 3 of Goethe's scientific writings. He begins his doctoral dissertation, which will become *Truth and Science* (CW 3). He also meets the poet and feminist Rosa Mayreder (1858–1938), with whom he can exchange his most intimate thoughts. In September, Rudolf Steiner moves to Weimar to work in the Goethe-Schiller Archive.

1891: Volume 3 of the Kurschner edition of Goethe appears. Meanwhile, Rudolf Steiner edits Goethe's studies in mineralogy and scientific writings for the *Sophien* edition. He meets Ludwig Laistner of the Cotta Publishing Company, who asks for a book on the basic question of metaphysics. From this will result, ultimately, *The Philosophy of Freedom* (CW 4), which will be published not by Cotta but by Emil Felber. In October, Rudolf Steiner takes the oral exam for a doctorate in philosophy, mathematics, and mechanics at Rostock University, receiving his doctorate on the twenty-sixth. In November, he gives his first lecture on Goethe's "Fairy Tale" in Vienna.

1892: Rudolf Steiner continues work at the Goethe-Schiller Archive and on his *Philosophy of Freedom*. *Truth and Science*, his doctoral dissertation, is published. Steiner undertakes to write introductions to books on Schopenhauer and Jean Paul for Cotta. At year's end, he finds lodging with Anna Eunike, née Schulz (1853–1911), a widow with four daughters and a son. He also develops a friendship with Otto Erich Hartleben (1864–1905) with whom he shares literary interests.

1893: Rudolf Steiner begins his habit of producing many reviews and articles. In March, he gives a lecture titled "Hypnotism, with Reference to Spiritism." In September, volume 4 of the Kurschner edition is completed. In November, *The Philosophy of Freedom* appears. This year, too, he meets John Henry Mackay (1864–1933), the anarchist, and Max Stirner, a scholar and biographer.

1894: Rudolf Steiner meets Elisabeth Förster Nietzsche, the philosopher's sister, and begins to read Nietzsche in earnest, beginning with the as yet unpublished *Antichrist*. He also meets Ernst Haeckel (1834–1919). In the fall, he begins to write *Nietzsche, A Fighter against His Time* (CW 5).

1895: May: *Nietzsche, A Fighter against His Time* appears.

1896: January 22: Rudolf Steiner sees Friedrich Nietzsche for the first and only time. Moves between the Nietzsche and the Goethe-Schiller Archives, where he completes his work before year's end. He falls out with Elisabeth Förster Nietzsche, thus ending his association with the Nietzsche Archive.

1897: Rudolf Steiner finishes the manuscript of *Goethe's Worldview* (CW 6). He moves to Berlin with Anna Eunike and begins editorship of the *Magazin fur Literatur*. From now on, Steiner will write countless reviews, literary and philosophical articles, and so on. He begins lecturing at the "Free Literary Society." In September, he attends the Zionist Congress in Basel. He sides with Dreyfus in the Dreyfus affair.

1898: Rudolf Steiner is very active as an editor in the political, artistic, and theatrical life of Berlin. He becomes friendly with John Henry Mackay and poet Ludwig Jacobowski (1868–1900). He joins Jacobowski's circle of writers, artists, and scientists—"The Coming Ones" (*Die Kommenden*)—and contributes lectures to the group until 1903. He also lectures at the "League for College Pedagogy." He writes an article for Goethe's sesquicentennial, "Goethe's Secret Revelation," on the "Fairy Tale of the Green Snake and the Beautiful Lily."

1898–99: "This was a trying time for my soul as I looked at Christianity. . . . I was able to progress only by contemplating, by means of spiritual perception, the evolution of Christianity. . . . Conscious knowledge of real Christianity began to dawn in me around the turn of the century. This seed continued to develop. My soul trial occurred shortly before the beginning of the twentieth century. It was decisive for my soul's development that I stood spiritually before the Mystery of Golgotha in a deep and solemn celebration of knowledge."

1899: Rudolf Steiner begins teaching and giving lectures and lecture cycles at the Workers' College, founded by Wilhelm Liebknecht (1826–1900). He will continue to do so until 1904. Writes: *Literature and Spiritual Life in the Nineteenth Century; Individualism in Philosophy*; *Haeckel and His Opponents; Poetry in the Present;* and begins what will become (fifteen years later) *The Riddles of Philosophy* (CW 18). He also meets many artists and writers, including Käthe Kollwitz, Stefan Zweig, and Rainer Maria Rilke. On October 31, he marries Anna Eunike.

1900: "I thought that the turn of the century must bring humanity a new light. It seemed to me that the separation of human thinking and willing from the spirit had peaked. A turn or reversal of direction in human evolution seemed to me a necessity." Rudolf Steiner finishes *World and Life Views in the Nineteenth Century* (the second part of what will become *The Riddles of Philosophy*) and dedicates it to Ernst Haeckel.

It is published in March. He continues lecturing at *Die Kommenden*, whose leadership he assumes after the death of Jacobowski. Also, he gives the Gutenberg Jubilee lecture before 7,000 typesetters and printers. In September, Rudolf Steiner is invited by Count and Countess Brockdorff to lecture in the Theosophical Library. His first lecture is on Nietzsche. His second lecture is titled "Goethe's Secret Revelation." October 6, he begins a lecture cycle on the mystics that will become *Mystics after Modernism* (CW 7). November–December: "Marie von Sivers appears in the audience...." Also in November, Steiner gives his first lecture at the Giordano Bruno Bund (where he will continue to lecture until May, 1905). He speaks on Bruno and modern Rome, focusing on the importance of the philosophy of Thomas Aquinas as monism.

1901: In continual financial straits, Rudolf Steiner's early friends Moritz Zitter and Rosa Mayreder help support him. In October, he begins the lecture cycle *Christianity as Mystical Fact* (CW 8) at the Theosophical Library. In November, he gives his first "Theosophical lecture" on Goethe's "Fairy Tale" in Hamburg at the invitation of Wilhelm Hubbe-Schleiden. He also attends a tea to celebrate the founding of the Theosophical Society at Count and Countess Brockdorff's. He gives a lecture cycle, "From Buddha to Christ," for the circle of the *Kommenden*. November 17, Marie von Sivers asks Rudolf Steiner if Theosophy does not need a Western-Christian spiritual movement (to complement Theosophy's Eastern emphasis). "The question was posed. Now, following spiritual laws, I could begin to give an answer...." In December, Rudolf Steiner writes his first article for a Theosophical publication. At year's end, the Brockdorffs and possibly Wilhelm Hubbe-Schleiden ask Rudolf Steiner to join the Theosophical Society and undertake the leadership of the German section. Rudolf Steiner agrees, on the condition that Marie von Sivers (then in Italy) work with him.

1902: Beginning in January, Rudolf Steiner attends the opening of the Workers' School in Spandau with Rosa Luxemberg (1870–1919). January 17, Rudolf Steiner joins the Theosophical Society. In April, he is asked to become general secretary of the German Section of the Theosophical Society, and works on preparations for its founding. In July, he visits London for a Theosophical congress. He meets Bertram Keightly, G.R.S. Mead, A.P. Sinnett, and Annie Besant, among others. In September, *Christianity as Mystical Fact* appears. In October, Rudolf Steiner gives his first public lecture on Theosophy ("Monism and Theosophy") to about three hundred people at the Giordano Bruno Bund. From October 19–21, the German Section of the Theosophical Society has its first meeting; Rudolf Steiner is the general secretary, and Annie Besant attends. Steiner lectures on practical karma studies. On October 23, Annie Besant inducts Rudolf Steiner into the Esoteric School of the Theosophical Society. On October 25, Steiner begins a weekly series of lectures: "The Field of Theosophy." During this year, Rudolf Steiner also first meets Ita Wegman (1876–1943), who will become his close collaborator in his final years.

1903: Rudolf Steiner holds about 300 lectures and seminars. In May, the first issue of the periodical *Luzifer* appears. In June, Rudolf Steiner visits London for the first meeting of the Federation of the European Sections of the Theosophical Society, where he meets Colonel Olcott. He begins to write *Theosophy* (CW 9).

1904: Rudolf Steiner continues lecturing at the Workers' College and elsewhere (about 90 lectures), while lecturing intensively all over Germany among Theosophists (about 140 lectures). In February, he meets Carl Unger (1878–1929), who will become a member of the board of the Anthroposophical Society (1913). In March, he meets Michael Bauer (1871–1929), a Christian mystic, who will also be on the board. In May, *Theosophy* appears, with the dedication: "To the spirit of Giordano Bruno." Rudolf Steiner and Marie von Sivers visit London for meetings with Annie Besant. In June, Rudolf Steiner and Marie von Sivers attend the meeting of the Federation of European Sections of the Theosophical Society in Amsterdam. In July, Steiner begins the articles in *Lucifer-Gnosis* that will become *How to Know Higher Worlds* (CW 10) and *Cosmic Memory* (CW 11). In September, Annie Besant visits Germany. In December, Steiner lectures on Freemasonry. He mentions the High Grade Masonry derived from John Yarker and represented by Theodore Reuss and Karl Kellner as a blank slate "into which a good image could be placed."

1905: This year, Steiner ends his non-Theosophical lecturing activity. Supported by Marie von Sivers, his Theosophical lecturing—both in public and in the Theosophical Society—increases significantly: "The German Theosophical Movement is of exceptional importance." Steiner recommends reading, among others, Fichte, Jacob Boehme, and Angelus Silesius. He begins to introduce Christian themes into Theosophy. He also begins to work with doctors (Felix Peipers and Ludwig Noll). In July, he is in London for the Federation of European Sections, where he attends a lecture by Annie Besant: "I have seldom seen Mrs. Besant speak in so inward and heartfelt a manner...." "Through Mrs. Besant I have found the way to H.P. Blavatsky." September to October, he gives a course of thirty-one lectures for a small group of esoteric students. In October, the annual meeting of the German Section of the Theosophical Society, which still remains very small, takes place. Rudolf Steiner reports membership has risen from 121 to 377 members. In November, seeking to establish esoteric "continuity," Rudolf Steiner and Marie von Sivers participate in a "Memphis-Misraim" Masonic ceremony. They pay forty-five marks for membership. "Yesterday, you saw how little remains of former esoteric institutions." "We are dealing only with a 'framework'... for the present, nothing lies behind it. The occult powers have completely withdrawn."

1906: Expansion of Theosophical work. Rudolf Steiner gives about 245 lectures, only 44 of which take place in Berlin. Cycles are given in Paris, Leipzig, Stuttgart, and Munich. Esoteric work also intensifies. Rudolf Steiner begins writing *An Outline of Esoteric Science* (CW 13). In January, Rudolf Steiner receives permission (a patent) from the Great Orient of the Scottish A & A Thirty-Three Degree Rite of the Order of the Ancient Freemasons of the Memphis-Misraim Rite to direct a chapter under the name "Mystica Aeterna." This will become the "Cognitive Cultic Section" (also called "Misraim Service") of the Esoteric School. (See: *From the History and Contents of the Cognitive Cultic Section* [CW 264].) During this time, Steiner also meets Albert Schweitzer. In May, he is in Paris, where he visits Edouard Schuré. Many Russians attend his lectures (including Konstantin Balmont, Dimitri Mereszkovski, Zinaida Hippius, and Maximilian Woloshin). He attends the General Meeting of the European Federation of the Theosophical Society, at which Col. Olcott is present for the last time. He spends the year's end in Venice and Rome, where he writes and works on his translation of H. P. Blavatsky's *Key to Theosophy.*

1907: Further expansion of the German Theosophical Movement according to the Rosicrucian directive to "introduce spirit into the world"—in education, in social questions, in art, and in science. In February, Col. Olcott dies in Adyar. Before he dies, Olcott indicates that "the Masters" wish Annie Besant to succeed him: much politicking ensues. Rudolf Steiner supports Besant's candidacy. April–May: preparations for the Congress of the Federation of European Sections of the Theosophical Society—the great, watershed Whitsun "Munich Congress," attended by Annie Besant and others. Steiner decides to separate Eastern and Western (Christian-Rosicrucian) esoteric schools. He takes his esoteric school out of the Theosophical Society (Besant and Rudolf Steiner are "in harmony" on this). Steiner makes his first lecture tours to Austria and Hungary. That summer, he is in Italy. In September, he visits Edouard Schuré, who will write the introduction to the French edition of *Christianity as Mystical Fact* in Barr, Alsace. Rudolf Steiner writes the autobiographical statement known as the "Barr Document." In *Luzifer–Gnosis*, "The Education of the Child" appears.

1908: The movement grows (membership: 1150). Lecturing expands. Steiner makes his first extended lecture tour to Holland and Scandinavia, as well as visits to Naples and Sicily. Themes: St. John's Gospel, the Apocalypse, Egypt, science, philosophy, and logic. *Lucifer-Gnosis* ceases publication. In Berlin, Marie von Sivers (with Johanna Mücke [1864–1949]) forms the *Philosophisch-Theosophisch* (after 1915 *Philosophisch-Anthroposophisch*) *Verlag* to publish Steiner's work. Steiner gives lecture cycles titled *The Gospel of St. John* (CW 103) and *The Apocalypse* (104).

1909: *An Outline of Esoteric Science* appears. Lecturing and travel continue. Rudolf Steiner's spiritual research expands to include the polarity of Lucifer and Ahriman; the work of great individualities in history; the

Maitreya Buddha and the Bodhisattvas; spiritual economy (CW 109); the work of the spiritual hierarchies in heaven and on Earth (CW 110). He also deepens and intensifies his research into the Gospels, giving lectures on the Gospel of St. Luke (CW 114) with the first mention of two Jesus children. Meets and becomes friends with Christian Morgenstern (1871–1914). In April, he lays the foundation stone for the Malsch model—the building that will lead to the first Goetheanum. In May, the International Congress of the Federation of European Sections of the Theosophical Society takes place in Budapest. Rudolf Steiner receives the Subba Row medal for *How to Know Higher Worlds*. During this time, Charles W. Leadbeater discovers Jiddu Krishnamurti (1895–1986) and proclaims him the future "world teacher," the bearer of the Maitreya Buddha and the "reappearing Christ." In October, Steiner delivers seminal lectures on "anthroposophy," which he will try, unsuccessfully, to rework over the next years into the unfinished work, *Anthroposophy (A Fragment)* (CW 45).

1910: New themes: *The Reappearance of Christ in the Etheric* (CW 118); *The Fifth Gospel* (CW 148); *The Mission of Folk Souls* (CW 121); *Occult History* (CW 126); the evolving development of etheric cognitive capacities. Rudolf Steiner continues his Gospel research with *The Gospel of St. Matthew* (CW 123). In January, his father dies. In April, he takes a month-long trip to Italy, including Rome, Monte Cassino, and Sicily. He also visits Scandinavia again. July–August, he writes the first mystery drama, *The Portal of Initiation* (CW 14). In November, he gives "psychosophy" lectures. In December, he submits "On the Psychological Foundations and Epistemological Framework of Theosophy" to the International Philosophical Congress in Bologna.

1911: The crisis in the Theosophical Society deepens. In January, "The Order of the Rising Sun," which will soon become "The Order of the Star in the East," is founded for the coming world teacher, Krishnamurti. At the same time, Marie von Sivers, Rudolf Steiner's coworker, falls ill. Fewer lectures are given, but important new ground is broken. In Prague, in March, Steiner meets Franz Kafka (1883–1924) and Hugo Bergmann (1883–1975). In April, he delivers his paper to the Philosophical Congress. He writes the second mystery drama, *The Soul's Probation* (CW 14). Also, while Marie von Sivers is convalescing, Rudolf Steiner begins work on *Calendar 1912/1913*, which will contain the "Calendar of the Soul" meditations. On March 19, Anna (Eunike) Steiner dies. In September, Rudolf Steiner visits Einsiedeln, birthplace of Paracelsus. In December, Friedrich Rittelmeyer, future founder of the Christian Community, meets Rudolf Steiner. The *Johannes-Bauverein*, the "building committee," which would lead to the first Goetheanum (first planned for Munich), is also founded, and a preliminary committee for the founding of an independent association is created that, in the following year, will become the Anthroposophical Society. Important lecture cycles include *Occult Physiology* (CW 128);

Wonders of the World (CW 129); *From Jesus to Christ* (CW 131). Other themes: esoteric Christianity; Christian Rosenkreutz; the spiritual guidance of humanity; the sense world and the world of the spirit.

1912: Despite the ongoing, now increasing crisis in the Theosophical Society, much is accomplished: *Calendar 1912/1913* is published; eurythmy is created; both the third mystery drama, *The Guardian of the Threshold* (CW 14) and *A Way of Self-Knowledge* (CW 16) are written. New (or renewed) themes include life between death and rebirth and karma and reincarnation. Other lecture cycles: *Spiritual Beings in the Heavenly Bodies and the Kingdoms of Nature* (CW 136); *The Human Being in the Light of Occultism, Theosophy, and Philosophy* (CW 137); *The Gospel of St. Mark* (CW 139); and *The Bhagavad Gita and the Epistles of Paul* (CW 142). On May 8, Rudolf Steiner celebrates White Lotus Day, H.P. Blavatsky's death day, which he had faithfully observed for the past decade, for the last time. In August, Rudolf Steiner suggests the "independent association" be called the "Anthroposophical Society." In September, the first eurythmy course takes place. In October, Rudolf Steiner declines recognition of a Theosophical Society lodge dedicated to the Star of the East and decides to expel all Theosophical Society members belonging to the order. Also, with Marie von Sivers, he first visits Dornach, near Basel, Switzerland, and they stand on the hill where the Goetheanum will be. In November, a Theosophical Society lodge is opened by direct mandate from Adyar (Annie Besant). In December, a meeting of the German section occurs at which it is decided that belonging to the Order of the Star of the East is incompatible with membership in the Theosophical Society. December 28: informal founding of the Anthroposophical Society in Berlin.

1913: Expulsion of the German section from the Theosophical Society. February 2–3: Foundation meeting of the Anthroposophical Society. Board members include: Marie von Sivers, Michael Bauer, and Carl Unger. September 20: Laying of the foundation stone for the *Johannes Bau* (Goetheanum) in Dornach. Building begins immediately. The third mystery drama, *The Soul's Awakening* (CW 14), is completed. Also: *The Threshold of the Spiritual World* (CW 147). Lecture cycles include: *The Bhagavad Gita and the Epistles of Paul* and *The Esoteric Meaning of the Bhagavad Gita* (CW 146), which the Russian philosopher Nikolai Berdyaev attends; *The Mysteries of the East and of Christianity* (CW 144); *The Effects of Esoteric Development* (CW 145); and *The Fifth Gospel* (CW 148). In May, Rudolf Steiner is in London and Paris, where anthroposophical work continues.

1914: Building continues on the *Johannes Bau* (Goetheanum) in Dornach, with artists and coworkers from seventeen nations. The general assembly of the Anthroposophical Society takes place. In May, Rudolf Steiner visits Paris, as well as Chartres Cathedral. June 28: assassination in Sarajevo ("Now the catastrophe has happened!"). August 1: War is declared. Rudolf Steiner returns to Germany from Dornach—he will travel back and forth. He writes the last chapter of *The Riddles of Philosophy*. Lecture cycles include: *Human and Cosmic Thought* (CW 151); *Inner Being of Humanity between Death and a New Birth* (CW 153); *Occult Reading and Occult Hearing* (CW 156). December 24: marriage of Rudolf Steiner and Marie von Sivers.

1915: Building continues. Life after death becomes a major theme, also art. Writes: *Thoughts during a Time of War* (CW 24). Lectures include: *The Secret of Death* (CW 159); *The Uniting of Humanity through the Christ Impulse* (CW 165).

1916: Rudolf Steiner begins work with Edith Maryon (1872–1924) on the sculpture "The Representative of Humanity" ("The Group"—Christ, Lucifer, and Ahriman). He also works with the alchemist Alexander von Bernus on the quarterly *Das Reich*. He writes *The Riddle of Humanity* (CW 20). Lectures include: *Necessity and Freedom in World History and Human Action* (CW 166); *Past and Present in the Human Spirit* (CW 167); *The Karma of Vocation* (CW 172); *The Karma of Untruthfulness* (CW 173).

1917: Russian Revolution. The U.S. enters the war. Building continues. Rudolf Steiner delineates the idea of the "threefold nature of the human being" (in a public lecture March 15) and the "threefold nature of the social organism" (hammered out in May–June with the help of Otto von Lerchenfeld and Ludwig Polzer-Hoditz in the form of two documents titled *Memoranda*, which were distributed in high places). August–September: Rudolf Steiner writes *The Riddles of the Soul* (CW 20). Also: commentary on "The Chemical Wedding of Christian Rosenkreutz" for Alexander Bernus (*Das Reich*). Lectures include: *The Karma of Materialism* (CW 176); *The Spiritual Background of the Outer World: The Fall of the Spirits of Darkness* (CW 177).

1918: March 18: peace treaty of Brest-Litovsk—"Now everything will truly enter chaos! What is needed is cultural renewal." June: Rudolf Steiner visits Karlstein (Grail) Castle outside Prague. Lecture cycle: *From Symptom to Reality in Modern History* (CW 185). In mid-November, Emil Molt, of the Waldorf-Astoria Cigarette Company, has the idea of founding a school for his workers' children.

1919: Focus on the threefold social organism: tireless travel, countless lectures, meetings, and publications. At the same time, a new public stage of Anthroposophy emerges as cultural renewal begins. The coming years will see initiatives in pedagogy, medicine, pharmacology, and agriculture. January 27: threefold meeting: " We must first of all, with the money we have, found free schools that can bring people what they need." February: first public eurythmy performance in Zurich. Also: "Appeal to the German People" (CW 24), circulated March 6 as a newspaper insert. In April, *Toward Social Renewal* (CW 23)—"perhaps the most widely read of all books on politics appearing since the war"—appears. Rudolf Steiner is asked to undertake the "direction and leadership" of the school founded by the Waldorf-Astoria Company.

Rudolf Steiner begins to talk about the "renewal" of education. May 30: a building is selected and purchased for the future Waldorf School. August–September: Rudolf Steiner gives a lecture course for Waldorf teachers, *The Foundations of Human Experience (Study of Man)* (CW 293). September 7: Opening of the first Waldorf School. December (into January): first science course, the *Light Course* (CW 320).

1920: The Waldorf School flourishes. New threefold initiatives. Founding of limited companies *Der Kommenden Tag* and *Futurum A.G.* to infuse spiritual values into the economic realm. Rudolf Steiner also focuses on the sciences. Lectures: *Introducing Anthroposophical Medicine* (CW 312); *The Warmth Course* (CW 321); *The Boundaries of Natural Science* (CW 322); *The Redemption of Thinking* (CW 74). February: Johannes Werner Klein—later a cofounder of the Christian Community—asks Rudolf Steiner about the possibility of a "religious renewal," a "Johannine church." In March, Rudolf Steiner gives the first course for doctors and medical students. In April, a divinity student asks Rudolf Steiner a second time about the possibility of religious renewal. September 27–October 16: anthroposophical "college course." December: lectures titled *The Search for the New Isis* (CW 202).

1921: Rudolf Steiner continues his intensive work on cultural renewal, including the uphill battle for the threefold social order. "College" arts, scientific, theological, and medical courses include: *The Astronomy Course* (CW 323); *Observation, Mathematics, and Scientific Experiment* (CW 324); the *Second Medical Course* (CW 313); *Color* (CW 291). In June and September–October, Rudolf Steiner also gives the first two "priests' courses" (CW 342 and 343). The "youth movement" gains momentum. Magazines are founded: *Die Drei* (January), and—under the editorship of Albert Steffen (1884–1963)—the weekly, *Das Goetheanum* (August). In February–March, Rudolf Steiner takes his first trip outside Germany since the war (Holland). On April 7, Steiner receives a letter regarding "religious renewal," and May 22–23, he agrees to address the question in a practical way. In June, the Clinical-Therapeutic Institute opens in Arlesheim under the direction of Dr. Ita Wegman. In August, the Chemical-Pharmaceutical Laboratory opens in Arlesheim (Oskar Schmiedel and Ita Wegman, directors). The Clinical-Therapeutic Institute is inaugurated in Stuttgart (Dr. Ludwig Noll, director); also the Research Laboratory in Dornach (Ehrenfried Pfeiffer and Gunther Wachsmuth, directors). In November–December, Rudolf Steiner visits Norway.

1922: The first half of the year involves very active public lecturing (thousands attend); in the second half, Rudolf Steiner begins to withdraw and turn toward the Society—"The Society is asleep." It is "too weak" to do what is asked of it. The businesses—*Die Kommenden Tag* and *Futura A.G.*—fail. In January, with the help of an agent, Steiner undertakes a twelve-city German tour, accompanied by eurythmy performances. In two weeks he speaks to more than 2,000 people. In April, he gives a "college course" in The Hague. He also visits England. In June, he is in Vienna for the East-West Congress. In August–September, he is back in England for the Oxford Conference on Education. Returning to Dornach, he gives the lectures *Philosophy, Cosmology, and Religion* (CW 215), and gives the third priest's course (CW 344). On September 16, The Christian Community is founded. In October–November, Steiner is in Holland and England. He also speaks to the youth: *The Youth Course* (CW 217). In December, Steiner gives lectures titled *The Origins of Natural Science* (CW 326), and *Humanity and the World of Stars: The Spiritual Communion of Humanity* (CW 219). December 31: Fire at the Goetheanum, which is destroyed.

1923: Despite the fire, Rudolf Steiner continues his work unabated. A very hard year. Internal dispersion, dissension, and apathy abound. There is conflict—between old and new visions—within the society. A wake-up call is needed, and Rudolf Steiner responds with renewed lecturing vitality. His focus: the spiritual context of human life; initiation science; the course of the year; and community building. As a foundation for an artistic school, he creates a series of pastel sketches. Lecture cycles: *The Anthroposophic Movement* (CW 258); *Initiation Science* (CW 227) (in England at the Penmaenmawr Summer School); *The Four Seasons and the Archangels* (CW 229); *Harmony of the Creative Word* (CW 230); *The Supersensible Human* (CW 231), given in Holland for the founding of the Dutch society. On November 10, in response to the failed Hitler-Ludendorf putsch in Munich, Steiner closes his Berlin residence and moves the *Philosophisch-Anthroposophisch Verlag* (Press) to Dornach. On December 9, Steiner begins the serialization of his *Autobiography: The Course of My Life* (CW 28) in *Das Goetheanum*. It will continue to appear weekly, without a break, until his death. Late December-early January: Rudolf Steiner refounds the Anthroposophical Society (about 12,000 members internationally) and takes over its leadership. The new board members are: Marie Steiner, Ita Wegman, Albert Steffen, Elizabeth Vreede, and Guenther Wachsmuth. (See *The Christmas Meeting for the Founding of the General Anthroposophical Society* [CW 260]. Accompanying lectures: *Mystery Knowledge and Mystery Centers* [CW 232]; *World History in the Light of Anthroposophy* [CW 233].) December 25: the Foundation Stone is laid (in the hearts of members) in the form of the "Foundation Stone Meditation."

1924: January 1: having founded the Anthroposophical Society and taken over its leadership, Rudolf Steiner has the task of "reforming" it. The process begins with a weekly newssheet ("What's Happening in the Anthroposophical Society") in which Rudolf Steiner's "Letters to Members" and "Anthroposophical Leading Thoughts" appear (CW 26). The next step is the creation of a new esoteric class, the "first class" of the "School for Spiritual Science" (which was to have been followed, had Rudolf Steiner lived longer, by two more advanced classes). Then comes a new language for anthroposophy—practical, phenomenological, and direct—and Rudolf Steiner creates the model for the second Goetheanum. He begins the series of extensive "karma" lectures (CW 235–40); and finally, responding to needs, he creates two new initiatives: biodynamic agriculture and curative education. After the middle of the year, rumors begin to circulate regarding Steiner's health. Lectures: January–February, *Anthroposophy* (CW 234); February: *Eurythmy as Visible Singing* (CW 278); June: *The Agriculture Course* (CW 327); June–July: *Eurythmy as Visible Speech* (CW 279); *Curative Education* (CW 317); August: (England, "Second International Summer School") *Initiation Consciousness: True and False Paths in Spiritual Investigation* (CW 243); September: *Pastoral Medicine* (CW 318). On September 26, for the first time, Rudolf Steiner cancels a lecture. On September 28, he gives his last lecture. On September 29, he withdraws to his studio in the carpenter's shop; now he is definitively ill. Cared for by Ita Wegman, he continues working, however, and writing the weekly installments of his *Autobiography* and *Letters to the Members/Leading Thoughts* (CW 26).

1925: Rudolf Steiner, while continuing to work, continues to weaken. He finishes *Extending Practical Medicine* (CW 27) with Ita Wegman.

On March 30, around ten in the morning, Rudolf Steiner dies.

INDEX

A

B

C

D

E

N

O

P

Q

R

T

U

V

W

Y

Z

RUDOLF STEINER'S BLACKBOARD DRAWINGS

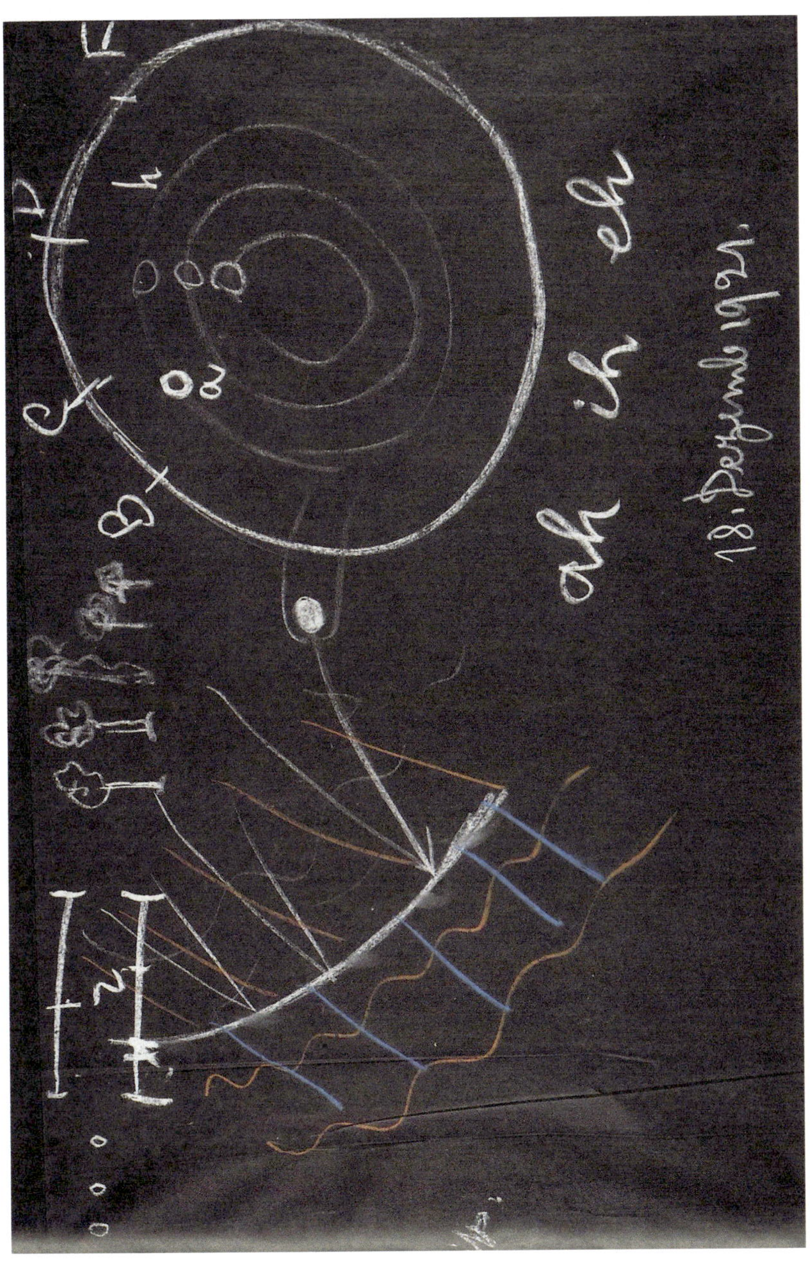

PLATE 1

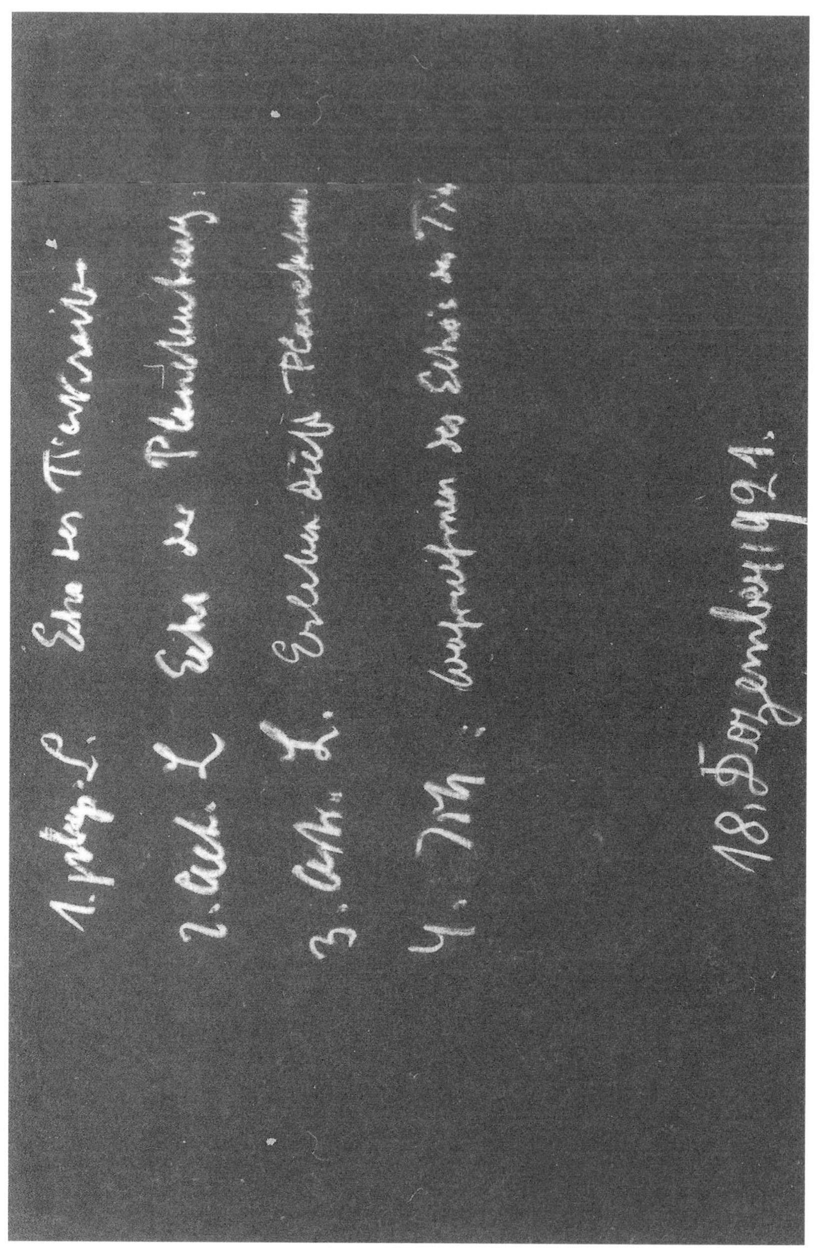

Plate 2

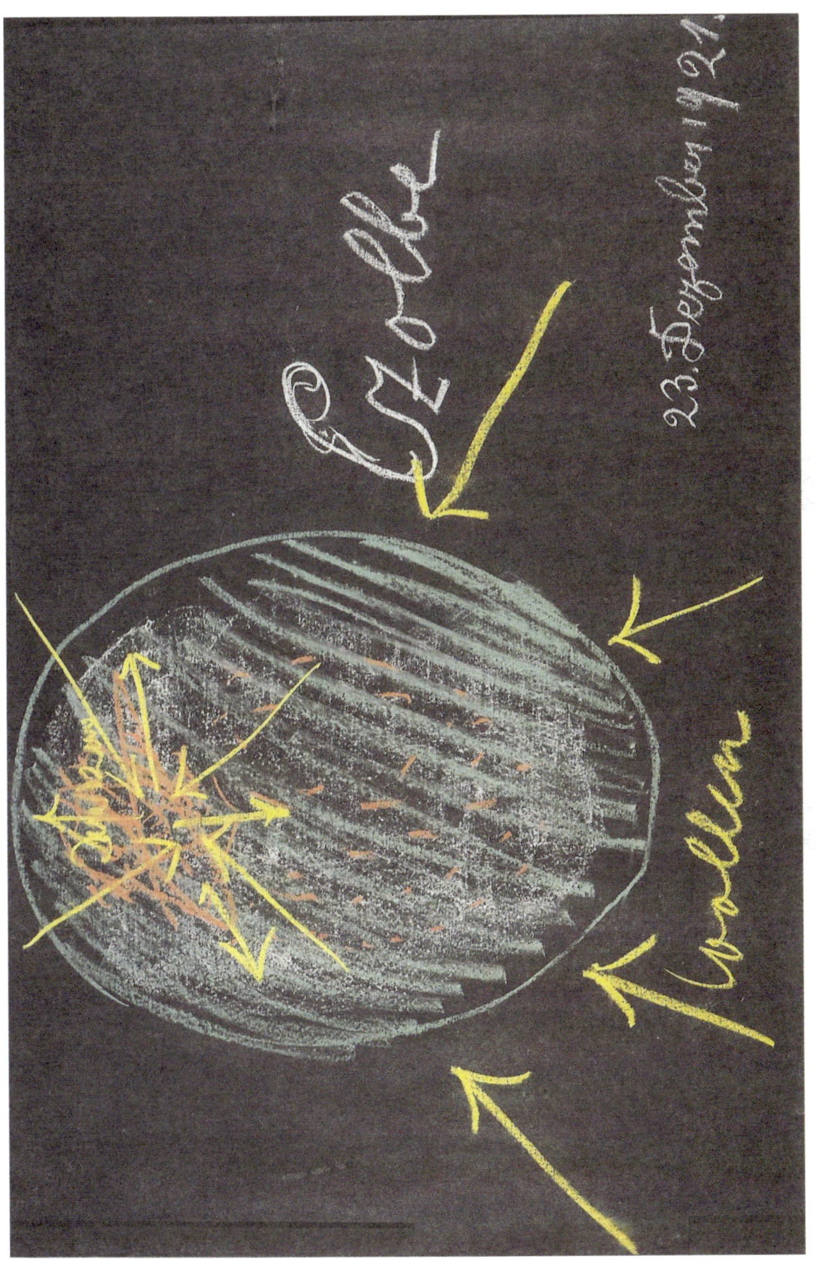

PLATE 3